DATE DUE

GAYLORD

PRINTED IN U.S.A.

Bioprediction, Biomarkers, and Bad Behavior

Oxford Series in Neuroscience, Law, and Philosophy

Series Editors
Lynn Nadel, Frederick Schauer, and Walter P. Sinnott-Armstrong

Conscious Will and Responsibility
Edited by Walter P. Sinnott-Armstrong and Lynn Nadel

Memory and Law
Edited by Lynn Nadel and Walter P. Sinnott-Armstrong

Neuroscience and Legal Responsibility
Edited by Nicole A. Vincent

Handbook on Psychopathy and Law
Edited by Kent A. Kiehl and Walter P. Sinnott-Armstrong

A Primer on Criminal Law and Neuroscience
Edited by Stephen J. Morse and Adina L. Roskies

Bioprediction, Biomarkers, and Bad Behavior
Edited by Ilina Singh, Walter P. Sinnott-Armstrong and Julian Savulescu

Bioprediction, Biomarkers, and Bad Behavior

Scientific, Legal, and Ethical Challenges

Edited By

Ilina Singh

Walter P. Sinnott-Armstrong

Julian Savulescu

OXFORD
UNIVERSITY PRESS

OXFORD
UNIVERSITY PRESS

Oxford University Press is a department of the University of Oxford.
It furthers the University's objective of excellence in research, scholarship,
and education by publishing worldwide.

Oxford   New York
Auckland   Cape Town   Dar es Salaam   Hong Kong   Karachi
Kuala Lumpur   Madrid   Melbourne   Mexico City   Nairobi
New Delhi   Shanghai   Taipei   Toronto

With offices in
Argentina   Austria   Brazil   Chile   Czech Republic   France   Greece
Guatemala   Hungary   Italy   Japan   Poland   Portugal   Singapore
South Korea   Switzerland   Thailand   Turkey   Ukraine   Vietnam

Oxford is a registered trademark of Oxford University Press
in the UK and certain other countries.

Published in the United States of America by
Oxford University Press 198 Madison Avenue, New York, NY 10016

Library of Congress Cataloging-in-Publication Data
Bioprediction, biomarkers, and bad behavior : scientific, legal, and ethical challenges / edited
by Ilina Singh, Walter P. Sinnott-Armstrong.
    pages cm. — (Oxford series in neuroscience, law, and philosophy)
Includes bibliographical references and index.
ISBN 978-0-19-984418-0 — ISBN 978-0-19-932144-5 — ISBN 978-0-19-932145-2
1. Criminal behavior—Genetic aspects.   2. Mental illness—Genetic aspects.
3. Genetic markers—Social aspects.   4. Psychology, Pathological.
I. Singh, Ilina.   II. Sinnott-Armstrong, Walter, 1955–
HV6047.B56 2014
362.2′4—dc23
2013011019

9 8 7 6 5 4 3 2 1
Printed in the United States of America
on acid-free paper

CONTENTS

FOREWORD

BIOPREDICTION HOPES AND HYPES

Each week, the journal *Nature* sends out press releases about its research papers to hundreds of journalists around the world. Press releases include the following preamble:

> We take great care not to hype the papers mentioned on our press releases, but are sometimes accused of doing so. If you ever consider that a story has been hyped, please do not hesitate to contact us at press@nature.com, citing the specific example.

Bioprediction is one topic around which there is recurring hype by scientists and nonscientists alike. The present book represents an excellent compendium of knowledge and research around bioprediction of forms of problematic behavior. If there is one recurring motif it is, indeed, "don't hype!"

Some of the hype to be found around bioprediction is blatant; some is more subtle. In cutting through the hype, this book surely succeeds in its principal intention: to provide a timely overview of newly emerging knowledge and uncertainties around the neuroscience, genetics, and psychology of 'bad behavior', and of the manner in which those in society are approaching or should be approaching such developments.

The end achievement is not to minimize or maximize the concerns about the use of biomarkers to predict "bad" behavior, but rather to place these concerns in their proper multidisciplinary context. And that multidisciplinarity is an unusual strength of this collection.

For example, anyone reading this book will understand how, in the United States at least, there is a likelihood that bioprediction techniques will be invoked in legal frameworks despite strong warnings from scientists about the limitations in our understanding of them. The grounding of this volume in that legal context is one of its particular strengths. I would guess that few researchers in psychology and in psychiatric biomarkers and perhaps even in bioethics are aware of how the U.S. deployment of risk indicators for offending and reoffending is structured and how it might variously develop in the different states and then affect the law in other countries. Another context that is briefly mentioned is the sheer cost of violence and therefore the power of the incentive to reduce it. The economic impacts of mental illness, criminality, and violence rightly have a place in discussions about the development of technologies to reduce or to prevent these societal problems. The difficulty, of course, is when economic projections are given overly much weight in calculations of the societal 'burden' of these issues, as compared to equally important understanding of the social drivers that, along with biological risk factors, shape pathways to mental illness, criminality, and violence.

Another value in this collection lies in the accounts of biomarker development. Complementary accounts of genetics and imaging—some general, some usefully focusing closely on case studies of particular biological clues—are replete with due warnings of difficulties in replication and uncertain chains of logic. Nevertheless, one can sense that the power seems to be potentially there for biomarkers that will eventually sit alongside age and gender as risk factors for violent behavior.

As a frequent reader of the ethical discussions that surround new technologies, and especially biomarkers, I am struck by how repeatedly concerns are appropriately aired about future scenarios and yet how seldom these concerns are elaborated and sharpened by active exploration. Perhaps philosophers and ethicists are suspicious of focus groups and polls, dismissing them as mere futurology. But imagine that one was to produce a serum biomarker that indicated that a particular 13-year-old child has a 30 percent possibility of developing, say, a psychotic disorder that would lead to full-blown schizophrenia at the age of 22. It would seem to me to be a worthwhile exercise to instigate a workshop in which this scenario is discussed by a group of people for whom children are a day-to-day professional preoccupation: parents, teachers, social workers, police, physical and mental health services, technology regulators.... And included in that room would be researchers into such biomarkers, so that their perspective can influence and be influenced by these potential worlds brought about by their interventions. And yet how often have such people been brought together to discuss such a scenario? Illuminated by that discussion, how might one sharpen ethical discussions, with the aim of broadening the range of biomarker research and of anticipating regulatory needs? There have been such participatory exercises in anticipatory governance, but such efforts do not seem to have developed traction despite claims that they can generate new perspectives (e.g., Guston, 2011).

Support for such deliberations, and perhaps support for biomarker research itself, can only be damaged by hype. So what are the various hypes one should beware of? This book contains alerts about the following:

Hyping biomarker signatures as measured
Hyping the certainty of scientific papers
Hyping the chain of inference that leads (or usually doesn't) from a statistical assessment to considerations of an individual
Hyping the clarity (in fact absent) in the links from genes to endophenotypes to phenotypes
Hyping the ethical concerns surrounding potential scientific and technological developments by omitting discussions of the positive ethical benefits
Hyping the importance of biomarkers by neglecting to inclusively consider other risk factors

No doubt some will plausibly argue that the competitive character of research encourages such hype, and certainly high-impact journals such as *Nature* need to be ever vigilant against overstated claims for the validity of biomarkers. What is more, despite many claims that multidisciplinary research needs encouragement, it has proved chronically difficult to bring the various disciplines together in a way that received due funding and due credit.

With these challenges in mind, this volume represents a valuable outcome of an admirably inclusive project.

Philip Campbell
Editor in Chief, *Nature*

REFERENCE

Guston, D. (2011). Participating despite questions: toward a more confident participatory technology assessment. *Science and Engineering Ethics*, *17*(4), 691–697.

CONTRIBUTORS

Mohammad R. Arbabshirani
The Mind Research Network,
Albuquerque, NM, USA
Department of ECE, University
of New Mexico, Albuquerque,
NM, USA

Matthew Baum
Oxford Centre for Neuroethics and
Oxford Uehiro Centre for Practical
Ethics, University of Oxford,
Oxford UK

Joshua W. Buckholtz
Department of Psychology, Harvard
University, Cambridge, MA, USA

Vince D. Calhoun
The Mind Research Network,
Albuquerque, NM, USA
Department of ECE, University
of New Mexico, Albuquerque,
NM, USA

Colin Campbell
Department of Forensic and
Neurodevelopmental Science,
Institute of Psychiatry, King's
College London, London, UK

John-Dylan Haynes
Bernstein Center for Computational
Neuroscience, Charité–
Universitätsmedizin, Berlin

Nigel Eastman
Emeritus Professor of Law and
Ethics in Psychiatry, St George's,
University of London, London, U.K.

Eamon McCrory
Reader in Developmental
Psychopathology, Consultant
Clinical Psychologist
Division of Psychology and Language
Sciences, University College,
London, UK

Andreas Meyer-Lindenberg
Central Institute of Mental Health,
Mannheim, Germany.
Department of Psychiatry and
Psychotherapy, University of
Heidelberg, Germany

John Monahan
University of Virginia School of Law,
Charlottesville, VA, USA

Michael Rutter
Centre for the History of Medicine,
University College, London, UK

Julian Savulescu
Oxford Centre for Neuroethics and
   Oxford Uehiro Centre for Practical
   Ethics, University of Oxford,
   Oxford UK

Ilina Singh
Department of Social Science,
   Health, and Medicine,
   King's College, London, UK

Walter P. Sinnott-Armstrong
Philosophy Department and
   Kenan Institute for Ethics, Duke
   University, Durham, NC, USA

Christopher Slobogin
Vanderbilt University Law School,
   Nashville, TN, USA

Essi Viding
Professor of Developmental
   Psychopathology
Division of Psychology and Language
   Sciences, University College,
   London, UK

Charlotte K. Walsh
School of Law, University of
   Leicester, UK

Paul Root Wolpe
Center for Ethics, Emory University,
   Atlanta, GA, USA

Introduction: Deviance, Classification, and Bioprediction

ILINA SINGH AND WALTER P. SINNOTT-ARMSTRONG

In August 2011, a Norwegian man, Anders Breivik, systematically planned attacks on government officials and a political youth group. He proceeded to execute 77 people, many of them teenagers tracked down and murdered at close range. Afterwards, there was much discussion of whether Breivik would be ruled insane. In pretrial hearings his demeanor was chillingly calm, even proud. He insisted that he was sane, and that his actions were intended.

Approximately 1 year later, a U.S. graduate student in neuroscience, James Holmes, systematically planned an attack on a local movie theater. He attended the midnight showing of a film, *The Dark Knight*, and opened fire from the front of the theater on the audience. Twelve people died. Again, there was much discussion afterwards about Holmes' sanity. However, in this case, by the time the court convened to set a trial date, there were already rumors of Holmes' gradual mental decline in the months before his murderous attack. At the court hearing, he looked bewildered and dazed.

After people do terrible things, energy focuses on *post hoc* explanations and assessments of the individual for purposes of punishment. For the moment, these assessments are still largely made using what some see as crude tools, including interviews with the person and reports from witnesses who observed the person's behavior during the crime and before. Rarely, but increasingly, scientific evidence in the form of biological assays, brain scans, and genetics penetrates the landscape of psychiatric and legal assessments to diagnose mental fitness, assess culpability, and ensure just punishment.

Now imagine that, instead of *post hoc* explanations, there was a robust and reliable scientific way to *predict* bad behavior of the sort that seriously violates social norms. If it were possible to take biological and social data points from individuals and calculate a risk for future antisocial or violent behavior, would it be a good idea to do so? In which cases? Who should be told about the risks? Which interventions are justified to minimize the risk that individuals are deemed to pose to society?

This book investigates how scientific evidence from brain scans, genetics, and other biological assays is likely to be used to diagnose and predict 'bad' behavior. We call this process 'bioprediction.' We focus on antisocial and violent behavior that is likely to result in criminal prosecution, on its theoretical precursors, and on a subset of mental disorders that can be—but are by no means inevitably— associated with an increased tendency to antisocial, criminal, or violent behavior. One set of chapters provides expert reviews of the state of the science in bioprediction of antisocial behavior and in diagnosis of mental disorders such as psychopathy and schizophrenia. Another set of chapters focuses on social, legal, and ethical analyses of the implications of translating the science into practice—in families, communities, clinics, schools, and courtrooms. These chapters simultaneously celebrate and interrogate scientific developments in bioprediction and serve as a reminder that these developments occur as part of a reciprocal relationship between science and those social institutions vested with the adjudication of morality and immorality, crime and punishment. It is this relationship that gives bioprediction its creative, material, and ethical force.

CLASSIFICATION OF BAD BEHAVIOR

Not all behaviors identified as 'bad' are as unambiguously awful as premeditated mass murder of innocent citizens. A book on bioprediction of bad behavior ought to consider how bad behaviors are identified, classified, and targeted as part of intersecting scientific, sociopolitical, and legal agendas. Indeed, a reader may have a reasonable concern about our emphasis on "bad behavior." This may indicate skepticism about the classification of deviant behaviors (a longstanding sociological concern) or a worry that biological evidence will be used to reify problematic classifications. We consider these to be important and relevant issues.

Classification of behaviors as deviant or criminal has shifted markedly over time and continues to vary significantly across different contexts. Marriage between persons of different races was once considered criminal behavior in the United States; sex acts associated with homosexuality are still outlawed in some areas; smoking, once a highly promoted social activity, is now illegal in public places in most Western countries.

Moreover, deviant behaviors are also symptoms in a mental illness classification system, such as the *Diagnostic and Statistical Manual of the American Psychological Association* (DSM) (APA, 2004). This method of classifying deviant behaviors has been criticized as a "medicalization" of deviance. Addiction serves as a useful current example. For a century or more, addicts were judged in moral terms and behaviors were thought to result from personally mutable traits, such as weak or bad character. In the intervening years, addictive behaviors have been increasingly linked to neuronal and genetic biomarkers. Today, the U.S. National Institute of Drug Addiction (NIDA) classifies addiction as a "chronic brain disease," and "addiction" is the preferred terminology (over "substance use disorder") for DSM 5 (O'Brien, 2011). This epistemological shift from "badness" to "sickness" has arisen in part from technological and scientific developments in genetics and neuroscience, including research into biomarkers.

These changing accounts of deviant behavior have significant social and economic consequences. When deviant behavior is classified under a contemporary DSM label, a gradual shift in the etiological narrative occurs, from an emphasis on the moral dimensions of the person to a focus on biological mechanisms and structures. DSM diagnoses have global impact in a way that moral accusations cannot: they inform public health models of well-being, in which mental disorders are viewed as "burdens" that carry significant social and economic costs. But a DSM diagnosis does not only provide a new means of classifying behavior; it is also meant to predict illness course and responsiveness to treatment. In an important sense, then, psychiatric diagnosis could be a useful form of bioprediction.

From this perspective, the classification of some deviant behaviors as mental disorders on the basis of valid evidence, and research into predictive biomarkers to aid in the diagnosis, treatment, and prevention of mental disorders, could be seen as straightforward goods. However, the significant scientific contestation over DSM classifications has recently come to a head in a statement by the Director of the National Institutes of Mental Health (NIMH) which declares that NIMH will move away from scientific research based on DSM categories, given their problematic validity (Insel, 2013). Indeed, in practice, DSM diagnosis of conditions that predict violent behavior is often problematic. Many of these conditions are ambiguously defined and differentiated and, hence, overdiagnosed in certain regions and in certain people and underdiagnosed in others. When this is coupled with the fact that violence statistics are often biased toward the poor and toward ethnic minorities, it becomes clear that the intersection of psychiatric classification and deviance does not make for morally neutral territory.

A further consequence of the move to classify deviant behaviors as psychiatric disorders is that it has become increasingly common to associate mental disorder with violent behavior. As we see in the two cases that open this chapter, the response to inexplicable violence by an individual is almost immediately to question both the actor's mental status at the time of the crime, and whether or not there is a longstanding but unrecognized mental illness. This easy connection between violent behavior and mental illness potentially increases the stigma of certain mental disorders, and indeed, the connection is reinforced in countless crime novels, films, and television shows. At the same time, it is in the public interest to know whether anyone could have predicted criminal behavior and prevented it. The "treatability" question—the extent to which the person's tendency to behave badly can be managed successfully with interventions—is answered in part by a valid diagnosis. Ideally, when we know enough, the diagnosis is supposed to tell us how the individual is likely to behave and what we can do about it.

CLASSIFICATION IN THE LAW

Some nonmedical classifications of 'bad behavior,' such as 'criminality' and 'violence,' are freed of these particular accusations. Criminal categories, such as first-degree murder, do not pretend to be predictions of future behavior. Instead, they are descriptions of past behavior. In addition, legal definitions of crimes refer to the agent's mental states but not to their biological features: the agent's brain, hormones, and heart rate are never mentioned in criminal codes. Thus, unlike medical categories, legal categories cannot be seen as a form of bioprediction.

Nonetheless, the law can use bioprediction at various points. Consider, for instance, sentencing (discussed by Slobogin in Chapter 5). If we could place convicted criminals into categories that reliably predict future criminal behavior, then we could prevent more crime at less cost by giving longer sentences to the dangerous few and shorter sentences to those who are not dangerous. The problem is to come up with such predictive categories. If such legal categories are overly inclusive and underly inclusive as well as ambiguously defined in the same way as psychiatric categories, then sentences based on such categories will not achieve their goals and could do much more harm than good. It is not clear whether science can help the law by constructing predictive categories that will be reliable enough.

BIOMARKERS AND BIOPREDICTION

We are not classificatory nihilists. We believe that the solution is not *no* classification but *better* classification. To the extent that bioprediction is developed and used appropriately, biology could help to deconstruct and to reorganize some of the classifications that have been based purely on behavior. If the science can be worked out, then it could lead to more accurate identification of persons at risk of unwanted social behavior, more accurate predictions of the behavior over the course of an individual's life and under different environmental conditions, and more targeted and effective interventions.

Of course, any system—medical, legal, educational, or otherwise—that classifies and predicts behavior needs to acknowledge that known biomarkers are probabilistic, not deterministic. Biological information is combined with social predictors in the hope that this will improve the overall risk algorithm. Indeed, rather than reasserting flawed hypotheses about genetically determined behaviors and traits, the probabilistic nature of biomarkers ideally encourages more systematic and more focused attention on environmental influences and gene–environment interactions. Moreover, epigenetic theory now suggests that this interplay between biomarkers and environmental factors is ongoing throughout the life of an individual and has heritable consequences.

The extraordinary complexity of the changing human organism over the life course is one of the reasons why the near future of biomarker research may be a period of more dark than light. Many scientists doubt that bioprediction of bad behavior can or should have translational impact in the near future. At the present time, most known biopredictors are weak, and bio-environmental pathways to bad behavioral outcomes are poorly understood. Both prediction and intervention are ill advised in such an uncertain landscape. Moreover, it is important to remember that the science of bioprediction is, like the science of risk assessment, founded upon population statistics. Statistical methods that are designed to predict what will happen on average in certain populations under certain conditions generally do not provide a good idea of what will happen for a given individual. However, new techniques bring new possibilities. Some statisticians are optimistic about the use of such tools as pattern classifiers and independent components analysis to predict individual responses. Some of these new methods are explained and explored in this volume (see Chapter 12).

CATEGORIES OF PERSONS AND THE APPLICATION OF BIOPREDICTION SCIENCE

Despite the significant problems outlined above, it is likely that the hoped-for developments in scientific understanding of biomarkers will eventually have significant consequences for efforts to predict bad behavior. These uses of bioprediction are targeted at four distinct (but not exclusive or exhaustive) categories of persons. Predicting who will *develop* bad behavior applies to persons who currently display limited or no bad behaviors, so they are innocent.

The second category includes persons who are already entangled in the legal system; or if we imagine the commercial use of predictive biomarkers, individuals who are guilty of transgressions that are not illegal but are nonetheless painful to others, such as infidelity to a spouse. Third is a category of individuals whose current behavior and/or cognitive profile indicates a higher level of risk of future antisocial or criminal behavior. Such individuals might be targeted as part of screening or prevention initiatives. An important fourth category, of course, involves persons who are evaluated for a psychiatric diagnosis. As we argued above, a psychiatric diagnosis is, ideally, a form of bioprediction, and psychiatric evaluations will benefit from the addition of biomarker information. Thus, we have four targets of bioprediction: the *innocent,* the *marked,* the *guilty,* and the *patient.* These categories indicate particular scientific, social, and ethical concerns that warrant some discussion here as an introduction to the chapters in this volume.

The innocent

In the online forum that accompanied the deliberations over diagnostic categories in DSM 5, there was much disagreement over the proposal for a new category, initially called "psychosis risk syndrome." After fiery real and virtual discussions, the DSM Psychotic Disorders Workgroup decided to change the name of the proposed category to "attenuated psychosis syndrome." The difference in nomenclature is important: psychosis risk syndrome was a category defined purely by *risk*; an individual need not have had any current clinical need or symptoms to receive a diagnosis. The definition of attenuated risk syndrome is, by contrast, "a condition with recent onset of modest, psychotic-like symptoms and clinically relevant distress and disability." The working group goes on to say:

> Based on a review of the data relatively early in the process, it was realized that it may be premature to recommend a new category primarily based on future risk (i.e., "Psychosis Risk Syndrome") and not on current clinical need. We recognized that a majority of individuals with this condition did *not* go on to develop a psychotic disorder and that most individuals with this condition had additional relevant clinical needs other than risk of conversion to psychosis.

> http://www.dsm5.org/proposedRevisions/Pages/
> proposedrevision.aspx?rid=412# accessed October 20, 2012

The example of psychosis risk syndrome identifies an important goal for the psychiatric profession: reliable risk assessment at the presymptomatic stage for future psychotic behavior in an individual. Attenuated psychosis syndrome is the penultimate step, when symptoms are at a low level, sufficient to make a diagnosis and to start interventions. Both of these disorders are part of an intense focus in psychiatry and public policy alike on identification of prodromal stages of mental disorders, intervention, and prevention.

Prodromal categories cannot strictly be called a diagnosis: symptoms are ambiguous or absent; and, as the psychosis workgroup states, course and outcome at this stage are not predictable. Even if the prodrome can be justified within a psychiatric classification system, there are numerous social and ethical concerns that arise from its use. Perhaps the stickiest problem is that the prodrome might be used as justification for what we might call 'womb management.' Technically, the presence of predictive biomarkers on a genetic test performed on an embryo could be interpreted as a sufficient "mark" of a prodromal stage of a disorder. Despite all the requisite cautions, it is likely that a significant proportion of parents-to-be will seek out biomarker risk information for highly stigmatized disorders. For example, despite scientific reservations, a biomarker-based screen, chromosomal microarray (CME), is now commercially available in America and has been publicized as a genetic test for autism (Walsh et al., 2011). Clinics report that the test is requested even by parents who carry no risk factors for autism. Such parental decisions, while they may be troubling to some, are at least free decisions (insofar as social norms allow parents to make free decisions about their offspring). Embryonic testing for biomarkers for bad behavior becomes much more problematic if it is coerced or made compulsory by the state, employers, insurers, or other institutions.

If bioprediction at a prodromal stage becomes possible, which interventions are justified? Several authors in this volume discuss the polymorphism MAOA-L (monoamine oxidase A, low repeat), a variant shown to correlate with antisocial behavior in adults who have a history of maltreatment in childhood. This correlation has been validated in several high-quality scientific studies, leading some observers to suggest that genetic testing should be used to identify those fetuses and children who may carry the relevant genetic and environmental risk factors. In Chapter 2 Baum and Savulescu carefully dissect the ethics of different potential uses of biomarkers, using MAOA-L as a case study. Their discussion considers interventions in those found to be at high risk of later antisocial behavior, including genetic enhancement and early removal of a child from an abusive family. While Baum and Savulescu are relatively optimistic that some uses of biomarkers like MAOA-L at the prodromal stage are ethical, Charlotte Walsh, in Chapter 3, is more critical of efforts to use biomarkers to predict antisocial and criminal behavior in young people. She notes that it has long been known that abusive conditions in early childhood negatively affect a child's development, and she argues that social exclusion and social inequities are more ethically urgent and more reliable predictors of child maltreatment and a criminal career than biomarkers.

These chapters suggest that whether social indicators, biological indicators, or a combination of the two are used to predict risk of antisocial and criminal behavior in young people, much thought still needs to be given to how this risk is managed at the level of social policy.

The guilty

The predictive power of biomarkers rises sharply if they are applied not to the general population but only to people who have already behaved badly. When the prevalence or base rate of a condition, such as violent behavior, is low enough, then even a very sensitive and specific test will yield an unacceptably large number of false positives. This lesson is taught by Bayes' theorem. Nonetheless, the same test can have much greater predictive power when applied only to a population with a higher prevalence or base rate. That is why an independent second medical test can be useful in confirming an initial screening test or in diagnosis when symptoms are present. The same calculations show that the biopredictors can have much greater predictive value when used not in the general population but only among those who have already been convicted of bad behavior—namely, the guilty. Their past bad behavior puts them in a special category of people who have a higher likelihood of future bad behavior. When used within such a category, a biopredictor may become a more reliable means of predicting future bad behavior.

Of course, no test will be perfect, so society needs to ask how many mistakes and which kinds of mistakes it is willing to live with. That depends, among other things, on the benefits and the costs of bioprediction. In the case of predicting violent crime, the benefits include prevention of devastating losses. Potential future victims, even if nameless, have lots to gain from accurate bioprediction. The costs, however, are also great when bioprediction is not accurate, because then criminals will be confined or restricted more than is needed. These people are guilty, but it is still clearly very undesirable to deprive them of freedom more than necessary.

The legal system faces this challenge at several points. Courts need to decide how much to sentence people after conviction. This decision is sometimes made at least partly on the basis of a prediction of how dangerous it will be to release them back into the public after a number of years in prison. Similarly, courts also need to determine who should receive probation. This assessment is made at least partly on the basis of which defendants will misbehave if released on probation. Again, if convicted defendants are sent to prison, then prison officials need to sort inmates into security levels on the basis of how they are likely to behave in prison. Then, when their sentences near the end, parole boards need to predict who is safe to release. Even after a full sentence is served, some courts have the power to order civil commitment as preventive detention. In all of these cases, the law bases decisions on predictions, so bioprediction might seem to be useful if it is workable and more accurate than current alternatives.

Several of these potential applications of bioprediction are discussed in this volume. Monahan (Chapter 4) focuses on civil commitment. Slobogin (Chapter 5) discusses bioprediction as a basis for sentencing. Then Campbell and Eastman (Chapter 6) survey the dangers of bioprediction in law, with some special attention to preventive detention. Wolpe (Chapter 7), in a more general critique of the ethics of biologically based approaches to criminal justice, points out that a system of early identification and preventive interventions in young people on the basis of bioprediction models may lead to a "self-fulfilling prophecy." Both labeling theory and the statistics on reoffending among those who enter the juvenile justice system suggest that criminality is a learned social behavior as well as having a biological dimension.

Monahan and Slobogin are more optimistic than Campbell, Eastman, and Wolpe, but they all recognize that bioprediction in criminal law could be useful if accurate and properly applied but also could become disastrous if abused.

Together these chapters discuss many of the benefits and costs—as well as scientific uncertainties—of various uses of bioprediction of bad behavior among the guilty.

The marked

If bioprediction can be said to be more useful in a population of individuals already convicted of a crime, then perhaps it can be hypothesized to be useful, too, in specified groups of individuals whose current socially aberrant behaviors are not at the level of criminality, but whose behavioral or cognitive profile is associated with future risk of dangerousness or criminality. What if, through testing or screening, some of these individuals are found to carry biomarkers associated with a higher risk of developing future antisocial or violent behavior? For some of our scientific authors, a primary question in such cases of "marked" individuals is whether the science is ready for translation into public use. The MAOA variant makes another appearance in Chapter 8, by Buckholtz and Meyer-Lindenberg, who systematically analyze the state of the science and argue strongly against the use of MAOA as a predictive biomarker in the public domain, at the present time. The authors emphasize the problem of making "person-level inferences" from population-level data, suggesting that the use of biomarkers to manage individuals is a "misapplication" of science. Viding and McCrory (Chapter 9) are also cautious about the translation of research on children with callous and unemotional traits (CU traits) into the law and into policy. However, they are optimistic that better understanding of the mechanisms underlying the development of CU traits will eventually translate into environmental interventions aimed at prevention. Another area in which there is a great deal of public interest is the potential to identify individuals whose *thoughts* indicate the risk of future violent behaviors. Dylan-Haynes (Chapter 10) describes scientific progress in "mind-reading," or the identification of neural patterns associated with intentions, of which individuals may or may not be aware. Mind-reading is posited as a technology with potential applications in national security contexts (e.g., airport screening); however, Dylan-Haynes notes the careful, precise, and subtle scientific investigations required to understand the cognitive architecture of intentionality and its relationship to action. Collectively this set of chapters suggests that it will be some time yet before we have robust and reliable neurobiological models of intentionality and antisocial behavior.

The patients

A good deal of research into predictive biomarkers has involved patient populations, with the goal of better identification, management, and treatment of mental illness and prevention of future mental illness. As we noted above, diagnosis of mental illness interacts in complicated ways with the assessment and management of bad behavior, such that developments in understanding biomarkers for some mental illness conditions would likely have significant implications both for societal programs of treatment and intervention into antisocial and criminal behavior, as well as for the law. Several years ago it was hoped that DSM 5 would be based around biomarkers, at least for some conditions. As Michael Rutter notes in Chapter 11, however, diagnosis of psychiatric illnesses based on biomarker evidence is still in its infancy, despite a good deal of research in this area. Investigation of psychiatric biomarkers has been akin to unraveling a knot made up of many subtly different colored strings: one promising biomarker turns out to be tangled up in the operations of a series of biomarkers, each of which have differential effects depending on how the system is organizing itself at a particular moment. Rutter's careful analysis of these technical as well as theoretical problems suggests that biomarker science will not be much help in the near future in making predictions of which individuals may go on to commit antisocial or violent crimes as a consequence of mental illness.

However, Calhoun and Arbabshirani end this volume on a more positive note, at least in relation to the potential of biomarker science to aid predictions of certain kinds of mental illness. They review research that uses machine learning and pattern recognition techniques to automatically classify schizophrenia patients. They are optimistic that biomarker-based diagnostic techniques could be clinically applicable, particularly in relation to the ability to identify subtypes of disease. As schizophrenia is, like most other psychiatric disorders, a complex, heterogeneous condition, the identification of subtypes would allow better understanding of illness course and, therefore, a more robust assessment of whether a person may go on to develop violent behaviors of the sort associated with some types of schizophrenia.

CONCLUSION

Much scientific work remains to be done in the area of predictive biomarkers, but this is not a reason to be complacent about its impact on and translation into the public domain. Public engagement should not lag behind in a scientific area that intersects with, and creates significant challenges to, collective democratic values of citizenship, justice, and well-being. Indeed, in putting together this collection we noted the lack of social science research among stakeholders likely to be affected by such technologies; for example, persons with mental illness diagnoses, those in the adult criminal system, and families and young people in the juvenile system. We also noted, alongside a good deal of media hype, a lack of sustained public dialog around justified uses of bioprediction technologies. We hope that this volume will inspire research, public conversation, and interdisciplinary engagements that shape the sociopolitical and legal landscapes into which bioprediction technologies are integrated, thus promoting responsible and ethical translation of these technologies into the public domain.

REFERENCES

American Psychiatric Association. (2000). *Diagnostic and statistical manual of mental disorders* (4th ed., text rev.). Washington, DC: Author.

Insel, T. (2013). Transforming Diagnosis. *NIMH Director's Blog* 29 April. http://www.nimh.nih.gov/about/director/index.shtml. Accessed 16 May 2013.

O'Brien, C. (2011). Addiction and dependence in DSM-V. *Addiction, 106*(5), 866–867.

Walsh, P., Elsabbagh, M., Bolton, P., & Singh, I. (2011). In search of biomarkers for autism: Scientific, policy and ethical challenges. *Nature Reviews Neuroscience, 12,* 603–612.

2

Behavioral Biomarkers: What Are They Good For?

Toward the Ethical Use of Biomarkers

MATTHEW BAUM AND JULIAN SAVULESCU

A technology that better predicts human behavior is a powerful tool. Increasingly, knowledge from biology and neuroscience allows us to identify biological states that are predictive, but not determinative, of human behavior in certain situations. These are called biomarkers of behavior.

Biomarkers range from metabolites, protein levels, and genetic variants to brain states and can target varied behaviors. We will focus on the MAOA gene × environment interaction and its use as a biomarker to predict criminally aggressive behavior. Only when a certain genetic variant is combined with childhood maltreatment is there an increase in the likelihood of future aggression. We choose the MAOA biomarker as an example because the science is comparatively well developed and the predicted behavior is socially undesired. Though we primarily discuss MAOA, we do so with the aim of highlighting ethical issues relevant also to other biomarkers; for example, biomarkers of susceptibility to posttraumatic stress disorder (PTSD) in soldiers.

Using MAOA as a case study, we ask how such behavioral biomarkers can ethically be used. We group potentially justifiable uses into four rough classes: (1) for the benefit of both the person with the biomarker and for others; (2) for the benefit of the person with the biomarker with acceptable costs to others; (3) for the benefit of others with no harm to the person with the biomarker; and (4) for the benefit of others with acceptable costs to the person with the biomarker. In discussing these categories, we touch on uses of a biomarker to minimize exposure of susceptible children to maltreatment, to allocate social services, to mitigate punishment in the justice system, to make reproductive choices, and to influence public health.

But first, it is important to embed bioprediction within its historical context and to review the relevant science of MAOA as a biomarker.

THE HISTORICAL CONTEXT AND SCIENCE OF MAOA AS A BIOMARKER[1]

The use of biomarkers of undesirable behavior has a tawdry history.

Lombroso: an early attempt to establish biomarkers of criminality

To [...] decide whether there is a force in nature that causes crime, we must [...] proceed to the direct physical and psychological study of the criminal, comparing the results with information on the healthy [.] (Author's preface, in Lombroso, Gibson, and Rafter, 2006, p. 44)

This was Cesare Lombroso's aim when, in 1876, he published *L'Uomo Deliquente* (*The Criminal Man*) (Lombroso, Gibson, & Rafter, 2006). This first "empirical" theory of the biology of criminal behavior became famous for the argument that some criminals were "born criminals" and could be identified by their enrichment in "primitive" or "atavistic" physical features—jug ears, cranial structure, jutting jaw, skin wrinkles, nose size, etc. But more relevant for the aims of this paper are the two thirds of criminals who, according to Lombroso, were not "born criminal." The "criminaloid," for example, possessed fewer physical features of criminality and consequently had a predisposition toward crime that could be activated by adverse environments (Lombroso, Gibson, & Rafter, 2006), an idea that on surface resembles biomarkers of behavior. Lombroso's early claims about atavistic traits as biomarkers, however, radically overstepped scientific support, echoed racist stereotypes, and fell out of favor.

The shadow of eugenics

Many would soon come to think that where Lombroso failed, the fledgling science of heredity could succeed. From the late 19th century until after the Second World War, the eugenics movement in Europe and North America aimed to apply the new science of heredity to enhancement of the genetic pool. Eugenicists argued that they knew enough to predict the undesirable behavior of future generations based on the traits of potential parents and that action based on this information was warranted. Eugenic policy encouraged those judged to have a good genetic constitution to reproduce (positive eugenics) and discouraged the "genetically unfit" from reproducing (negative eugenics). Much of negative eugenics was geared toward those believed to be at risk of passing on criminality, psychiatric disease, and mental retardation.

Again, racist and other stereotypes spread and sustained bad science behind the eugenics movement. One chart at a Kansas Free Fair, typical for the time, read: "Unfit human traits such as feeblemindedness, epilepsy, criminality, insanity, alcoholism, pauperism and many others run in families and are inherited in exactly the same way as color in guinea pigs" (Kevles, 1985). It is now hard to imagine how people ever believed such claims.

Even more surprising is the influence of similar claims beyond the fairgrounds. In the United States, the first eugenic sterilization law was passed in Indiana in 1907. By 1917, 15 more states had passed legislation in favor of sterilization of the "feebleminded," "habitual or confirmed criminals, or persons guilty of some particular offense, like rape" (Savulescu, 2001b). Although these laws were challenged, they were unambiguously supported in *Buck v. Bell* (1927) by the Supreme Court. Justice Holmes, presiding, concluded, "It is better for all the world if, instead of waiting to execute degenerate offspring for crime or to let them starve for their imbecility, society can prevent those who are manifestly unfit from continuing their kind." (274 U.S. 200, LII, accessed 2012).

It is sobering to remember that influential intellectuals at the time not only aligned themselves with this eugenics movement, but also believed it to be progressing carefully and in accord with evidence. In a speech to the Eugenics Council during the interwar period, Yale psychologist Robert Yerkes claimed that "one of the most encouraging features of this modern movement for racial improvement is the insistence by its leaders upon the need for a thorough investigation of the facts of human heredity and the relations of means to ends." Later he argued that "the safe development of eugenics is indeed assured by this insistence that we should not let application outstrip knowledge" (Robert Means Yerkes Papers [MS 569]).

But application *did* outstrip knowledge. Eugenics was to become an important tool in the Nazi program of racial purification and extermination.

Modern efforts

In light of the dark past of behavioral genetics, many continue to question whether there will ever be any correlation between genes and complex behaviors such as criminality. Criminality is, as we have seen, a socially and historically relative concept. We raise this history not to suggest that knowledge of genetics cannot ever be used, but rather how important it is that we think and debate deeply the ethics of the new, more scientifically supported behavioral biomarkers.

As the functions of the roughly 30,000 human genes are identified, we may see that certain genetic mutations or polymorphisms (variants) will make it more likely that certain behaviors occur. This possibility becomes more realistic when we break free of simple genetic determinist thinking, begin to think probabilistically, and separate complex behavior into lower-level related components rather than looking simply for "the gene for criminality." Even Lombroso differentiated among the types of crime; he posited different biological factors for murderers and thieves, for example. Increasing understanding of epigenetics (how different environments can lead to chemical modifications of genes and thereby change how and when the genes are expressed) reinforces the importance of context.

One area that has received increasing attention and that is taking a sophisticated, nuanced approach is bioprediction of violent behavior. By violent behavior, we mean impulsive violence produced in reaction to anger, irritation, threat, etc. We will sometimes call this "aggression" as shorthand. Although this type of violence can be socially accepted, as it is in self-defense (a reaction to a perceived threat), it is most often both socially unacceptable and criminal. It is also an important social problem: according to a World Health Organization estimate, 560,000 people die in a single year due to homicide (more than one person each minute you spend reading this chapter) (Brown et al., 2007). Most of these homicides represent impulsive, not premeditated, violence (Siever, 2008); premeditated violence will not be discussed here. It is important to remember that in each case of loss of life, the effects also tear through friends, families, and communities.

A case study of a rare familial genetic variant associated with violence

Early modern evidence that genetic variation can predispose to undesirable behavior is provided in the extreme case of a Dutch family (Brunner et al., 1993a, 1993b, see also ch. 8 of this volume). For over 30 years, this family recognized that a disproportionate number of males in the maternal family line exhibited aggressive behavior. This behavior was extreme, characterized by violent outbursts, arson, attempted rape, and exhibitionism (Brunner et al., 1993b). Brunner, the scientist who worked with the family, noted that the "aggressive behavior was usually triggered by anger and was often out of proportion to the provocation." For example, one "affected male tried to run over his boss with a car at the sheltered workshop where he was employed, after having been told that his work was not up to par" (Brunner et al., 1993b, 1035).

None of the women, however, and only roughly half of the men of the maternal family line exhibited such behavior. Male relatives who did not display this aggressive behavior did not express any type of abnormal behavior and reported difficulty understanding the criminal behavior of their brothers and cousins. An unaffected maternal grandfather, for example, was so perplexed that he documented the behavior for almost 40 years. Sisters of the males who demonstrated these aggressive outbursts reported intense fear of their brothers.

What was going on? The behavior appeared unrelated to environment, social context, or degree of social contact and appeared throughout the branches of the maternal line. Whatever it was, it was more complex than just the aggression. All affected males were also mildly mentally retarded, with a typical IQ of about 85 (females had normal intelligence). When a family tree was constructed to systematically investigate the pattern of inheritance, the aberrant behavior was clearly X-linked recessive. This means, roughly, that the behavior is associated with gene variants on the X chromosome, and one needs only one normally functioning copy to avoid the condition. Because females inherit one X chromosome from each parent (two total), the women in this family always inherited one normal X chromosome from the parent who married into the family and consequently were never affected. Women can carry one copy of the genetic variant without being affected, but still pass the variant to children; these women are called carriers. Since males inherit only one X chromosome (from the mother), roughly half of the sons of a carrier would inherit the dysfunctional variant and exhibit the disordered behavior, while the other half would inherit the normally functioning variant and be unaffected. Since most of the sons on the maternal side of this Dutch family came from such carrier mothers, roughly half of males were affected but none of the females.

Genetic analysis suggested dysfunction in the MAO region of the X chromosome. The MAO region codes for two enzymes, MAOA and MAOB, which assist in the breakdown of monoamine neurotransmitters. Neurotransmitters are substances that play a key role in the communication of signals in our brains. Monoamine neurotransmitters are a subset of neurotransmitters that include serotonin, dopamine, and norepinephrine. Urinalysis showed a higher-than-normal amount of molecules normally eliminated (broken down) by MAO and a lower-than-normal amount of the products from the breakdown activity MAO being excreted in the urine of affected males, results consistent with reduced functioning of one of the enzymes. Follow-up enzymatic activity tests showed that lack of function was specific to MAOA (Brunner et al., 1993b).

With molecular techniques, Brunner et al. (1993a) found that a single nucleotide (the coded building blocks of DNA) was changed from a C to a T at the 936th base pair in the MAOA genetic sequence of affected males; this mutation led to the premature termination of the MAOA protein during synthesis such that affected males completely lacked functional MAOA protein. This is called a "nonsense mutation." This was the first evidence of a strong association between disruption of a single gene and aggressive behavior in humans.

MAOA's primary role is in degradation of the neurotransmitter serotonin (although it also degrades to a lesser extent noradrenaline and dopamine). Since lower levels of the serotonin degradation product, 5-HIAA, in the cerebrospinal fluid have been previously associated with impulsive violence (not premeditated violence) (Coccaro, 1989, 52–62), dysregulation of serotonin degradation in these Dutch men was a potential model for their violent behavior. Also, mice genetically engineered to lack MAOA protein have been shown to have decreased serotonin turnover, increased levels of serotonin, and increased aggression (Buckholtz & Meyer-Lindenberg, 2008, 120–129). A role in aggression for the MAOA gene, because it is X-linked, also suggested a potential explanation for the increased aggression in men.

Not by genes alone: common variation in MAOA and a gene × environment interaction

The Dutch family's MAOA mutation was found to be exceedingly rare and thus of limited use for bioprediction of aggressive behavior in the general population. Certain less-extreme variations in MAOA were soon discovered to be common in the general population. People vary in the number of trains of a repeated nucleotide sequence they have in the gene's promoter, the region that controls transcription; this variation is called a variable number tandem repeat (VNTR). Approximately 30 percent of the MAOA alleles (gene copies) contain three repeats and 65 percent contain four (Kim-Cohen et al., 2006). Because in vitro studies suggested that the variant with three repeats is less efficiently expressed than the variant with four repeats (Caspi et al., 2002, 851–854), the three-repeat variant became referred to as MAOA-low (MAOA-L) and the four-repeat as MAOA-high (MAOA-H), a terminology we adopt here.

Caspi et al. (2002) were the first to investigate the hypothesis that MAOA-L would correlate with antisocial behavior. They followed at regular intervals 1,037 New Zealand male children as they grew to 26 years of age. The children spanned the range of socioeconomic diversity in their home of Dunedin, New Zealand. Antisocial behavior was estimated using third-party reports of antisocial personality disorder symptoms, psychological assessment of violence acceptance, diagnosis of conduct disorder, and convictions related to violent crime.

Neither MAOA-L nor MAOA-H correlated significantly with later antisocial behavior alone. Childhood maltreatment did correlate (8 percent of boys experienced severe maltreatment and 23 percent probable maltreatment between ages 3 to 11), but this was unsurprising as the maltreatment effect was concordant with previous research.

A deeply surprising result emerged when the maltreated boys were further grouped according to MAOA variant. Childhood maltreatment had its expected increase in risk of later antisocial behavior in boys who possessed the MAOA-L variant, but maltreated boys with MAOA-H were not statistically more likely to exhibit future antisocial behavior than boys who were not maltreated. Maltreatment significantly predisposed the boys to later antisocial behavior *if and only if* they possessed MAOA-L. If the boys were not maltreated, genotype had no effect.

While only 12 percent of the boys possessed the MAOA-L genotype AND were maltreated (or probably maltreated), this small group was responsible for 44 percent of convictions for violent crime. The authors point out that the effect size was similar in magnitude to "major risk factors associated with cardiovascular disease" (Caspi et al., 2002, 854). This was the first case of violent behavior correlating with a gene × environment interaction.

The gene × environment interaction remained after controlling for several confounding variables, such as IQ and socioeconomic status (Caspi et al., 2002, 851–854). Because the aggressive males in the Dutch family had low IQ, and low IQ had previously been linked with aggression (Lynam, Moffitt, & Stouthamer-Loeber, 1993), an IQ effect was particularly important to investigate. Although there *was* a significant association between low IQ and antisocial behavior in these boys (suggesting a role for IQ *in general*), low IQ was *not* significantly associated with genotype alone or maltreatment combined with genotype, suggesting it did not explain the gene × environment interaction. Moreover, possessing the MAOA-L genotype did not predispose the boys to receive maltreatment. Rather, MAOA-L seemed to increase susceptibility to the effect of maltreatment on antisocial behavior, while MAOA-H protected against it.

In follow-up studies to Caspi (2002), some groups confirmed the interaction while others failed to find it (Taylor & Kim-Cohen, 2007). To address these conflicting results, two key papers (Kim-Cohen et al., 2006; Taylor & Kim-Cohen, 2007) pooled data from up to eight studies to increase statistical power and worked to standardize their variables to conduct a meta-analysis (an analysis of previous analyses). Such a strategy allows one to better test whether different results were due to sample size (low statistical power) or different definitions (of target group, aggression, maltreatment, etc.). It also allows differential weighting of effect size according to the quality of data. Importantly, MAOA-L gene × environment predisposition to aggressive behavior continued to be seen even after the data were subjected to these meta-analyses (Kim-Cohen et al., 2006; Taylor & Kim-Cohen, 2007). That the interaction persisted is important and surprising, as other gene × environment interactions in behavioral genetics lost statistical significance when similarly analyzed.[2]

This population genetics and statistical work stimulated work in cognitive and molecular neuroscience, some of which we will discuss later.

ETHICAL USE OF THE MAOA BIOMARKER

How should the MAOA biomarker be used? Through human history, alleged biomarkers, like those identified by Lombroso, have been uniformly abused to inflict harm and loss of liberty on innocent people. However, that need not be so.

The first step toward ethical use of biomarkers is to ensure that good scientific research establishes a reliable probabilistic relationship between the marker and behavior, in a given set of environmental and social circumstances. There have been noticeable mathematical methodological advancements in statistical validation of biomarkers in other fields of medicine that may be helpful in biomarkers of behavior (Buyse et al., 2010; Weir & Walley, 2006). We focus on the ethical issues assuming a validated probabilistic biomarker or set of biomarkers.[3] Our aim is to use the MAOA gene × environment interaction as an illustrative case study for the ethical use of a broader set of biomarkers. For the purposes of the initial discussion that follows, we will imagine the case where many of the questions and uncertainties remaining about MAOA have been resolved; several important caveats will be raised later in this chapter (see also Chapter 8 of this volume, where Buckholtz & Meyer-Lindenberg stress, e.g., that the use of MAOA *geneotypes alone* for bioprediction of aggression is not supported by sound data; and Zammit et al. 2010, 65–68 for other limitations).

We propose that there are good moral reasons to pursue the use of biomarkers for the following general applications:

1. For the benefit of both the person with the biomarker and for others
2. For the benefit the person with the biomarker, with acceptable costs to others
3. For the benefit of others, with no harm to the person with the biomarker
4. For the benefit of others, with acceptable costs to the person with the biomarker

Some specific applications of biomarkers will be appropriately controversial. That there will be disagreement, however, does not mean that we should abandon using biomarkers in all circumstances. In what follows, we flag cases in each of the four categories above that might, with the proper moral deliberation, be candidates for the moral use of biomarkers of behavior (Table 2.1).[4]

Table 2.1 Possible Cases for Children with MAOA-L

Case 1	Higher priority for child protection services (lower threshold to send a social worker to investigate the household situation)
Case 2	Earlier removal from abusive households into foster or adoptive care
Case 3	Harsher punishments for those who knowingly maltreat a child with MAOA-L
Case 4	Priority placement with specially trained foster caregivers
Case 5	Free provision of mindfulness training, omega-3 fatty acid dietary supplementation, or self-control tutoring

Biomarkers for the benefit of the person with the biomarker and for others: early identification, prevention of maltreatment, and provision of social care

ALLOCATION OF RESOURCES THAT HAVE CERTAIN BENEFITS, BUT ALSO RISK OF HARM

Prioritized child protection to prevent or minimize maltreatment

The UN Convention on Rights of the Child specifies that no child should experience maltreatment. Following this belief, many societies have established structures and social services to minimize the occurrence of maltreatment. These include social surveillance and, if necessary, removal of a child to foster or adoptive care. These services, however, are chronically underfunded and have limited resources.[5] They cannot practically keep an eye out for all at-risk children. Importantly, these services themselves are not unambiguously beneficial; rather, they have significant risks for child and family. Surveillance and removal from abusive households, for example, can disrupt and fragment the family.

One of the assumptions embedded in child protection services is that abuse and maltreatment have similar effects on all children regardless of their genetics or other features specific to them. The research on the MAOA biomarker challenges that assumption by suggesting that abuse or maltreatment leads to a predisposition toward aggression, primarily in children with MAOA-L variants. Thus, if the risk/benefit ratio of these social services is justified in part because of the possible enormous cost to the well-being of children of later being imprisoned, then long-term considerations of child welfare are likely to prioritize the treatment of children with the MAOA-L variant.[6] Note that one need not make the controversial claim that social costs should be included in the cost/benefit analysis, but only that the future well-being of a child should be included; however, if one *were* to consider the potential benefit to society, given the association of abuse with antisocial behavior, this would further shift the risk/benefit ratio further toward prioritizing MAOA-L.

If there is a higher risk of harm from non-intervention in one group and a lower risk in the other, then the current threshold level of maltreatment used to deem intervention justifiable might be too high for MAOA-L and too low for MAOA-H. If the MAOA variant were known, therefore, it would be especially important to follow children with MAOA-L to identify early abuse or deprivation and to correct this through social means. Such children could be placed at a higher priority for child protection. This might translate into early removal from abusive households into foster or adoptive care. MAOA-H children, more resilient to this particular effect of maltreatment, may conversely be prioritized for slower-acting, "riskier" interventions to improve the family situation, rather than removal to care. Some data suggest that the resulting predisposition to antisocial behavior might be proportional to the severity and duration of the exposure to the adverse environment rather than an all-or-nothing situation (Tremblay & Szyf, 2010; Weder et al., 2009), but further research is needed. If a single episode of abuse can reliably predispose a child to antisocial behavior, for example, then prevention rather than removal at first exposure would be necessary.

Enhanced responsibility

While all child abuse or maltreatment harms the child, the MAOA story suggests that different children react in different ways. When the child has the MAOA-L variant, there is a risk of harm to others, due to the predisposition to impulsive aggression, that is not created if the child has the MAOA-H variant. Thus, the harm an abusing parent causes is not only to his child but also potentially to society, insofar as others are put at increased risk of harm due to the resulting predisposition in the child. Punishment could take some account of these "follow-on" harms of child abuse.

One possibility is to amend legislation and/or child protection services procedures to make it clear that someone who knowingly maltreats a child with MAOA-L will be punished more harshly. While the requirement that the abuser know the status of the child avoids objections from procedural unfairness, it also creates a moral hazard: purposeful ignorance to avoid punishment. The moral hazard could be constrained if someone (the child, social services, relatives, etc.) knew and informed the potential abuser of the MAOA status. Since the MAOA-L variant is very common, however, it might be possible to avoid both the objections from procedural unfairness and those from moral hazard by making it clear that any case of abuse risks (in about 1 out of 3 cases) harsher punishment if the child does happen to be MAOA-L; such a strategy would be similar to holding someone responsible for reasonably foreseeable but unintended consequences[7] and have the add-on benefit of discouraging maltreatment of any child.

Mitigation of effects of maltreatment

After suspected abuse or maltreatment, MAOA genotyping could be used to help decide how to distribute social services and foster care, and to decide what type of care to provide. A maltreated child with MAOA-L might benefit from a foster caregiver with special training to deal appropriately with impulsive, aggressive behavior (i.e., mindfulness training etc.), while such a specially trained caregiver may not benefit a child with MAOA-H to the same extent.

While it would be ideal if all children enjoyed an adequate upbringing, and we should certainly aim for that, social support services are a limited resource. The dual importance of protecting the child and future others may justify granting priority to the social support of children at higher risk of becoming aggressive under conditions of deprivation.

Special provision of resources that are recommended for everyone

Perhaps one of the most uncontroversial uses of the MAOA biomarker would be in the distribution of resources that are both (1) recommended for everyone to promote health *and* (2) potentially useful in the prevention or amelioration of impulsive aggression. For example, mindfulness training, which helps individuals recognize and manage emotional impulses and stress, is being recommended for general use in schools to deal with life stresses (Williams & Penman, 2011) but also shows promise specifically for helping individuals deal with violent impulses (Wright, Day, & Howells, 2009). Omega-3 fatty acids (found in oily fish) are recommended for general healthy brain development and for heart health, but they similarly show potential for specifically addressing aggression (Hibbeln, Ferguson, & Blasbalg, 2006).

Other techniques for self-control/impulse control could also be taught and tested. One of us (Savulescu) has previously argued that self-control is an "all-purpose" good, a capacity that can help one achieve one's goals in life no matter what those goals are (Savulescu, 2012). The psychology of self-control is generating strategies for enhancing self-control (Baumeister, Vohs, & Tice, 2007).

In each of these cases, the resource—mindfulness training, omega-3 fatty acid supplementation, or self-control tutoring—would be beneficial to anyone. Usually, however, none of them is provided by a social service; there would be reason to subsidize or provide such resources to those at social risk.

Resources not currently provided: tailored pharmacological treatment

Novel strategies for preventing the development of impulsive violent patterns of behavior should be pursued, as evidence accumulates for their effectiveness.

More detailed understanding of the neuropharmacology of the MAOA-L variant opens the door to the development of tailored pharmacological interventions.

For example, one group showed that high testosterone levels may interact with the MAOA-L variant to predispose to aggression, raising the possibility of pharmaceutically disrupting that interaction (Ducci & Goldman, 2008). High testosterone levels correlated with antisocial personality disorder and aggression in males who also possessed MAOA-L, but not those with MAOA-H. Moreover, the group showed that (1) testosterone and glucocorticoids (stress hormones) compete for binding to certain sequences in the MAOA gene promoter region called "response elements" to trigger transcription of the gene and (2) testosterone binding leads to less new MAOA transcription than does glucocorticoid binding, which suggests (3) high testosterone levels may mean low transcription of MAOA. Lowering testosterone levels or targeting these response elements directly could be investigated for beneficial behavioral outcomes.

Other research suggests that blocking certain serotonin receptors might be promising. A certain brain region, the perigenual anterior cingulate, which is unusually rich in the 5-HT2a subtype of serotonin receptors, was shown to increase its functional activity in MAOA males during the completion of an emotion face-matching task (Buckholtz et al., 2008, 313–324). Upregulation of the 5-HT2a receptor in this region had previously been shown in those who have committed violent crime (Siever, 2008, 429–442), and pharmacological inhibition of the 5-HT2a receptor decreases aggression in animal models (Tsiouris, 2010, 1–16).[8] This suggests a potential for 5-HT2a antagonists as pharmacological modulators of aggression.

Buckholtz et al. (2008) also produced evidence that suggests that the MAOA-L variant might be associated with a specific dysregulation of an emotional brain center. In males with the MAOA-L gene who performed the task, there was a decrease in activity in a region implicated in impulse control (the ventromedial prefrontal cortex [vmPFC]) and an increase in activity in a region implicated in emotional salience (the amygdala). The authors point out that decreased activity of the vmPFC and increased activity in the amygdala had previously been correlated with conviction for violent crime and self-reported violence. Modifying this connectivity through real-time magnetic resonance imaging (MRI) by neurofeedback or other means might also be therapeutic.

These are merely suggestive examples. The science is young. While no clinical pharmacological interventions are available now, neuropharmacology may one day enable strategic modification of underlying neurochemistry with widely beneficial behavioral effects.

Biomarkers for the benefit of the person with the biomarker: mitigation of responsibility

One example of a use of a biomarker for the benefit only of the person with the biomarker would be to mitigate responsibility in legal proceedings. The use of a genetic predisposition to violence in criminal court has been controversial and permitted in only a handful of cases. We will introduce key cases here, first descriptively without comment. After all have been introduced, we will then briefly address the appropriateness of this use of the MAOA biomarker. As will become obvious, these cases show the urgent requirement of research into (1) what counts as an adverse childhood environment, (2) the time window of exposure, and (3) generalizability.

THE LEGAL CASES

Mobley: first attempts
The first attempt to use the MAOA biomarker in court failed. In *Mobley v. State* (1995), the defense requested MAOA genotyping for the Dutch family's rare MAOA nonsense mutation. Because the defendant, a 29-year-old man named Mobley who was accused of murder, did not have a family tree with the proper X-linked inheritance pattern, the judge decided genotyping was not warranted. Mobley was executed (Bernet et al., 2007, 1362–1371).

Since then, however, the MAOA-L gene × environment interaction has been identified, and the MAOA-L biomarker has been offered in courts several times (Bernet et al., 2007).[9] Only in three very recent cases has it had an effect on the outcome of the trial, and in these three it was referenced in reduction of the severity of the charge or sentence.

Bayout: Reduction of sentence
On Sept. 18, 2009, an Italian appeals court (in Trieste) reduced by 1 year a defendant's sentence for killing a man. The court controversially cited MAOA-L as particularly relevant (Ahuja, 2009; *Bayout v. Francesco*, 2009 Feresin, 2009; Forzano et al., 2010).

Earlier in the day of the killing, Bayout had been physically beaten by a group of young South Americans. After changing his clothes and buying a knife, Bayout followed a South American man down a street, falsely believing the man to have been one of his attackers (the man was, in reality, uninvolved), and cut the victim's throat. The killing occurred approximately 1.5 hours after the accused had been assaulted.

Because the defendant had a history of mental disorder, had discontinued medical treatment half a year ago, and had killed the wrong person, the trial judge in the original trial had decided that on the balance of probabilities there was some diminution of rational capacity. He had therefore given Bayout a reduced sentence of 9 years. The appeal argued that the MAOA-L biomarker offered a new mitigating factor. The case report (translated from Italian) explains the appeal court's reasoning in further reducing the sentence: "In particular, carrying the low activity MAOA gene (MAOA-L) could make the subject more prone to express aggression if provoked or socially excluded. It should be stressed that such `genetic vulnerability' turns out to carry even more significant weight in cases in which an individual grew up in a negative domestic social context, and was, especially in the early decades of life, exposed to adverse, psychologically traumatic environmental factors" (*Bayout*, 2009).

There was no mention of childhood abuse in Bayout's history, although the defense went to great lengths to argue that Bayout's cultural uprooting from Algeria to Italy caused him significant alienation and distress. This uprooting occurred when Bayout was 24 years old.

Waldroup: the liability phase

In the United States, also in 2009, a jury considered MAOA-L biomarker evidence when reducing a charge in the trial of Davis Bradley Waldroup from first-degree murder (a capital offense) to voluntary manslaughter (a maximum sentence of 6 years). The judgment claimed MAOA-L was not the specific reason for the reduced sentence (Hagerty, July 1, 2010; Polk News, 2009a, 2009b). Waldroup was convicted of voluntary manslaughter, especially aggravated kidnapping, and attempted second-degree murder, which resulted in a 32-year total prison sentence.

On the day in question, Waldroup's ex-wife had asked a female friend to drive with her to Waldroup's home to retrieve her children. Waldroup and his wife were experiencing significant marital problems. Once the women arrived, a discussion between Waldroup and his wife became heated. Abruptly, Waldroup fired his rifle into the vehicle, killing his wife's friend. He then shot his wife in the back as she attempted to escape. She managed to kick away the gun, at which point the attack was continued with a knife, a shovel, and finally a machete. Eventually, the wife submitted and was forcefully taken inside the home. Shortly thereafter the police arrived, arrested Waldroup, and saved the wife (Polk News, 2009a). There was evidence both that Waldroup was abused as a child and possessed the MAOA-L variant (Hagerty, July 1, 2010). The violence followed immediately from a triggering stressful event.

Albertani: combination of genetic and imaging biomarkers

In the court of Como, Italy, Stefania Albertani was tried in 2011 for the murder of her sister and the attempted murder of her parents (*Albertani* Gip di Como,

Aug. 20, 2011; Feresin, 2011). The sentence was reduced from 30 to 20 years (3 years of which to be spent in a mental institution) by the weight of a combination of traditional psychiatric analysis, structural brain imaging, memory tests, and genetic testing, which showed that Albertani possessed the MAOA-L variant as well as two other genes weakly associated with impulsive violence.

Albertani had administered benzodiazepine sedatives to her sister over a period of several days, which caused her sister to be in a confused state. Neighbors called the police and the sister was taken to the hospital, but Albertani convinced the sister to return home without consulting the doctors. Albertani then murdered the sister and burned her body in the back yard, after first telling the neighbors she was about to burn some paper so that they would neither be worried by the smoke nor call the police. Albertani then took identification and credit cards off the body and used them for some time. During this time, she also created threatening letters, impersonating her sister, and sent them to various family members. In a separate incident, Albertani had attempted to set fire to her parents' car with them inside. She had also on another occasion given her father a harmful dose of medication.

Albertani was arrested, however, upon the attempted murder of her mother. After the disappearance of the sister, the police had "bugged" the parents' house and entered the scene after hearing screams and sounds of struggle. They found the mother partially unconscious with her clothes on fire and were able to remove her to a hospital.

There were initially two expert psychiatric testimonies, but they came to opposite conclusions. As such, the judge permitted the defense to bring in a third expert, and neuroimaging, behavioral, and genetic tests were done. Besides the genetic polymorphisms already mentioned, Albertani was shown to have abnormalities in the anterior cingulate gyrus and the insula as compared with 10 female controls (Feresin, 2011). The former is particularly interesting because the perigenual cingulate, mentioned previously as potentially important in the mechanism of MAOA-L–mediated behavior, is a component of the anterior cingulate gyrus. The experts also used behavioral tests to estimate dissociation from memories (as Albertani claimed not to remember attacking her mother) and by the combination of these measures assigned Albertani a dissociative identity disorder.[10]

GAPS IN EMPIRICAL KNOWLEDGE, OBLIGATION TO RESEARCH, AND PRACTICALITIES

While we will not go into the details here of the appropriateness of these decisions, we will make general points. Before entering the complexity of the real-world cases, it will be helpful if we consider the case for mitigation in the abstract, canonical form of the MAOA gene × environment interaction.

For mitigation, it is essential to establish the relationship between biomarkers and some important aspect of responsibility. One of us has considered this at length (Baum, 2011) in relation to the partial defense of provocation. The strength of this approach is that it enables the incorporation of MAOA-L into middle principles already in use and relevant to mitigation.

We will briefly review and respond to the main objections raised against the use of genetic predispositions in trials and propose the conditions in which this biomarker may appropriately lead to mitigation. Then we will return to the messy cases of Bayout, Waldroup, and Albertani to point out important limitations given the current state of the science. Finally we will argue that if we admit a theoretical case for mitigation in the canonical interaction, then we should accept an obligation to address and minimize these limitations.

On involuntariness and "proneness to violence:" the importance of the mechanism of the MAOA predisposition to violence

Involuntariness is not required for a biomarker to be relevant

In an editorial objecting to the use of the MAOA data in the Bayout case, Forzano et al.'s (2010) main argument against genetic biomarkers is as follows: "There is no scientific support to declare that gene variants, claimed to predispose to aggression, would make the carriers incapable of repressing an aggressive behavior and thus unable to choose appropriate socially acceptable behaviors."

However, most factors that are commonly thought relevant to moral responsibility do not demand this type of incapability of repression; only the small set of defenses of involuntariness do so. The main body of criminal law is devoted to defenses dealing with the *mens rea* (intent), the numerous partial defenses, and existing mitigating factors that do not depend on involuntariness.

There may be a relevant mechanism behind the proneness to violence

Eastman et al. suggest that neuroscientific evidence of a predisposition to violent behavior would not fit into a provocation defense because "the mental characteristics cannot be 'proneness to violence' but must be characteristics that made the defendant more susceptible to the particular provocation emitted. This seems infertile ground for neuroscientific evidence" (Eastman & Campbell 2006). One of us (Baum) has argued elsewhere that the MAOA gene × environment interaction fits into the provocation defense *precisely because of the mechanism by which it might operate to make one prone to violent reactions.* Eastman et al.'s statement can be grounded by the appeal to the "reasonable man" standard in cases of provocation. As *Camplin* (1978) explained, "the reasonable man is a person having the power of self-control to be expected of an ordinary person of the sex and age of the accused, but in other respects sharing such of the accused's characteristics as they think would affect the gravity of the provocation to him" (Padfield, 2008).

It is, then, the subjective gravity of the provocation to the person that could legitimately make him or her more susceptible to the particular provocation. Interestingly, the cognitive and behavioral research on the general population with MAOA-L suggests that those with this variant may have (1) stronger emotional reactions to aversive stimuli, such as emotional faces or exclusion from a laboratory game and (2) decreased control over violent impulses. These combine to make it more likely that a person will respond with aggression, and with a higher degree of aggression (increased likelihood and extent of choosing to punish). The first of these (stronger emotional reactions) would be relevant to the reasonable man.

These cognitive science results, however, are from the general population (not those who were maltreated) and the effect sizes are small. Although it is hypothesized that these differences increase in size when the MAOA-L variant interacts with childhood maltreatment (Buckholtz & Meyer-Lindenberg, 2008, 120–129) the hypothesis is untested. This is the most important gap in empirical knowledge that needs to be supported if the MAOA interaction is to be fitted into a strong provocation defense. It is a reasonable hypothesis, however, and should be considered in the balance of probabilities similarly to other types of evidence of uncertain nature.

Stronger emotional reactions would increase the subjective gravity of the provocation to the person. The self-control embodied in the concept of the reasonable man might bar effects of the MAOA biomarker on self-control from legal consideration. However, forbidding the consideration of variations in impulse control is difficult to morally defend and indeed has been flip-flopping back and forth from permissible to impermissible in U.K. law: it was allowed by *Luc Thiet Thuan v. R* (1997), overturned in *Campell* (1997), allowed again by a 3–2 split decision in *Smith* (2000), upheld by *Rowland* (2003) and *Weller* (2003), and controversially overturned again by *A-G for Jersey v. Holley* (2005) and the overturn was upheld by *R v. James; Karimi* (2006); reviewed in Padfield (2008). If variations in impulse control are again permitted, the mechanism would be even more relevant.

LIMITATIONS OF THE CURRENT STATE OF RESEARCH LIMIT ETHICALLY PERMITTED USE OF THE BIOMARKER

If a canonical case of MAOA-L interaction is relevant to moral responsibility, it is crucial to better understand when, how, and to whom it would apply. Also, someone might have the variant and the right environment without the predisposition to *impulsive* aggression being relevant to that particular case—for example, in a case of premeditation and planned murder. *Albertani* is closest to the latter case, *Bayout* is at the midrange (violence occurring at 1.5 hours after provocation), and *Waldoup* displays canonically impulsive violence.

There needs to be evidence linking the gene × environment interaction with the cognitive neuroscience work on mechanism in order to fit the biomarker into existing law

Although a putative mechanism is supported by work in cognitive neuroscience, as discussed above, it remains to be shown that the increased emotional response and decreased impulse control in those with MAOA-L alone are increased in magnitude when combined with an adverse childhood environment. If lack of impulse control were increased alone, for example, then the provocation partial defense would not currently be available.

The definition and of the adverse environment needs to be better defined, as does the valid time window of susceptibility to that environment

Waldroup is the classic case of physical child abuse and fits into the canonical gene × environment interaction. *Bayout* does not. Bayout's claimed adverse environment was social exclusion. Does social exclusion count for the same as abuse? Or could onset of schizophrenia around age 16 to 21 be a relevant adverse environment? Buckholtz (Buckholtz & Meyer-Lindenberg, 2008, 120–129) suggests a very inclusive definition of adverse environment, "one typified by persistent uncertainty, unpredictable threat, poor behavioral modeling and social referencing, and inconsistent reinforcement for prosocial decision making." Some research suggests even prenatal exposure to cigarette smoke may be a relevant adverse environment (Wakschlag et al., 2010). And at what age does the adverse environment no longer combine with genotype in the same way? Bayout moved to Italy when he was 24; is this past that critical period? To be practically relevant, further research needs to better establish which environments in which age groups lead to a predisposition to impulsive violence and which do not.

The population in which this predisposition is valid needs to be defined

The majority of MAOA gene × environment work has been conducted with white males. This is especially relevant to the *Albertani* case (since Albertani is female). So far, male preference has been pragmatic. Males only have one X chromosome and so are easily separated into groups of either MAOA-L or MAOA-H. Females, on the other hand, can have (1) two copies of MAOA-L, (2) two copies of MAOA-H, or (3) one copy of MAOA-L and one copy of MAOA-H. Do the variants have the same effect in females? The data are scarce and underpowered compared to that on males. The data that exist are certainly more complicated and not necessarily comparable (females were excluded from the meta-analyses mentioned earlier). Caspi (2002) mention (in a footnote) a possible predisposition in females with two copies of MAOA-L and maltreatment in a very small sample (looking at just females with two copies of MAOA-H or MAOA-L). A different group found a correlation between females carrying two copies of MAOA-L with low or no maltreatment and future conduct disorder (Prom-Wormley et al., 2009). Another group found some evidence that females with one or two copies of MAOA-H (not MAOA-L) and adverse childhood environment may be predisposed to delinquent behavior, but these studies have significant technical limitations; one (Sjoberg et al., 2007) includes multifamily households as an adverse childhood environment and the other (Aslund et al., 2011), while a larger sample, relies exclusively on one-time self-reports of childhood environment and aggressive behavior. More data will need to be gathered to see if this latter, opposite effect in females holds true.[11] More research in general on females and diverse ethnicities is needed.[12]

SUMMARY OF BIOMARKERS AND THE LAW
The MAOA-L biomarker has the strongest case for a plausible role in legal proceedings if:

1. There is an established history of evidence-based adverse environment.
2. The person falls within a population category for which there is evidence of vulnerability.
3. Evidence exists of possible provocation within valid timeframe of the crime (and lack of premeditation).
4. Evidence exists of enhanced emotional reaction to the provocation (enhanced gravity of provocation).
5. Evidence exists of loss of impulse control.[13]

Under these conditions, it is reasonable to believe that those with the MAOA-L activity variant have reduced responsibility and are candidates for a provocation partial defense, in that they are more liable to be provoked and less likely to be able to control their responses. A partial defense of provocation would decrease a charge from murder to manslaughter. As all potentially relevant factors are considered during the sentencing phase, even weak evidence of these five items might in that phase continue to be relevant. The strength of the case for sentence mitigation would decrease proportionally to an increase in uncertainty in an item.

THE PROBLEM OF UNKNOWN INTERACTIONS
If we accept that the canonical case of the MAOA gene × environment interaction would be relevant to mitigation of responsibility, what should we do

if we have noncanonical cases? Think about a defendant of an ethnicity on which there has been no MAOA research, but who has been abused and has MAOA-L. Right now, an effect in such a population is an untested hypothesis. Imagine that the defendant's lawyer moves to bring this information in, the jury considers it, and it leads to reduction of a murder charge to manslaughter. One response is to angrily shout down this case as a misuse of research and an abuse of justice, as the science is not yet there. But is such a response justified if there is also no evidence that it *should not count* in his population? If the interaction does hold in his population, then we will have punished too harshly, which is also an abuse of justice. Depending on how much weight one puts on preventing or correcting miscarriages of justice, an equally weighty commitment to developing the research that pushes back the shroud of ignorance may be required. In the absence of such research, uncertainty could be incorporated similarly to the uncertainty inherent in ALL evidence: the uncertainty in eyewitness testimony, circumstantial evidence, expert testimony, etc., that is dealt with on a daily basis in the courts. That is, the farther the actual case strays from the canonical, the more that its weight in the argument is discounted. This is of course an imperfect solution, with its own risks (one would need to be science savvy to help the jury avoid overweighting or underweighting the evidence).

Benefit to others without harm to the person with the biomarker

Biomarkers of behavior could also possibly be used in the selection of embryos. Since the person who will arise from the embryo is neither benefited nor harmed by selection (rather she exists or doesn't exist), the benefit of this use of biomarkers would be to others (parents, family, or community).

One of us (Savulescu) has previously defended a principle called Procreative Beneficence (PB): couples (or single reproducers) should select the child, of the possible children they could have, who is expected to have the best life, or at least as good a life as the others (Savulescu, 2001a; Savulescu & Kahane, 2009).

In these papers, Savulescu has argued that this is a principle of rationality applied to reproduction and applies even when there are weak probabilistic connections between genes and well-being. Savulescu previously defended the application of this principle to selection against the full mutation variant found in the Brunner study. But the argument extends to low-activity variants of MAOA (Savulescu, 2001b). He argued that in vitro fertilization (IVF) and preimplantation genetic diagnosis (PGD) or prenatal diagnosis could be used by couples or single reproducers to have offspring without low-activity variants of MAO. He argued that criminal behavior does make a life go worse, in virtue of the consequent incarceration, social deprivation, and loss of independence.

Thus PB would support selection in favor of the high-activity mutation, which would translate to resilience to an adverse environment.[14,15]

However, there is a stronger argument than PB in favor of genetic selection against low-activity MAOA. Buchanan, Brock, Daniels, and Wikler, in their influential book *From Chance to Choice*, claim:

> …there is already some evidence of genes associated with dispositions to violent criminal behavior. Just as the criminal law is a justified coercive social means aimed at preventing or reducing such behavior, society might in the future attempt genetic interventions to do so as well. These interventions would not be made for the benefit of the subject of the genetic intervention…, but for the benefit of the broader society and to protect the rights of its members against violent assault. (Buchanan et al., 2000, 173)

Buchanan et al. go on to say:

> While violent behavior is not a disease, these genes would be similar to genes that transmit diseases in that they dispose individuals who have them to deviations from the social norm for violence.

We might go further, incorporating what we have argued above, that the deviation from the social norm of tendency to violence makes the person's life go worse. Buchanan et al. go on to tentatively support not only the pharmacological intervention we mentioned earlier, but also genetic manipulation, including "gene therapy," to prevent criminal behavior. They say: "It is not at all clear why it would be wrong for a society to support or undertake these genetic interventions for the benefit of society."

Imagine that a couple from the Dutch kindred previously described, or a couple living in a potentially adverse environment over which they have little control, came forward asking if there is any way they can have a child without the nonsense mutation or the MAOA-L variant, both of which increase the risk of predisposition to criminal behavior. There are two ways in which a couple might have a child without a predisposition to this behavior: genetic selection or gene therapy.

With genetic selection, they could select, from the range of possible children they could have, a child without the genetic predisposition (the MAO mutation). This could be done by doing mutational analysis of embryos created by IVF, or by prenatal testing and termination of pregnancy if the fetus has the mutation.

With genetic enhancement, they could genetically enhance an embryo or fetus, if it is found to carry the mutation. This would require gene therapy, as Buchanan et al. suggest, but this is not possible at the present.

While the outcome of these two interventions is the same—a child without the predisposition to criminal behavior—the means are very different. Genetic selection is superior, we believe, to genetic manipulation in the following way.

SELECTION ENABLES A GENETIC INTERVENTION TO "PROTECT THE RIGHTS OF ITS MEMBERS AGAINST VIOLENT ASSAULT" WITHOUT HARMING THE CHILD

First, harm to the child is often taken to be the foremost consideration in discussion of these issues. A child could be harmed by genetic (or other) manipulation. Gene therapy may have risks, such as risks of introducing other mutations, or it may be only partially effective. The same is true of nongenetic therapies, such as drug therapy.

Second, there is the phenomenon of "pleiotropy": the gene variant that contributes to a predisposition to criminal behavior may also predispose or contribute to other behaviors, which are desirable. There is some weak evidence that the MAOA-L confers resilience to depression in stressful circumstances (Beach et al., 2010; Rivera et al., 2009). Let's assume for argument's sake that this is true. Treating a person's MAOA deficiency would then harm the person for the sake of protection of others, trading risk to the well-being of others for the risk to well-being of the self.

Genetic selection avoids this type of harm to the person with the biomarker. Imagine a couple that wants to have a child with MAOA-H. They have in vitro fertilization. It produces six embryos. These are all genetically tested, and four are found to have MAOA-H. One of these is selected. The embryo grows to be a child, who grows to be an adult, Rudy. Rudy becomes depressed occasionally but lives an otherwise orderly and ordinary life. Can he raise a valid moral claim against his parents for what they did in selecting an embryo that resulted in him, a man with few violent tendencies but a disposition to some depression? If they chose any other embryo, it would not have been him. It would have been someone else. Insofar as his life is overall worth living, even if he is not as happy and joyful as his siblings, he has no complaint about the selection procedure.

If we are concerned to minimize harm to the offspring, genetic selection has an advantage over genetic enhancement, or other therapies. Because the predisposition may operate through a mechanism of inappropriately strong emotional responses and poor impulse control, selection of MAOA-H might be thought of as associated with increased emotional balance and impulse control; these two qualities could be argued to be the kind of "natural primary goods—capabilities that are general-purpose means [...] broadly valuable across a wide array of life plans and opportunities typically pursued in a society like our own" that Buchanan et al. describe as the only enhancements "that would be compatible with a strong liberal commitment to neutrality between different comprehensive conceptions of the good" and thus permitted in a liberal democracy.

This argument in favor of genetic selection is strongest in the case of couples having IVF and PGD for other reasons. In this case, testing for MAOA and selecting in favor of high-activity variants add no extra risk or cost to the procedure, and there are likely significant upsides for both the family and society.

For those not contemplating either IVF or PGD, the strength of the overall reason to have selection depends on other factors that must be weighed, like cost and the risks of IVF and PGD. As those risks and costs come down, there is more reason to select against low-activity variants of MAOA. Society is a winner, and no one is a loser.[16]

Benefit to others but harm to the person with the biomarker

Historically, the largest and most ethically troubling class of applications has been those that benefit others but *harm* the person with the biomarker. Examples include the involuntary sterilizations that continued into the 1970s as a part of the eugenics movement (Buchanan et al., 2000). Unjust surveillance, over-investigation, preventive detention, and harsher sentencing of those suspected of being prone to criminal behavior might be appealed to for, as Lombroso put it, the protection of society; he argued that "born criminals" should be punished not in proportion to the magnitude of their crimes, but rather according to the threat of future crime (Lombroso, Gibson, & Rafter, 2006).

According to John Stuart Mill's harm principle, significant harm or loss of liberty to an individual is only justified where that individual harms others or is at clear risk of harming others. The liberty restriction in the criminal justice system is one example. What counts as "clear risk" is a difficult but important question. In recent years the United Kingdom has debated whether to create a new category for a person assessed to pose a greater than 50 percent risk of future violence: dangerous and severe personality disorder (DSPD). DSPD would allow an optional extension of a criminal sentence to life in prison or permanent monitoring (Corbett & Westwood, 2005; Maden & Tyrer, 2003). As biomarkers become more finely tuned and prevalent, the debate about whether such a category can be ethically justified will be all the more real.

While not addressing the issue in detail, we note that public health or public safety goals can be achieved using a variety of means; these exist on a spectrum of liberty restriction, from zero to complete. An example of near-zero restriction of liberty is the mere provision of information to the individual (i.e., telling someone that the biomarker exists). At the other end there is involuntary surgery, medical treatment, or incarceration. Along this spectrum, there are a variety of methods that apply intermediate levels of force, such as rational argument, persuasion, manipulation of psychological limitations, biases and heuristics (e.g., so-called "nudge" strategies in public health), incentives, taxes, and so on.

The reduction in the undesired behavior can be achieved by many methods, with biological intervention being only one method. As a general rule, the least harmful and liberty-restricting method of promising efficacy should be employed first to explore whether a reasonable reduction in the undesired behavior can be achieved. For example, dedicated efforts were made to reduce violent crime in the United States in the 1970s and 1980s, employing a range of strategies, some liberty restricting. A large drop in violence occurred in the 1990s, but Donohue and Levitt found that one statistically significant factor that correlated with this drop in violence was the provision of free abortion services to poor, disadvantaged populations over a quarter of a century ago (Donohue & Levitt, 2001). This finding caused considerable debate. The authors claim that the finding survives statistical reanalysis.

Let us assume that this research was well conducted, controlled for confounding variables, and was able to demonstrate causation as well as correlation. In this case, offering free abortion might be justifiable. Moreover, the intervention could offer an advantage to a woman insofar as it allows her to have increased control over her own life. Since no person's liberty is restricted, and there are other good ethical reasons to provide abortion services, it is hard to see how providing free abortion services could be unethical. In a similar way, offering people (without attempted coercion or even persuasion) free sterilization or long-term contraception increases their options and is potentially life enhancing. When dealing with vulnerable populations, such as the affected males of the Dutch family (who had an IQ of approximately 85), it would be especially important to guard against lack of information or misinformation. It is also important that such services are distributed equally and do not close off other valuable options.

Consider the parallel case of testing for the carrier state of thalassemia, an inherited deficit in functional hemoglobin in the blood. In Cyprus, the Church must authorize marriage, but prior to such authorization couples must have thalassemia carrier testing. There is no obligation to have prenatal diagnosis on the basis of the result. However, the vast majority of those tested choose to have prenatal diagnosis, and today virtually no babies are born in Cyprus with thalassemia. Currently (in Cyprus) around 50 percent of the supply of blood for transfusion is used to treat people with thalassemia, and this accounts for about 20 percent of the "drug budget." If screening for thalassemia had not been introduced, there would have been more than twice as many people in Cyprus with thalassemia today.

There is an element of coercion in the carrier testing program in Cyprus, as people who want to marry must have such testing. However, the program increases informed decision making about reproduction and thus increases autonomy. In one way, it might be similar to requiring that a patient be "informed" before consenting to any medical procedure. The carrier testing program is also in the public interest. Some would argue that coercion may be justified in the public interest if and only if:

- There is a significant health, legal, or social problem.
- The intervention will be an effective way of promoting the public interest.
- There is no effective, less coercive alternative..

A FUTURE OF BIOMARKERS

In many cases, there are ways of tackling our greatest social problems without employing biomarkers, but increasing knowledge of biomarkers may change the moral landscape. Once a biomarker is developed, it is no longer a morally neutral decision to act without that information. Rather, one is required to justify why it is acceptable *not* to gain that information. This is illustrated elsewhere with the advance of tissue typing in organ transplantation. We began this chapter by asking how biomarkers like MAOA could potentially be used ethically. We finish with the thought that we may soon be asking when it is ethically justifiable *not* to use biomarkers or at least not to contemplate their ethical use.

NOTES

1. One of us (Baum) recently published in the journal *Neuroethics* (Baum 2011) on MAOA and the provocation defense, in which he reviews Lombroso and the science of MAOA and the Mobley, Waldroup, and Bayout trials as related to the mechanism of provocation. The review of the science and law of MAOA presented here draws upon and adapts the ideas developed in that paper as elements of the extended discussion of the general ethical uses of biomarkers that is the topic of this chapter.
2. The other well-studied gene × environment interaction, between the 5HTT-LPR (the gene coding for the serotonin transporter), stressful life events, and depression, did not pass a similar meta-analytical method (Risch et al., 2009, 2462–2471).
3. Because even validated biomarkers could have low predictive power, it is worth considering how much of this ethical analysis would change as the predictive power changes. This is an important area of inquiry but beyond this paper. We will, however, mention three points: (1) we seem logically committed to care equally about magnitude in context of biomarkers and of other predictive markers like smoking, lifestyle, fatty food, poverty, provocation, etc; (2) we have set up a series of institutions and practices (legal defenses, for example) implicitly reliant on predictions of

behavior of low or unquantified predictive power; and (3) by 1 and 2, either (a) having low or unquantified predictive power is acceptable as a basis for social, medical, and legal policy and should also apply to biomarkers or (b) we should be concerned about all areas of social practice that involve using measures of low or unquantified predictive power. It may be the case that the MAOA interaction, even if these significant issues are resolved, will be shown to contribute only minorly to overall incidence of impulsive aggression in comparison to other factors, and as such may not merit special attention from the perspective of public health or society.

4. A note on the timing of testing: While we will focus on the ethical use of the information gained from testing and not on the testing itself, the two are interrelated, and we will say a few brief points on timing. Testing for MAOA could happen at five major time points: (1) before birth, (2) after birth or during early childhood, (3) at the first sign of possible maltreatment, (4) after maltreatment, or (5) during criminal trials of defendants who experienced childhood maltreatment. Testing at each stage raises unique ethical issues: the numbers of individuals involved vary drastically, for example, from the entire population in 1 and 2 to a miniscule fraction in 4. So does whether the person is able to give valid consent. Certain types of preventive interventions would only be possible with testing earlier in the timescale, but earlier testing might come with an increased risk of stigmatization, discrimination, and self-fulfilling prophecy.

5. One might object that the financial cost of testing would pull resources away from social services. The cost, however, is fast decreasing and the advance of platform genotyping techniques may soon make it as costly to test for one variant as for hundreds or thousands. MAOA testing might "piggyback" on other tests for pennies that would do little directly put toward social services.

6. A range of consequentialist and nonconsequentialist moral theories posit that we should give priority to benefiting/avoiding harming the worse off, even if doing so leads to less net benefit with the given resources. These theories would again give priority to MAOA-L children, as one could argue that children who are maltreated and have the MAOA-L are worse off because of the increased likelihood of future loss of liberty.

7. For an interesting discussion, see George Sher, *Who Knew? Responsibility Without Awareness*. Oxford University Press, 2009.

8. Activation of the 5-HT2a receptor increases aggression.

9. For a digest of interesting legal cases involving bioscience, see Nita Farahany's website at http://lawandbiodigest.com/author/nfarahan/

10. A disorder characterized by the alternation of (often subtly) distinct personalities within the same person accompanied by amnesia of the events and actions of the other personality. Often accompanied by childhood trauma, and hypothesized to be a defense mechanism.

11. If one version turns out to be generally beneficial to one sex and vice versa, then it might be impossible to get rid of the "bad" gene variant because it will be bad for males and good for females. It would be possible through selection, however, to choose the beneficial variant in each individual while applying procreative beneficence as discussed below.

12. If the biomarker can benefit some people but not others due to differential research, we might become concerned with issues of distributive justice.
13. Only legally relevant if the reasonable man standard is subjectified, but circumstantially relevant in building evidence that the MAOA mechanism is operating in that person.
14. Should the differential effect of MAOA on females, for which the first evidence was found after this publication, be supported, then one would have the opposite reason for selection in females. Until this evidence is substantiated, the case for selection is stronger for boys. This qualification applies to the entirety of the section.
15. If the bad effects of MAOA-L could be avoided by the strategies suggested in the first section (child protection), then there would no longer be reason to select against MAOA-L. Conversely, if everyone selected against the susceptible version of MAOA, then there would be no reason to have other strategies. The higher practical feasibility of the former might be a reason to prefer it, but we merely wish to present selection as another possibility.
16. There is a normative judgment here that a predisposition to depression, which also has many costs to others (especially in societies with a national health care system), is preferable from society's point of view to a predisposition to violence. This view may be contested, but is, we believe, defensible.

REFERENCES

A-G for Jersey v. Holley. (2005) UKPC 23; (2005) Crim LR 966.

Albertani, Gip di Como. Giudice per le le indagini preliminary di Como, Maria Luisa Lo Gatto decisione del 20 agosto 2011. Full transcript http://static.ilsole24ore.com/DocStore/Professionisti/AltraDocumentazione/body/12600001-12700000/12693249.pdf *In:* Machiochhi, P. Gip di Como: le neuroscienze entrano e vincono in tribunale. 30.08.2011 http://www.diritto24.ilsole24ore.com/guidaAlDiritto/penale/primiPiani/2011/08/le-neuroscienze-entrano-e-vincono-in-tribunale.html

Ahuja, A. (2009). The Get Out of Jail Free Gene. *The Sunday Times (UK).*

Aslund, C., Nordquist, N., Comasco, E., Leppert, J., Oreland, L., & Nilsson, K. W. (2011). Maltreatment, MAOA, and delinquency: sex differences in gene–environment interaction in a large population-based cohort of adolescents." *Behavioral Genetics, 41,* 262–272.

Bayout V. Francesco, Public Law RGAssise App. 6/2008 RGNR 1685/2007, RG. sent 5, dd 18 settembre 2009, (2009):. http://www.personaedanno.it/cms/data/articoli/files/016153_resource1_orig.pdf.

Baum, M. L. (2011). The monoamine oxidase A (MAOA) genetic predisposition to impulsive violence: is it relevant to criminal trials? *Neuroethics,* 1–20, doi:10.1007/s12152-011-9108-6.

Baumeister, R. F., Vohs, K. D., & Tice, D. M. (2007). The strength model of self-control. *Current Directions in Psychological Science 16* (6): 351–355.

Beach, S. R. H., Brody, G. H., Gunter, T. D., Packer, H., Wernett, P., & Philibert, R. A. (2010). Child maltreatment moderates the association of MAOA with symptoms of depression and antisocial personality disorder. *Journal of Family Psychology, 24*(1), 12–20.

Bernet, W., Vnencak-Jones, C. L., Farahany, N., & Montgomery, S. A. (2007). Bad nature, bad nurture, and testimony regarding MAOA and SLC6A4 genotyping at murder trials. *Journal of Forensic Sciences, 52*(6), 1362–1371.

Brown, D., Butchart, A., Harvey, A., Bartolomeos, K., Meddings, D., & Sminkey, L. (2007). *World Health Organization: Third Milestones of a Global Campaign for Violence Prevention Report 2007: Scaling Up.* Geneva: World Health Organization.

Brunner, H. G., Nelen, M. R., Breakefield, X. O., Ropers, H. H., & Van Oost, B. A. (1993a). Abnormal behavior associated with a point mutation in the structural gene for monoamine oxidase A. *Science, 262*(5133), 578–580. doi:10.1126/science.8211186.

Brunner, H. G., Nelen, M. R., van Zandervoort, P., Abeling, N. G., van Gennip, A. H., Wolters, E. C., Kuiper, M. A., Ropers, H. H., & van Oost, B. A. (1993b). X-linked borderline mental retardation with prominent behavioral disturbance: phenotype, genetic localization, and evidence for disturbed monoamine metabolism. *American Journal of Human Genetics, 52*(6), 1032–1039.

Buchanan, A. E., Brock, D. W., Daniels, N., & Wikler, D. (2000). *From chance to choice: genetics and justice.* Cambridge, U.K., and New York: Cambridge University Press.

Buck v. Bell, 274 U.S. 200, available at LII, http://www.law.cornell.edu/supct/html/historics/USSC_CR_0274_0200_ZS.html (last visited July 21, 2012).

Buckholtz, J. W., Callicott, J. H., Kolachana, B, Hariri, A. R., Goldberg, T. E., Genderson, M., Egan, M. F., Mattay, V. S., Weinberger, D. R., & Meyer-Lindenberg, A. (2008). Genetic variation in MAOA modulates ventromedial prefrontal circuitry mediating individual differences in human personality. *Molecular Psychiatry, 13*(3), 313–324.

Buckholtz, J. W. & Meyer-Lindenberg, A. (2008). MAOA and the neurogenetic architecture of human aggression. *Trends in Neurosciences, 31*(3), 120–129.

Buyse, M., Sargent, D. J., Grothey, A., Matheson, A., & De Gramont, A. (2010). Biomarkers and surrogate end points: the challenge of statistical validation. *Nature Reviews Clinical Oncology, 7*(6), 309–317.

Campbell. (1997) 1 Cr App Rep 1999, (1997) Crim LR 227, CA.

Camplin. (1978) AC 705, (1978) 2 WLR 679, 67 Cr App Rep 14, (1978) 2 All ER 168, HL

Caspi, A., McCray, J., Moffitt, T. E., Mill, J., Martin, J., Craig, I. W., Taylor, A., & Poulton, R. (2002). Role of genotype in the cycle of violence in maltreated children. *Science, 297*(5582), 851–854.

Coccaro, E. F. (1989). Central serotonin and impulsive aggression. *British Journal of Psychiatry Supplement* (8) (8), 52–62.

Corbett, K., & Westwood, T. (2005). 'Dangerous and severe personality disorder': a psychiatric manifestation of the risk society. *Critical Public Health, 15*(2), 121–133.

Donohue, J. D., & Levitt, S. D. (2001). The impact of legalized abortion on crime. *Quarterly Journal of Economics*, 379–420.

Ducci, F., & Goldman, D. (2008). Genetic approaches to addiction: genes and alcohol. *Addiction, 103*(9), 1414–1428.

Eastman, N., & Campbell, C. (2006). Science and society: neuroscience and legal determination of criminal responsibility. *Nature Reviews Neuroscience, 7*(4), 311–318.

Feresin, E. (2009). Lighter sentence for murderer with 'bad genes'. *Nature.* doi:10.1038/news.2009.1050

Feresin, E. (2011). Italian court reduces murder sentence based on neuroimaging data. *Nature News Blog,* http://blogs.nature.com/news/2011/09/italian_court_reduces_murder_s.html.

Forzano, F., Borry, P., Cambon-Thomsen, A., Hodgson, S. V., Tibben, A., De Vries, P., Van El, C., & Cornel, M. (2010). Italian Appeal Court: a genetic predisposition to commit murder. *European Journal of Human Genetics, 18*(5), 519–521.

Hagerty, B. Can your genes make you murder? *National Public Radio*.http://www.npr.
    org/templates/story/story.php?storyId=128043329.
Hibbeln, J. R., Ferguson, T. A., & Blasbalg, T. L. (2006). Omega-3 fatty acid deficiencies
    in neurodevelopment, aggression and autonomic dysregulation: opportunities for
    intervention. *International Review of Psychiatry, 18*(2), 107–118.
Kevles, D. J. (1985). *In the name of eugenics: genetics and the uses of human heredity*,
    1st ed. New York: Knopf.
Kim-Cohen, J., Caspi, A., Taylor, A., Williams, B., Newcombe, R., Craig, I. W., &
    Moffitt, T. E. (2006). MAOA, maltreatment, and gene–environment interaction
    predicting children's mental health: new evidence and a meta-analysis. *Molecular
    Psychiatry, 11*(10), 903–913.
Lombroso, C., Gibson, M., & Rafter, N. H. 2006. *Criminal man* [Uomo delinquente.].
    Durham, NC, and London: Duke University Press.
Luc Thiet Thuan v. R. (1997) AC 131, (1996) 2 All ER 1033, (1996) 3 WLR 45, (1996) 2
    Cr App Rep 178, (1996) Crim LR 820, PC.
Lynam, D., Moffitt, T., & Stouthamer-Loeber, M. (1993). Explaining the relation
    between IQ and delinquency: class, race, test motivation, school failure, or self-
    control? *Journal of Abnormal Psychology, 102*(2), 187–196.
Maden, T., & Tyrer, P. (2003). Dangerous and severe personality disorders: a new per-
    sonality concept from the United Kingdom. *Journal of Personality Disorders, 17*(6),
    489–496.
Mobley v. State 455 S.E.2d 61 (Ga. Sup. Ct. 1995)
Padfield, N. (2008). *Criminal law*, 6th ed. New York: Oxford University Press.
Polk News (2009a). Waldroup Guilty, Will not Face Death Penalty. http://www.
    polknewsonline.com/2009/03/25/Top_News/Waldroup_guilty,_will_not_face_
    death_penalty/4158.html.
Polk News (2009b). Waldroup Gets 32 Years. http://www.polknewsonline.com/2009/
    05/13/Top_News/Waldroup_gets_32_years/4493.html.
Prom-Wormley E. C., Eaves, L. J., Foley, D. L., Gardner, C. O., Archer, K. J., Wormley, B.
    K., Maes, H. H., Riley, B. P., & Silberg, J. L. (2009). Monoamine oxidase A and child-
    hood adversity as risk factors for conduct disorder in females. *Psychological Medicine,
    39*, 579–590.
R v. James; Karimi. (2006) EWCA Crim 14.
Risch, N., Herrell, R., Lehner, T., Liang, K-Y., Eaves, L., Hoh, J., Griem, A., Kovacs, M.,
    Ott, J., & Merikangas, K. R. (2009). Interaction between the serotonin transporter gene
    (5-HTTLPR), stressful life events, and risk of depression: a meta-analysis. *Journal of
    the American Medical Association, 301*(23), 2462–2471. doi:10.1001/jama.2009.878.
Rivera, M., Gutiérrez, B., Molina, E., Torres-González, F., Belión, J. A., Moreno-
    Küstner, B., King, M., et al. (2009). High-activity variants of the uMAOA polymor-
    phism increase the risk for depression in a large primary care sample. *American
    Journal of Medical Genetics, Part B: Neuropsychiatric Genetics, 150*(3), 395–402.
Robert Means Yerkes Papers (MS 569). Manuscripts and Archives, Yale University
    Library.
Rowland. (2003) EWCA Crim 3636, 148 Sol Jo LB 26, (2003) All ER (D) 237 (Dec).
Savulescu, J. (2001a). Procreative Beneficence: why we should select the best children.
    Bioethics, 15(5–6), 413–426.

Savulescu, J. (2001b). Why genetic testing for genes for criminality is morally required. *Princeton Journal of Bioethics, 4,* 79–97.

Savulescu, J.(2012). 'Enhancing equality'. In K. Lippert-Rasmussen, M. Rosendahl, & J. Wamberg (Eds.), *The posthuman condition: ethics, aesthetics and politics of biotechnological challenges* (pp. 184–203). Aarhus: Aarhus University Press.

Savulescu, J., & Kahane, G. (2009). The moral obligation to create children with the best chance of the best life. *Bioethics, 23*(5), 274–290.

Siever, L. J. (2008). Neurobiology of aggression and violence. *American Journal of Psychiatry, 165*(4), 429–442.

Sjoberg, R. L., Nilsson, K. W., Wargelius, H. L., Leppert, J., Lindstrom, L., & Oreland, L. (2007). Adolescent girls and criminal activity: role of MAOA-LPR genotype and psychosocial factors. *American Journal of Medical Genetics B, 144B,* 159–164.

Smith (Morgan James). (1999) QB 1079, affd (2001) 1AC 146, (2000) 4 All ER 289, (2000) 3 WLR 654, (2001) 1 Cr App Rep 31, (2000) Crim LR 1004, HL.

Taylor, A., & Kim-Cohen, J. (2007). Meta-analysis of gene–environment interactions in developmental psychopathology. *Development and Psychopathology, 19*(4), 1029–1037.

Tremblay, R. E., & Szyf, M. (2010). Developmental origins of chronic physical aggression and epigenetics. *Epigenomics, 2*(4), 495–499.

Tsiouris, J. A. (2010). Pharmacotherapy for aggressive behaviors in persons with intellectual disabilities: treatment or mistreatment? *Journal of Intellectual Disability Research, 54*(1), 1–16.

Wakschlag, L. S., Kistner, E. O., Pine, D. S., Biesecker, G., Pickett, K. E., Skol, A. D., Dukic, V., et al. (2010). Interaction of prenatal exposure to cigarettes and MAOA genotype in pathways to youth antisocial behavior. *Molecular Psychiatry, 15*(9), 928–937.

Weder, N., Yang, B. Z., Douglas-Palumberi, H., Massey, J., Krystal, J. H., Gelernter, J., & Kaufman, J. (2009). MAOA genotype, maltreatment, and aggressive behavior: the changing impact of genotype at varying levels of trauma. *Biological Psychiatry, 65*(5), 417–424.

Weir, C. J., & Walley, R. J. (2006). Statistical evaluation of biomarkers as surrogate endpoints: a literature review. *Statistics in Medicine, 25*(2), 183–203.

Weller. (2003) EWCA Crim 815, (2004) 1 Cr App Rep 1, (2003) Crim LR 724.

Williams, M., & Penman, D. (2011). *Mindfulness: a practical guide to finding peace in a frantic world* (D. Penman, Ed.). London: Piatkus.

Wright, S., Day, A., & Howells, K. (2009). Mindfulness and the treatment of anger problems. *Aggression and Violent Behavior, 14*(5), 396–401.

Zammit, S., Owen, M. J., & Lewis, G. (2010). Misconceptions about gene-environment interactions in psychiatry. *Evid Based Mental Health, 13*(3), 65–68.

3

Bioprediction in Youth Justice

CHARLOTTE K. WALSH

[T]here is a small number of children, 0.1 per cent, about whom we should be very worried. These are the youngsters who at times want to kill and who hunger for savage power over others. Chronic maltreatment has weakened their pre-frontal cortex, the part of the brain responsible for restraining our emotions and impulses. Instead, in the service of survival, the earlier-evolved regions of the brain, those that generate the more primitive responses—such as kill or be killed—exercise greater influence…Neuroscience is now demonstrating that, without doubt, maltreatment alters the neuronal pathways, producing developmentally traumatised children. Brain research being undertaken by scientists working with Kids Company demonstrates that many of the children who come to us are suffering from post-traumatic stress disorder. Even though they are as traumatised as soldiers who have gone to war, they don't receive a medal or care fit for heroes. Instead, they are dismissed as "scum." (Batmanghelidjh, 2012, 18)

This quote from Camilla Batmanghelidjh—founder of the children's charity Kids Company—encapsulates many of the themes that this chapter seeks to explore: a longstanding concern about the very small percentage of young people who go on to cause a disproportionate amount of violent harm; a growing belief that these children are neurologically damaged in a detectable way; increased understanding that these impairments occur (at least partially) as a result of abuse or neglect, generally parental; along with the implicit hope that science, predominantly neuroscience, can help in doing something about this unhappy situation.

Young people are incommensurately involved in recorded criminality: in 2009-2010, 17 percent of all arrests in the United Kingdom were of those aged 10 to 17 years old, in spite of this age group accounting for only 11 percent of the population (Youth Justice Board/Ministry of Justice, 2012, 2). While the bulk of youth offending is trivial and adolescence-limited—with most young people growing out of crime—some is not: identifying (and intervening with) those who will persist with serious criminality can be seen as the Holy Grail of youth justice policy. Influential longitudinal research—such as that carried out by Farrington and West (1993)—has cemented the idea that there is a hard-core group of males who are physically aggressive in childhood and remain so into later life. This small group is seen to be disproportionately responsible for offending, including grave transgressions (cf. Hales et al., 2009). In this group, certain childhood conduct disorders are increasingly seen as predictors of more severe adult conditions, which are, in turn, associated with criminality (cf. Moffitt et al., 2002; Odgers et al., 2008). However, assertions that amount to a claim that those who continue to offend are of a different "type" are controversial (cf. Skardhamar, 2010).

Crucially, there is a corresponding and growing belief that diagnosed conduct disorders have genetic underpinnings, and/or correlative structural and functional brain "abnormalities," rendering them potential targets for bioprediction, whether through genetic screening or neuroimaging (cf. von Polier et al., 2012). As this body of work grows, so too does the conviction that successful interventions may become possible, effectively preventing crime before it occurs. Such measures could be targeted either at "risky" parents—seen to play a crucial role in the development of many such disorders—and/or at their "risky" children. Both options will be considered in this chapter. The temptation to intervene with these groups, while certainly not new, is arguably enhanced by perceptions of risk being coated with a shiny new neuroscientific gloss. Bioprediction—along with any subsequent intervention—constitutes a classic dual-use dilemma: there may be enormous gains to be had here, both for the individual concerned and for society, but there is also a serious danger of causing unimaginable harm. Accordingly, the social, ethical, and public policy dilemmas that will accompany any such intercession are explored in the discussion that follows.

"RISKY" PARENTS

A belief that "poor" parenting is criminogenic is already central to governmental theorizing in the field of youth crime prevention: hence, the Parenting Order, a combination of compulsory parenting classes and requirements to control one's child, backed up by threat of criminal sanctions for failure to comply (Crime and Disorder Act 1998, ss. 8–10). These orders, while initially restricted to those parents whose children had offended, have since been broadened considerably to include the parents of children deemed to have behaved antisocially (though not necessarily criminally) (Antisocial Behaviour Act 2003, s. 26). Thus, already embedded in the youth justice system is an inclination to use the law to intervene in the parenting sphere, along with an established focus on "pre-crime."

It is salient to consider how bioprediction, using neuroscientific data, could be slotted into this context, potentially generating another layer of surveillance and control in a system that has already been described as "an extension of punitiveness underpinned by stigmatising and pathologising constructions of working class families" (Goldson & Jamieson, 2002, 82). As is so often the case with neuroscience research, it does not introduce an entirely novel argument, but rather can be incorporated to shore up positions in an age-old debate. Goldson and Jamieson trace the history of positing parents as a significant causal factor in youth crime from the Victorian age to the present day: for instance, they discuss the mid-twentieth-century work of Bowlby (1944), who found "that 'maternal deprivation' led to the development of 'affectionless characters' with a propensity to commit criminal offences in later years" (Goldson & Jamieson, 2002, 84). Emerging neuroscientific research tells a similar story, using a different discourse, illustrating the tale with brightly colored pictures: it is as though the (bio)markers of the aberrant behavior of the parent are now to be found in the brain of the child.

Interest in the neurological impact of abusive parenting—and its potentially criminogenic consequences—is strongly emerging in UK policy-shaping discourse. As an illustration, *Breakthrough Britain: The Next Generation*, a 2008 report from the Conservative think tank the Centre for Social Justice, features numerous references to neuroscience. The relationship between caregiver and child is described as being of paramount importance: "In the early years, the brain is still forming. Due to this period of rapid brain development, adult–infant interaction can affect the architecture and long-term chemical balance in a child's brain, for better or worse. Key stress response systems, and foundational systems for emotional regulation, kindness, empathy and concern are very immature at birth. How they will unfold is dramatically affected by the infant's relational experiences" (Centre for Social Justice, 2008, 14–15). The publication discusses how being raised in the context of a stressful or impoverished relationship—one that involves continuous criticism and verbal abuse, for instance—can actually damage brain tissue, due to the "toxic levels of stress hormones 'cascading' over the brain" (Centre for Social Justice, 2008, 43). The Centre's report situates this within the crucial concept of epigenetics, the increasing understanding that gene expression is highly dependent upon environmental—including relational—factors (Centre for Social Justice, 2008, 44).

The claim is made therein that "[p]arental beliefs about what constitutes good parenting...may be significantly at odds with...brain science research"

(Centre for Social Justice, 2008, 36). There are some controversial ideas packed within this seemingly innocuous statement. In a departure from postmodern relativism, the potential for brain pictures to be used to (allegedly) illustrate which parenting has "good" and which "bad" effects on the infant brain carries with it the notion that science can be used to answer—or at least to heavily contribute to—what have traditionally been seen as moral questions, exempt from the empirical realm (cf. Harris, 2010). Significantly, the Centre's report emphasizes that, by the time current interventions are triggered, it is typically too late: "[p]olicy is currently focused on dealing with the consequences of early adversity...The most effective intervention strategy...requires helping parents to get it right at the antenatal, postnatal and infant stages" (Centre for Social Justice, 2008, 13).

Where might all this lead? "The ultimate hope is that such information will contribute to the design of more effective prevention and intervention strategies as well as social policies pertaining to the support of families in raising their children" (Twardosz & Lutzker, 2010, 59–68). This is certainly the ambition of the liberal think tank CentreForum, as evidenced in their recent report *Parenting Matters: Early Years and Social Mobility*, which decisively links poor parenting with reduced chances of social mobility in the future (Paterson, 2011). (As an aside, the CentreForum report is heavily influenced by Frank Field's independent review on poverty and life chances, itself infused with neuroscientific research, as yet another example of the steadily increasing power of this particular narrative in such documentation; Field, 2010.)

Much of CentreForum's publication is devoted to a consideration of neuroscientific research into the effects of substandard parenting on the infant brain, along with discussion of what can be done to forestall or counterbalance them. Again, CentreForum's report stresses the importance of intervention at the earliest possible opportunity, namely with parents of those aged 5 years and under, as did the Centre for Crime and Justice Studies. It is interesting that those from different political positions appear to be coalescing on this issue. While acknowledging that their proposal for state interposition in parenting seems counterintuitive, somewhat "nanny-statish," when contrasted with classic laissez-faire liberalism, the CentreForum report views it as vital: "[i]ndeed, if we consider a core element of liberalism to be allowing each individual to realise their full potential, such squandering is in fact itself deeply and fundamentally *illiberal*" (Paterson, 2011, 6).

CentreForum's paper wrestles with the perennial dilemma of how to target "at risk" groups without further stigmatizing an already marginalized population, noting the importance of how such interventions are framed. An obvious way to avoid the stigma attaching to parental education and support is universalization, and, indeed—inspired by CentreForum's report—the Coalition

Government is currently launching national parenting classes through their CANparent initiative (http://www.canparent.org.uk/). To avoid placing undue weight on the shoulders of struggling parents, such endeavors will need to be acutely cognizant of the fact that parenting is an activity that takes place within—and is severely affected by—broader social structures. Regardless, sweeping measures such as these do not negate the perceived need for more directed, intensive interventions with those parents thought to be most at risk of helping to create the "riskiest" children, those with tenacious conduct disorders. Identifying such "conduct-disordered" children, so that they themselves become targets for intervention, is the second key domain where bioprediction looks set to have an impact upon youth justice practice and policy.

"RISKY" CHILDREN

What, precisely, does it mean to say that a child has a conduct disorder? "Conduct disorder in children is best described as a pattern of repetitive behaviour... where the rights of others or social norms are violated" (Baird in Farahany, 2009, 115). Thus, in its very definition, ethical difficulties inherent in pathologizing deviation from social standards begin to emerge. Personalities are seen as becoming "disordered" not solely through parental abuse and neglect but rather "through a multifaceted matrix of interactions between somatic and societal factors—genes and environment—which act together and upon each other in complex ways that shape the brain" (Pickersgill, 2009, 51).

Certain childhood conduct disorders are increasingly being coupled with adult criminality. For instance, Frick and White (2008) point to the display of callous and unemotional traits as being particularly prescient when predicting which offending young people will persist into adulthood. These characteristics can be crudely conceptualized as a sort of "switching off" of empathy, both for oneself and others: "[F]ailing to experience extant physiological arousal in the face of danger or stress or emotions has a certain appeal in a world that seems stressed and afraid all the time" (Shirtcliff et al., 2009, 163).

As a second example, psychopathy—as (controversially) diagnosed using Hare's Checklist (Hare 1991)—is considered highly relevant in the context of the adult criminal justice system: "Psychopathy is a serious personality disorder characterised by emotional and behavioural abnormalities... Psychopaths tend to lack feelings of empathy, guilt, and remorse; they often lack fear of punishment, are impulsive, have difficulty regulating their emotions, and display antisocial and violent behaviour" (Glenn & Raine, 2008, 163). Although psychopathy is, by its constructed definition, an adult disorder, Hare has devised a youth version of his checklist to help predict where conduct disorders in young people may develop into this condition (Forth, Kosson, & Hare, 2003).

Biopredictive techniques seem increasingly likely to be co-opted into facilitating such prognoses due to a growing belief that there are a number of distinguishable structural and functional differences in the brain that correlate with psychopathy. In their literature review of the subject, Glenn and Raine (2008) discuss a neurogenetic propensity to the disorder, along with dissimilarities in the makeup of the prefrontal cortex and with the functioning of the amygdala. The complexity of mapping the neural architecture of psychopathy (even assuming it exists) should not be underestimated: "[I]t is becoming increasingly clear that understanding the neurobiology of psychopathy goes far beyond identifying brain regions that may be involved. Genetics, neurotransmitters, and hormones all impact the functioning of brain structures and the connectivity between them" (Glenn & Raine, 2008, 471).

Similarly, the intricacy of the posited association between conduct disorders and criminality should not be underplayed, given that both the asserted disorder itself and criminal behavior are bound up with a multitude of factors that range far beyond the biological: "The association between [conduct disorders] and antisocial behavior is influenced by several factors such as parental psychopathology, socioeconomic status, neurocognitive impairment, school failure, substance abuse, and other psychiatric disorders as mediators" (von Polier et al., 2012, 133). Further, the essential cultural and societal dimensions of what are delineated as conduct disorders—and, indeed, what are designated as crimes—must not be forgotten (cf. Metzl, 2010).

As in the sphere of parenting, there are already a number of youth justice interventions operational in the United Kingdom that seek to target the "riskiest" children, such as Youth Inclusion Programmes, running in deprived and high-crime areas, directed at those young people deemed most likely to become involved in criminal or antisocial behavior (http://www.justice.gov.uk/youth-justice/prevention/youth-inclusion-programme-yip). At present, these "targets" are chosen through collating information from multiple different sources, such as Youth Offending Teams, the police, children and family services, local education authorities, and schools.

Given the hope that scientists will discover distinct biomarkers for conduct disorders (Moffitt, 2008, 10), a future in which genetic screening or neuroscience plays a role in helping to isolate this alleged subgroup—specifically those involved in violent, aggressive, and antisocial behavior—is far from fantastical. Indeed, risk assessment tools such as Onset for "pre-crime" (http://www.justice.gov.uk/youth-justice/assessment/onset) and Asset for post-offending (http://www.justice.gov.uk/youth-justice/assessment/asset-young-offender-assessment-profile), both of which are routinely deployed in the youth justice system, already include information regarding whether or not a young person has a conduct disorder judged to have an impact upon his or her life as a risk factor. The ubiquity of such technologies demonstrates that risk is the dominant discourse in youth justice policy.

While neuroimaging is not yet at the point where it can be used in risk prediction—with "the mappings from brain activity to mental process to behavior, remain[ing] complex and poorly understood" (Royal Society, 2011, 13)—fMRI scanning of children with a view to learning more about the development of conduct orders associated with antisocial behavior is under way (cf. Crowe & Blair, 2008). In the field of behavioral genetics, research is focusing on purported heritable susceptibility to conduct disorders, particularly with regard to the genes involved in the serotonergic and dopaminergic pathways, most notably MAOA and the serotonin transporter 5HTT (cf. Gunter et al., 2010). However, it is worth remembering that "[d]espite the considerable amount of scientific energy focused on identifying specific genetic factors operant in the genesis of antisocial spectrum disorders... behavioral genetics has yet to elucidate particular genetic pathways that lead to the development of the disorders, or devise molecular tests that may inform diagnosis or treatment" (Gunter et al., 2010, 148). No doubt this is due to the "long and tortuous path from the genome to behavior" (Gunter et al., 2010, 164), with an adverse early environment thought to be a crucial factor in the equation, reciprocally interacting with any biological inheritance (cf. Caspi et al., 2002).

Should biopredictive screening become possible in the future—whether through neuroimaging or genetic testing—the "neuro-molecular gaze" will potentially add another dimension to risk prediction in the youth justice system (cf. Abi-Rached & Rose, 2010). Some of the ethical issues such developments might generate are now considered in greater depth.

RISKY PREDICTIONS

The risk-focused approach to youth justice—even minus any biopredictive element—has been lambasted on multiple grounds: "Risk-factor based research largely ignores fundamental definitional issues. It automatically undergirds its own approach with a set of uninterrogated, supposedly culture- and jurisdiction-free assumptions about what is harm, what is crime and what risks need to be managed... [B]y side-stepping definitional issues and ignoring socio-cultural and temporal variations, [it] tends to support the legal and political status quo and to marginalise radical discourses that question fundamental definitions and mainstream values and practices in all cultures" (O'Mahony, 2009, 107). In short, the risk paradigm is ultimately directed at predicting a certain *kind* of crime, namely the predatory violence more prominent among marginalized groups, rather than, for instance, the crimes of the powerful, such as state crimes, green crimes, or white-collar crimes.

Undeniably, all prediction involving systems as richly complex (and fundamentally unpredictable) as human beings carries with it the unavoidable problem of identifying false positives, along with the concomitant danger of the adverse effects of labeling, of self-fulfilling prophesies: labels do not come with much higher potential for detriment than "psychopath." It is foreseeable that, once a person has been branded as a risk through a positive (or rather negative) genetic test or brain scan for predisposition to antisocial behavior, state overreactions to normal childhood transgressions become "justified," with every minor infraction held up as "proof" of dangerousness. Conversely, it can reasonably be argued that basing predictions on both behavior *and* biology might help to *avoid* a disproportionate response. No predictive system is without its pitfalls, yet at least some degree of prediction is an unavoidable aspect of all legal systems. Although the inability to infallibly identify those—and only those—who will go on to seriously offend will remain, regardless of advances in knowledge, the situation may feasibly be improved by using all the different strands of information available. However, to avoid falling victim to dichotomous thinking, it is important to remember ultimately that criminal risk exists on a spectrum: there is no "them and us," there is only us.

Singh and Rose strike a note of caution: "[I]nformation about a biomarker can help to build a risk profile for a particular condition or set of behaviours. But biomarkers alone, taken out of context of environmental influences, are unlikely ever to provide complete explanations for children's behaviour or a forecast of how children's lives will unfold. Biology is not destiny: biology provides information about potentials" (Singh & Rose, 2009). Tellingly, even eminent criminologist David Farrington—whose research is routinely deployed by politicians to justify the risk-based approach—has sounded the following warning: "[C]aution is ... required. In particular, any notion that better screening can enable policy makers to identify the young children destined to join the 5 per cent of offenders responsible for 50–60 per cent of crime is fanciful. Even if there were no ethical objection to putting 'potential delinquent' labels round the necks of young children, there would still continue to be statistical barriers. Research into the continuity of antisocial behaviour shows substantial flows out of—as well as in to—the pool of children who develop chronic conduct problems. This demonstrates the danger of assuming that antisocial five-year-olds are the criminals ... of tomorrow, as well as for highlighting the undoubted opportunities that exist for prevention" (Sutton et al., 2005, 5).

By focusing on biomarkers—which, taken alone, will remain poor predictors of risk—one danger is that more salient (and possibly even more intransigent) factors, such as social inequality, may be sidelined, their corrosive effects medicalized. However, this is by no means an inevitability, and the converse danger also holds true: namely, that there may be an unhelpfully narrow focus on social factors, at the expense of relevant biological ones. It is important to remain watchful for over-simplified solutions to complex problems, regardless of whether they emanate from the sociological or the biological realm, especially given the inextricable entwinement of these two fields.

A related concern with current predictive tools is that, while they exhibit a *theoretical* appreciation of the multicausal nature of criminalized behavior, *practically* they frequently culminate in responses that focus on the individual responsibility of the (potential) transgressor (cf. O'Mahony, 2009). Bioprediction risks taking this propensity to focus on individuals to new depths, delving into their craniums. As has been pointed out: "While it is still unclear whether individual predictions will ever be possible, in the current political and social climate, the assumption that an individual would benefit from…testing seems naïve when the test in question would be providing information about a susceptibility to violence and antisocial behaviour in a young person" (Levitt & Pieri, 2009, 192). Such procedures are ultimately aimed at protecting society from young people designated as "risky" and thus create a biopolitical conflict between individual human rights and wider public security that will require sensitive resolution.

The human rights most obviously threatened by incorporating a biopredictive element into actuarial risk assessment instruments (already utilitarian at heart) are those ostensibly protected by Articles 8 and 9 of the European Convention on Human Rights. Potential issues in relation to Article 8, the right to privacy, include those such as who would be authorized to order collection of biological data and in what circumstances, alongside questions of ownership and access (cf. Foundation for Information Policy Research, 2006). Significantly, even if this information is gathered with benign intent, this does not guarantee how it may be commandeered in some unforeseen future. There are also potential incursions into Article 9, the right to freedom of thought: An expanded concept of cognitive liberty, more tightly defining the limits of state power in relation to the individual, has been advanced as necessary in the face of developments that have the potential both to view—and ultimately to alter—neural pathways (cf. Boire, 2000). It is to this issue of where risk prediction may lead that this chapter now turns.

RISKY INTERVENTIONS

Controversies surrounding risk prediction are compounded by the interventions they may instigate, particularly if these are neuropharmacological. Returning to psychopathy: "[W]hile psychopathy has thus far been found to be intransigent to treatment attempts, an understanding of the neural substrates of psychopathy will likely be a major contributor to future treatment and prevention" (Glenn & Raine, 2008, 463).[1] The hope is that by understanding contributors to the etiology of such afflictions at the molecular level, novel treatment pathways will open up. A pivotal issue—both practically and ethically—is at what point in time any intervention should take place. In one study, a number of top working neuroscientists (though by no means all) advocated intervention with "fledgling psychopaths" (Pickersgill, 2009, 53). The general consensus is that such measures would need to take place with very young children in order to be effectual (Beauchaine, 2009), due to this age group's increased neural pliability: "The plasticity of brain development over the first decades of life may...mean that personality (and by extrapolation personality disorder) has the ability to change and that it is not set in stone by late adolescence. If this is the case, there may be grounds for optimism in terms of early identification of high-risk/high-harm children and therapeutic intervention to remove them from adverse developmental trajectories" (Vizard, 2008, 393).

In short, "interventions with children at risk of antisocial behavior may be effective if they begin when children are young, more malleable and without an entrenched history of indifference to the problems of others" (Shirtcliff et al., 2009, 162). Certain researchers are recommending that intercession may need to take place before these "future criminals" are even born: "[I]f serious offending is in part neurodevelopmentally determined, successful prevention efforts would be most effective if they began prenatally" (Raine et al., 2010, 191). The ethical issues in play here are stark, magnified as the age of those concerned drops, especially if the children involved are asymptomatic, and—for reasons already explored—only somewhat spuriously "pre"-symptomatic: "Whilst predictions are always probabilistic, decisions and actions are determinate" (Rose, 2010, 80).

A question that arises in tandem with that of when interventions should take place is whether (and whose) consent will be required. Leading neuroscientists and neuroethicists have posed an aspect of this dilemma in the following terms: "[I]f we were to develop pharmacological therapies for psychopathy...would the state be justified in forcibly medicating pre-psychopathic children who will otherwise likely go on to injure or kill innocent members of society?" (Nadelhoffer et al., 2012, 94). This is an extreme example, as interventions may be proposed in situations where the concern falls far short of suspected psychopathy. To what extent will (and should) the children in question have the power to accept or refuse any such intercessions? It is worth remembering that, were interventions to be offered in the youth justice context, it is often the least powerful (of an already largely powerless group) that are involved here, with the children being targeted almost incontrovertibly drawn from the most marginalized communities. Children in general rarely have a true say in the development of the processes that can so fundamentally affect them, in spite of the United Kingdom's ostensible commitment to such participation under the United Nations Convention on the Rights of the Child (1989). The potential repercussions such developments could have in terms of how children see themselves—and how others perceive them—need to be reflected upon. These issues—already arising in relation to bioprediction of physical disorders—are significantly amplified when they relate to predictions of behavior, being even more bound up with an individual's sense of self, of identity.

Exceptionally, a fascinating research project in Holland recently gathered the views of young people who had offended in relation to the implications of genetic screening and neuroimaging for the prevention and treatment of antisocial behavior (Horstkötter et al., 2012). Their voices were considered important to "enrich the debate, because as experiential experts they have a rather specific perspective that may throw another light on the issues discussed or that may introduce new elements hitherto overlooked or neglected" (Horstkötter et al., 2012, 290). Those interviewed had mixed opinions on these developments, with some regarding them as potentially supportive, as helping them (and their parents) to avoid the pains of future punishment, while others were understandably concerned about the aforementioned dangers of labeling, of stigmatization, of false positives (Horstkötter et al., 2012, 289).

Interestingly, these young people expressed concern about interventions potentially having a flattening effect, robbing them of their individual capacities, such as anger and aggression, that—while often socially disapproved of— they themselves valued and saw as potentially instrumental in getting what they wanted (Horstkötter et al., 2012, 292). They voiced their fears that "therapeutic" interventions may mean longer periods of confinement and that they were less likely to be efficacious where coerced. "Treatments" were often viewed as a form of punishment and thus seen as unjust, especially when targeted at "pre-crime" (Horstkotter et al., 2012, 293).

Some of those interviewed professed a reticence toward taking drugs, on the pretext of health, for reasons of bodily integrity, and because they felt it meant that they were not working through their issues "naturally" (Horstkötter et al., 2012, 293). Of course, neural engineering, measures that seek to "rewire" the brain, will not necessarily be solely (or indeed in any way) drug-based: as demonstrated in the literature on the development of conduct disorders, environmental factors are equally as capable of shaping neurochemistry. As an example, the Kids Company's research collaboration with neuroscientists, mentioned at the beginning of this chapter, seeks to establish whether therapeutic interventions such as surrogate parenting and loving care can reverse brain-based ill effects (http://www.kidspeaceofmind.org/).

Notably, the young people interviewed in the Dutch study were on the whole skeptical about the power of biological (and, indeed, psychiatric) narratives to explain their involvement in crime; they saw the functional, psychological, and social dimensions as being far more pivotal. By focusing on individuals—rather than on the interrelationships, cultures, and epochs within which they exist—there is much that "hard" science cannot reveal: humanity is a network that resists being coherently broken down into isolated units. Tellingly, these young people stressed their normality, their agency, the fact that they are simply part of the human continuum: "And I know that, I am just a normal boy... We are also normal humans, you know?" (J8 in Horstkötter et al., 2012).

CONCLUDING REMARKS

It was not necessary to develop neuroimaging to appreciate that early child-hood abuse and neglect can have a lasting negative impact on development; however, perhaps the existence of such pictures adds urgency to the perceived need to create social policies to support parents who are struggling, to provide children with nurturing experiences that counteract the corrosive encounters they have had to endure, and hopefully to thereby reverse the brain-based deficiencies that have resulted (cf. Perry, 2006). Along with being an exer-cise in humanity, such measures could indirectly have preventive benefits for the youth justice system, where many of these children might otherwise find themselves.

Using bioprediction in this way—to inform broad social policy and to advo-cate for loving care for those deemed to be *at risk*—is far less problematic than actively targeting and potentially compulsorily drugging (often the same) chil-dren because they are seen to be *a risk* to society. Neither genetic testing nor neuroscience are at a point where they can be used to screen individuals and predict childhood conduct disorders that will develop into more serious adult conditions, associated with criminal risk. Nor may they ever be. However, should such a position be deemed to have been reached in the future, it will be vital to proceed with extreme caution, paying full mind to the extremely sensi-tive issues that are provoked and were touched upon within this chapter.

"Crime," "conduct disorders," and even neuroimages and their interpretation are all human constructions, so this is far more complicated, far more ethically messy, than an "objective" exercise in prediction. Further, it is dangerously easy to injure when trying to help: brain development is nonlinear, an intricate web of recursive (and often strange) loops, and it may be difficult to foresee the ultimate outcome of any "therapeutic" intervention. Yet, there are also dangers in too easily dismissing new discoveries on the basis of such fears. The cluster of behaviors that are referred to as psychopathy, or one of the other serious conduct disorders, can have horrendous consequences, both for sufferers and their victims: "[I]t remains to be seen whether these attempts to translate from the molecular understanding of the nervous system to the molar management of human affairs represent a genuine advance in our understanding of the kinds of creatures we human beings are, or a premature and unwise extrapolation to society of the modest and always uncertain and correctible knowledge of the laboratory sciences" (Abi-Rached & Rose, 2010, 32).

As a parting observation, the system cannot justly have it both ways: As factors beyond a young person's control—such as the development of a brain-based conduct disorder, partially as a result of inadequate parenting—are increasingly regarded as integral to the genesis of offending, the current youth justice focus on individual responsibility, rooted in a conception of free will, may need to be tempered (cf. Greene & Cohen, 2004). Indeed, how neurobiological advances might affect issues of sentencing and punishment in the youth justice system are important questions for the future.

NOTE

1. Given the extreme resistance of extreme conduct disorders—such as psychopathy—to treatment, a future whereby individuals can be biologically identified as likely to develop this condition but where there is no efficacious treatment available is a distinct possibility, bearing with it the question of what the response would then be.

REFERENCES

Abi-Rached, J., & Rose, N. (2010). The birth of the neuromolecular gaze. *History of the Human Sciences, 23*(1), 11–36.

Batmanghelidjh, C. (2012). These kids are terrified, not morally flawed; don't dismiss gang members as scum. They are as traumatised as soldiers who go to war. *The Times,* March 29, p. 18.

Beauchaine, T. (2009). Role of biomarkers and endophenotypes in prevention and treatment of psychopathological disorders. *Biomarkers in Medicine, 3*(1), 1–3.

Boire, R. (2000). On cognitive liberty (part 1). *Journal of Cognitive Liberties, 1*/1, 7–13.

Bowlby, J. (1944). Forty-four juvenile thieves: their characters and home life. *International Journal of Psychoanalysis, 25,* 19–52.

Caspi, A., McClay, J., Moffitt, T., Mill, J., Martin, J., Craig, I., Taylor, A., & Poulton, A. (2002). Role of genotype in the cycle of violence in maltreated children. *Science, 297,* 851–853.

Centre for Social Justice (2008). *Breakthrough Britain: the next generation.* London: Centre for Social Justice.

Crowe, S., & Blair, R. (2008). The development of antisocial behavior: what can we learn from functional neuroimaging studies. *Development and Psychopathology, 20,* 1145–1159.

Farahany, N. (Ed.). (2009). *The impact of behavioral sciences on criminal law.* Oxford: Oxford University Press.

Farrington, D., & West, D. (1993). Criminal, penal and life histories of chronic offenders: risk and protective factors and early identification. *Criminal Behaviour and Mental Health, 3,* 492–523.

Field, F. (2010). *The foundation years: preventing poor children becoming poor adults.* London: HM Government.

Forth, A., Kosson, D., & Hare, R. (2003). *Hare Psychopathy Checklist: Youth Version.* Canada: MHS.

Foundation for Information Policy Research (2006). *Children's databases—safety and privacy. A Report for the Information Commissioner.* Bedfordshire: FIPR.

Frick, P., & White, S. (2008). The importance of callous-unemotional traits for developmental models of aggressive and antisocial behavior. *Journal of Child Psychology and Psychiatry, 49*(4), 359–375.

Glenn, A., & Raine, A. (2008). The neurobiology of psychopathy. *Psychiatric Clinics of North America, 31,* 463–475.

Goldson, B., & Jamieson, J. (2002). Youth crime, the "parenting deficit" and state intervention: a contextual critique. *Youth Justice, 2/2,* 82–99.

Greene, J., & Cohen, J. (2004). For the law, neuroscience changes nothing & everything. *Philosophical Transactions of the Royal Society of London Part B Biological Science, 359*(1451), 1775–1785.

Gunter, T., Vaughn, M., & Philibert, R. (2010). Behavioral genetics in antisocial spectrum disorders and psychopathy. *Behavioral Sciences and the Law, 28,* 148–173.

Hales, J., Nevill, C., Pudney, S., & Tipping, S. (2009). *Longitudinal analysis of the Offending, Crime and Justice Survey 2003-06.* London: Home Office.

Hare, R. (1991). *The Hare Psychopathy Checklist—Revised.* Toronto, Ontario: Multi-Health Systems.

Harris, S. (2010). *The moral landscape: how science can determine human values.* London: Bantam Press.

Horstkötter, D., Berghmans, R., de Ruiter, C., Krumeich, A., & de Wert, G. (2012). "We are also normal humans, you know?" Views and attitudes of juvenile delinquents on antisocial behavior, neurobiology and prevention. *International Journal of Law and Psychiatry, 35*(4), 289–297.

Levitt, M., & Pieri, E. (2009). "It could just be an additional test couldn't it?" Genetic testing for susceptibility to aggression and violence. *New Genetics and Society, 28*(2), 189–200.

Metzl, J. (2010). *Protest psychosis: how schizophrenia became a black disease.* Boston: Beacon Press.

Moffitt, T., Caspi, A., Harrington, H., & Milne, B. (2002). Males on the life-course-persistent and adolescence-limited antisocial pathways: follow-up at age 26 years. *Development and Psychopathology, 14*(1), 179–207.

Moffitt, T. (2008). Research review: DSM-V conduct disorder: research needs for an evidence base. *Journal of Child Psychology and Psychiatry, 49/1,* 3–33.

Nadelhoffer, T., Bibas, S., Grafton, S., Kiehl, K., Mansfield, A., Sinnott-Armstrong, W., & Gazzaniga, M. (2012). Neuroprediction, violence, and the law: setting the stage. *Neuroethics, 5,* 67–99.

Odgers, C., Moffitt, T., Broadbent, J., Dickson, N., Hancox, R., Harrington, H., Poulton, R., Sears, M., Thomson, W., & Caspi, A. (2008). Female and male antisocial trajectories: from childhood origins to adult outcomes. *Development and Psychopathology, 20*(2), 673–716.

O'Mahony, P. (2009). The risk factors prevention paradigm and the causes of youth crime: a deceptively useful analysis? *Youth Justice, 9/2*, 99–114.

Paterson, C. (2011). *Parenting matters: early years and social mobility.* London: CentreForum.

Perry, B. (2006). Applying principles of neurodevelopment to clinical work with maltreated and traumatized children: the neurosequential model of therapeutics. In N. Webb (Ed.), *Working with traumatized youth in child welfare* (pp. 27–52). New York: Guilford Press.

Pickersgill, M. (2009). Between soma and society: neuroscience and the ontology of psychopathy. *Biosocieties, 4,* 45–60.

Raine, A., Lee, L., Yang, Y., & Colletti, P. (2010). Neurodevelopmental marker for limbic maldevelopment in antisocial personality disorder and psychopathy. *British Journal of Psychiatry, 197,* 186–192.

Rose, N. (2010). 'Screen and intervene': governing risky brains. *History of the Human Sciences, 23*(1), 79–105.

Royal Society (2011). *Neuroscience and the law.* London: Royal Society.

Shirtcliff, E., Vitacco, M., Graf, A., Gostisha, A., Merz, J., & Zahn-Waxler, C. (2009). Neurobiology of empathy and callousness: implications for the development of antisocial behavior. *Behavioral Sciences and the Law, 27,* 137–171.

Skardhamar, T. (2010). Reconsidering the theory on adolescent-limited and life-course persistent antisocial behaviour. *British Journal of Criminology, 49,* 863–878.

Singh, I., & Rose, N. (2009). Biomarkers in psychiatry. *Nature,460,* 202–207.

Sutton, C., Utting, D., & Farrington, D. (2005). *Support from the start: working with young children and their families to reduce the risks of crime and antisocial behaviour.* London: Home Office.

Twardosz, S., & Lutzker, J. (2010). Child maltreatment and the developing brain: a review of neuroscience perspectives. *Aggression and Violent Behavior, 15*(1), 59–68.

Vizard, E. (2008). Emerging severe personality disorder in childhood. *Psychiatry,7/9,* 389–394.

von Polier, G., Vloet, T., & Herpertz-Dahlmann, B. (2012). ADHD and delinquency—a developmental perspective. *Behavioral Sciences and the Law, 30,* 121–139.

Youth Justice Board/Ministry of Justice (2012). *Youth justice statistics: executive summary.* London: YJB/MOJ.

4

The Inclusion of Biological Risk Factors in Violence Risk Assessments

JOHN MONAHAN

> Appellees claim, and the district court agreed, that it is virtually impossible to predict future criminal conduct with any degree of accuracy.... The procedural protections are thus, in their view, unavailing because the ultimate decision is intrinsically arbitrary and uncontrolled. Our cases indicate, however, that from a legal point of view there is nothing inherently unattainable about a prediction of future criminal conduct. Such a judgment forms an important element in many decisions, and we have specifically rejected the contention, based on the same sort of sociological data relied upon by appellees and the district court, "that it is impossible to predict future behavior and that the question is so vague as to be meaningless." (*Schall v. Martin,* 1984, at 278–279)

As the existence of biological risk factors for violence becomes increasingly plausible (Raine, 2013; Aharoni, Vincent, Harenski, Calhoun, Sinnott-Armstrong, Gazzaniga, & Kiehl, 2013), it appears inevitable that courts will be confronted with evidence of biological risk factors in cases in which the assessment of violence risk is a central issue. In this chapter, I reflect on what the use of "bioprediction" in American[1] law might learn from the law's extensive experience with the use of psychosocial risk factors to anticipate harm. The chapter proceeds in three parts. In Part I, I describe three legal contexts that rely explicitly and heavily on the assessment of an individual's likelihood of future violence: the civil commitment of people with serious mental illness, the civil commitment of "sexually violent predators," and—in an increasing number of jurisdictions—the criminal sentencing of convicted offenders. In Part II, I review the science of violence risk assessment and a range of current approaches to the task of assessing violence risk. In Part III, I discuss one legal issue that will confront neuroscientists—as it has confronted other behavioral scientists—who offer estimates of violence risk in the courtroom: to what constitutional standard of review will the admissibility of biological risk factors for violence be held, and will their use survive this review?

PART I. THE LAW OF VIOLENCE RISK ASSESSMENT

Civil commitment

All states have statutes allowing certain people with a mental disorder to be involuntarily hospitalized in a psychiatric facility.[2] Prior to the late 1960s, involuntary commitment to psychiatric hospitals was justified primarily by a concern for people who were seen to be "in need of treatment." Beginning at that time, however, public safety began to dominate as a rationale for commitment, and risk of harmful behavior—called "dangerousness" in statutes and court decisions—became a primary focus of legal attention (Appelbaum, 1994). Typically, to qualify for involuntary civil commitment as a hospital inpatient, the individual had to have a mental illness and because of this illness be either "dangerous to others" or "dangerous to self" (Perlin, 2006). Gostin (2008) has placed the involuntary hospitalization of people with mental illness in legal context:

> Civil commitment is the detention (usually in a hospital or other specially designated institution) for the purposes of care and treatment. Civil commitment, like isolation and quarantine, is both a preventive measure designed to avert risk, and a rehabilitative measure designed to benefit persons who are confined. Consequently, persons subject to commitment usually are offered, and sometimes are required to submit to, medical treatment. Civil commitment is normally understood to mean confinement of persons with mental illness or mental retardation, but it is also used for containing persons with infectious diseases, notably tuberculosis, for treatment. (p. 210)

While there was a flurry of interest during the 1970s in the constitutionality of civil commitment statutes, the U.S. Supreme Court left no doubt that it would uphold such laws provided that adequate procedural safeguards were in place, such as proof of disorder and "dangerousness" by clear and convincing evidence (*Addington v. Texas*, 1979).

State civil commitment statutes enacted in recent years have attempted to clarify the often-vague "mentally ill and dangerous" standard. For example, Virginia thoroughly revised its commitment standard in 2008 (Virginia Code § 37.2-817C) to read as follows:

[If] the judge or special justice finds by clear and convincing evidence that

(a) the person has a mental illness and there is a substantial likelihood that, as a result of mental illness, the person will, in the near future,
  (1) cause serious physical harm to himself or others as evidenced by recent behavior causing, attempting, or threatening harm and other relevant information, if any, or
  (2) suffer serious harm due to his lack of capacity to protect himself from harm or to provide for his basic human needs, and
(b) all available less restrictive treatment alternatives to involuntary inpatient treatment have been…determined to be inappropriate,

the judge or special justice shall [order] that the person be admitted involuntarily to a facility for a period of treatment not to exceed 30 days.

Cohen, Bonnie, and Monahan (2008), in an article written to train mental health professionals in performing civil commitment evaluations under this new standard, operationalized the phrase "substantial likelihood" as follows:

In our view, a 'one-in-four' estimated risk of serious harm in the near future is sufficient, particularly when the harm being threatened is potentially fatal, as opposed to cutting, burning, or punching oneself. A 'substantial risk' is *not* meant to mean 'more likely than not' (51%). (p. 8)

This recommendation of Cohen et al. is consistent with Monahan and Wexler's (1978) position that the legal *standard of proof*—in this case, "clear and convincing evidence" (*Addington v. Texas*, 1979)—is separable from the probabilistic *standard of commitment*—in this case, a "'one-in-four' [i.e., .25] estimated risk of serious harm." It is also consistent with the results of a survey of state and federal judges finding that the lowest likelihood of violence that most judges would accept as fulfilling the "dangerousness" standard of civil commitment was approximately 0.25 (Monahan & Silver, 2003).[3]

Sexually violent predators

In *Kansas v. Hendricks* (1997), the U.S. Supreme Court upheld for the first time a "sexually violent predator" law. Under the Kansas statute at issue, an offender, after being convicted of a specified sexual crime and serving the prison sentence associated with that criminal conviction, can be found to be a sexually violent predator, and this finding can serve as the predicate for civil commitment to a mental hospital for an indefinite period. The Act defined a sexually violent predator as "any person who has been convicted of or charged with a sexually

violent offense and who suffers from a mental abnormality or personality disorder which makes the person likely to engage in repeat acts of sexual violence."
A mental abnormality was defined in the Act not as a serious mental illness, such
as schizophrenia, but rather as a "congenital or acquired condition affecting the
emotional or volitional capacity which predisposes the person to commit sexually violent offenses in a degree constituting such person a menace to the health
and safety of others." In upholding Hendricks's civil commitment, the Supreme
Court emphasized two facts in the case: Hendricks's own admission of his
uncontrollable urges, and Hendrick's risk of future violence. The Court noted:

> Hendricks even conceded that, when he becomes "stressed out," he cannot
> "control the urge" to molest children. This admitted lack of volitional control,
> coupled with a prediction of future dangerousness, adequately distinguishes
> Hendricks from other dangerous persons who are perhaps more properly
> dealt with exclusively through criminal proceedings. (p. 360)

Sixteen states and the District of Columbia have now enacted sexually violent
predator statutes that provide for the post-imprisonment civil commitment of
sex offenders who have a mental abnormality and are believed to be at high risk
of violent recidivism (Beecher-Monas & Garcia-Rill, 2009).

Note that some states now not only affirmatively require the use of named
risk assessment instruments in sexually violent predator evaluations, but also
specify the exact cutoff score on these instruments required to proceed in the
evaluation process. The Virginia Sexually Violent Predator Act (Virginia Code
§37.2-900 et seq. (2013)), for example, reads as follows:

> [E]ach month, the Director [of the Department of Corrections] shall review
> the database [of prisoners incarcerated for sexually violent offenses] and
> identify all [p]risoners who are scheduled for release from prison within
> 10 months from the date of such review [(i)] who receive a score of five or
> more on the Static-99 or a similar score on a comparable, scientifically vali-
> dated instrument as designated by the Commissioner [of the Department of
> Behavioral Health], or (ii) who receive a score of four on the Static-99 or a
> similar score on a comparable, scientifically validated instrument if the sex-
> ually violent offense mandating the prisoner's evaluation [was one] where
> the victim was under the age of 13, or (iii) whose records reflect such aggra-
> vating circumstances that the Director determines the offender appears to
> meet the definition of a sexually violent predator.

The Static-99 is an actuarial risk assessment instrument consisting of ten
empirically derived risk factors: (1) young (less than 25 years old), (2) ever lived

with a lover for at least 2 years, (3) index nonsexual violence, (4) prior non-sexual violence, (5) prior sex offenses, (6) prior sentencing dates, (7) any convictions for noncontact sex offense, (8) any unrelated victims, (9) any stranger victims, and (10) any male victims (Anderson & Hanson, 2010). (On the issue of clinical vs. actuarial prediction, see Part II below.)

Criminal sentencing

In *Barefoot v. Estelle* (1983), the U.S. Supreme Court considered the constitutionality of using predictions of violence for the purpose of determining whom to sentence to death. In an opinion upholding the Texas statute, Justice White wrote:

> It is urged that psychiatrists, individually and as a group, are incompetent to predict with an acceptable degree of reliability that a particular criminal will commit other crimes in the future and so represent a danger to the community…The suggestion that no psychiatrist's testimony may be presented with respect to a defendant's future dangerousness is somewhat like asking us to disinvent the wheel. In the first place, it is contrary to our cases…and if it is not impossible for even a lay person sensibly to arrive at that conclusion, it makes little sense, if any, to submit that psychiatrists, out of the entire universe of persons who might have an opinion on the issue, would know so little about the subject that they should not be permitted to testify. (pp. 896–897)

While the constitutionality of risk assessment in criminal sentencing has not been challenged since *Barefoot*, the use of risk assessments as a matter of sentencing policy has been much more controversial. For example, the federal Sentencing Commission created by the Sentencing Reform Act of 1984 confronted what it referred to as a "philosophical problem" when it set out to draft guidelines for use in sentencing convicted offenders. The problem had to do with determining "the purposes of criminal punishment."

> Some argue that appropriate punishment should be defined primarily on the basis of the principle of "just deserts." Under this principle, punishment should be scaled to the offender's culpability and the resulting harms. Others argue that punishment should be imposed primarily on the basis of practical "crime control" considerations. This theory calls for sentences that most effectively lessen the likelihood of future crime, either by deterring others or incapacitating the defendant. (*U.S. Sentencing Guidelines Manual*, § 1A3, 2000)

Assessing the likelihood of future crime and violence is jurisprudentially irrelevant to sentencing under the backward-looking principle of punishment as just deserts but is a central task of sentencing under the forward-looking principle of crime control. With one exception, risk assessment in sentencing is not allowed under the backward-looking federal sentencing guidelines. The exception is that a defendant's criminal history can be relied upon as a risk factor in sentencing, since, in the words of one of the reports that led to the creation of the Sentencing Commission, "[a] record of prior offenses bears *both* on the offender's deserts *and* on the likelihood of recidivism" (von Hirsch, 1976, p. 87, emphasis added).

The assessment of an offender's risk of recidivism was once a central component of criminal sentencing in the United States. In California, for example, indeterminate sentencing—whereby an offender is given a low minimum sentence and a high maximum sentence and is released from prison whenever he or she is believed to no longer present a risk of committing new crime—was introduced in 1917 (Messinger & Johnson, 1978). In the 1970s, however, indeterminate sentencing based on forward-looking assessments of offender risk was abolished in California and in many other American jurisdictions in favor of set periods of confinement based on backward-looking appraisals of offender culpability. Sentencing systems now vary greatly at the state level. As Michael Tonry (1999, p. 1) has noted, "there is no longer anything that can be called 'the American system' of sentencing and corrections." Many state sentencing guidelines, like the federal ones, "typically reduce authorized sentencing criteria solely to the offender's crime and to some measure of his or her criminal history" (Tonry, 1999, p. 9; see also Tonry, 2010).

This situation is rapidly changing, however. Remarkably, after a hiatus of almost 40 years, there has recently been a resurgence of interest in risk assessment as an essential part of criminal sentencing in many American states. For example, as of 2010, all California prisoners convicted of nonviolent offenses are being administered the California Static Risk Assessment Instrument, which consists of the offender's age, gender, and numerous aspects of his or her prior criminal record (e.g., number of weapons offenses, number of drug offenses) (Turner, Hess, & Jannetta, 2009). Prisoners who are determined by this instrument not to pose a high risk of reoffense are eligible for placement into "Non-Revocable Parole," defined as "a non-supervised version of parole where you do not report to a Parole Agent."

Three factors, alone or in combination, may explain the remarkable return of risk assessment in criminal sentencing. First, the fiscal state of many American jurisdictions is so dire that maintaining an enormous prison population is simply not a sustainable option. California spends over $8 billion a year—11 percent of the entire state budget—on prisons, and at the time of this writing the state is experiencing a deficit of over $25 billion. What better way to reduce prison budgets than by releasing from prison those determined by risk assessment to be the least likely to return to it (Bergstrom & Mistick, 2010)? Second, the crime rate in the United States in 2009 was at its lowest level since 1969 (Austin, 2010). When better to effectively shorten prison sentences, or to try noninstitutional forms of sanction, than when the crime rate—and therefore public concern about crime—is significantly down? Finally, the science and technology of risk assessment is much more highly developed now than it was in the 1970s and 1980s, when culpability replaced risk as the principal driver of sentencing policy (Heilbrun, 2009). Why not take advantage of recently validated risk assessment instruments if the use of such instruments could simultaneously reduce prison costs *and* recidivism rates (Scott-Hayward, 2009)? It is to these instruments that we now turn.

PART II. THE SCIENCE OF VIOLENCE RISK ASSESSMENT

Much flows from the definition of "risk assessment" that one chooses. The definition of risk assessment given by Kraemer, Kazdin, Offord, Kessler, Jensen, and Kupfer (1997) is the one I have found most useful: "The process of using risk factors to estimate the likelihood (i.e., probability) of an outcome occurring in a population." Importantly, Kraemer et al. (1997) define a risk factor simply as (a) any variable that statistically correlates with the outcome and also (b) precedes the outcome in time. There is no implication in this definition that the risk factor in any sense "causes" the occurrence of the outcome.[4]

Approaches to violence risk assessment

No distinction in the history of risk assessment has been more influential than Paul Meehl's (1954) cleaving the field into "clinical" and "actuarial" (or statistical) approaches. In recent years, however, a plethora of instruments has been published that are not adequately characterized by a simple clinical–actuarial dichotomy. Rather, the risk assessment process now exists on a continuum of rule-based structure, with completely unstructured ("clinical") assessment occupying one pole of the continuum, completely structured ("actuarial") assessment occupying the other pole, and several forms of partially structured assessment lying between the two (Monahan, 2008; for reviews of the comparative validity of instruments based on these approaches, see Kroner, Mills, & Morgan, 2005; Singh, Grann, & Fazel, 2011).

The violence risk assessment process, in this regard, might usefully be seen as having four components: (1) identifying empirically valid risk factors, (2) determining a method for measuring ("scoring") these risk factors, (3) establishing a procedure for combining scores on the risk factors, and (4) producing an estimate of violence risk (Skeem & Monahan, 2011). It is possible to array five current approaches to violence risk assessment according to whether the approach structures (i.e., specifies rules for generating) none, one, two, three, or all four components of this process. Purely "clinical" risk assessment structures *none* of the components. The clinician selects, measures, and combines risk factors and produces an estimate of violence risk, as his or her clinical experience and judgment indicate.

Performing a violence risk assessment by reference to a standard list of risk factors that have been found to be empirically valid (e.g., age, past violence), such as the lists provided in psychiatric texts, structures *one* component of the process. Such lists function as an *aide mémoire* to identify which risk factors the clinician should attend to in conducting his or her assessment, but they do not further specify a method for measuring these risk factors.

The "structured professional judgment" (SPJ) approach exemplified by the HCR [Historical-Clinical-Risk Management]-20 (Webster, Douglas, Eaves, & Hart, 1997) structures *two* components of the process: the identification and measurement of risk factors, which may be scored as 0 if absent, 1 if possibly present, or 2 if definitely present. Structured professional judgment instruments do not go further and structure how the individual risk factors are to be combined in clinical practice. As Webster et al. (1997, p. 22) have stated: "it makes little sense to sum the number of risk factors present in a given case... [I]t is both possible and reasonable for an assessor to conclude that an assessee is at high risk for violence based on the presence of a single risk factor." A direct verbal threat of imminent violence is usually taken as the paradigmatic "single risk factor" that could trigger an estimate of high violence risk.

Approaches to risk assessment that structure *three* components of the process are illustrated by the Classification of Violence Risk (COVR; Monahan et al., 2001; Sturup, Kristiansson, & Monahan, in press). These instruments structure the identification, measurement, and combination of risk factors (via a classification tree design or summing scores). But those who developed the instruments do not recommend that the final risk assessment reflect *only* the combined scores on the assessed risk factors. Given the possibility that rare factors influence the likelihood of violence in a particular case—and that, precisely because such factors rarely occur, they will never appear on an actuarial instrument—a professional review of the risk estimate is advised.

The best-known forensic instrument that structures all *four* of the components of the violence risk assessment process is the Violence Risk Appraisal Guide (VRAG; Quinsey, Harris, Rice, & Cormier, 2006; Rice, Harris, & Lang, in press). This instrument not only structures the identification, measurement, and combination of risk factors but also specifies that once an individual's violence risk has been actuarially characterized, the risk assessment process is complete. As Quinsey et al. (2006) have stated, "What we are advising is not the *addition* of actuarial methods to existing practice, but rather the *replacement* of existing practice with actuarial methods" (p. 197).

Group data and individual risk assessments

One issue that has generated much controversy is the argument of Hart, Michie, and Cooke (2007) that the margins of error surrounding individual risk assessments of violence are so wide as to make such predictions "virtually meaningless" (p. 263). Cooke and Michie (2010) concluded, "it is clear that predictions of future offending cannot be achieved, with any degree of confidence, in the individual case" (p. 259).

This position has been vigorously contested. For example, Hanson and Howard (2010) demonstrate that the wide margin of error for individual risk assessments is a function of having only two possible outcomes (violent/not violent) and therefore conveys nothing about the predictive utility of a risk assessment tool. Because all violence risk assessment approaches, not just actuarial ones, yield some estimate of the likelihood that a dichotomous outcome will occur, none are immune from Hart et al.'s (2007) argument. Instead, their argument "if true,... would be a serious challenge to the applicability of any empirically based risk procedure to any individual for anything" (Hanson & Howard, 2010, p. 277).

My view (Skeem & Monahan, 2011) is that group data theoretically can be, and in many areas empirically are, highly informative when making decisions about individual cases. Consider two examples from other forms of risk assessment. In the insurance industry, "until an individual insured is treated as a member of a group, it is impossible to know his expected loss, because for practical purposes that concept is a statistical one based on group probabilities. Without relying on such probabilities, it would be impossible to set a price for insurance coverage at all" (Abraham, 1986, p. 79). In weather forecasting, a wealth of data is available on given events occurring under specified conditions. Therefore, when meteorologists "predict a 70 percent chance of rain, there is measurable precipitation just about 70 percent of the time" (National Research Council, 1989, 46). Finally, consider the revolver analogy of Grove and Meehl (1996, 305–306):

Suppose you are a political opponent held in custody by a mad dictator. Two revolvers are put on the table and you are informed that one of them has five live rounds with one empty chamber, the other has five empty chambers and one live cartridge, and you are required to play Russian roulette. If you live, you will go free. Which revolver would you choose? Unless you have a death wish, you would choose the one with the five empty chambers. Why?

Because you would know that the odds are five to one that you will survive if you pick that revolver, whereas the odds are five to one you will be dead if you choose the other one. Would you seriously think, "Well, it doesn't make any difference what the odds are. Inasmuch as I'm only going to do this once, there is no aggregate involved, so I might as well pick either one of these two revolvers; it doesn't matter which"?

Although the probabilities associated with risk assessment clearly will never be as certain as those associated with bullets being in firing chambers, I find compelling Grove and Meehl's point that group data can powerfully inform individual assessments of violence risk.

PART III. THE INCLUSION OF BIOLOGICAL RISK FACTORS IN VIOLENCE RISK ASSESSMENT INSTRUMENTS

If research demonstrated that a given biological variable functions as a risk factor for violence—that is, that the biological variable statistically correlates with the likelihood of future violence and that the biological variable can be measured before the violence occurs (Kraemer et al., 1997)—under what Fourteenth Amendment Equal Protection Clause test will the inclusion of the biological variable in a violence risk assessment instrument be reviewed? Much can be learned about the constitutional future of "bioprediction" by considering the current constitutional status of three partially[5] biological variables in violence risk assessments: age, gender, and race. We consider here first the empirical relationship between these risk factors and violence, and then the Fourteenth Amendment standard of review to which the risk factor is held.

Age

Few would dispute the conclusion that Sampson and Lauritsen (1994) offered in their definitive review for the National Research Council's Panel on the Understanding and Control of Violent Behavior: "Age is one of the major individual-level correlates of violent offending. In general, arrests for violent crime peak around age 18 and decline gradually thereafter" (p. 18). Age is a risk factor for crimes of sexual violence as well as violence more generally. For example, one review considered ten studies from the United States, the United Kingdom, and Canada involving a total sample of over 4,600 male sex offenders. The review concluded:

On average, the rate of sexual recidivism decreased with age.... For rapists, the highest risk age period was between 18 and 25 years, with a gradual decline in risk for each older age period. There were very few old rapists (greater than age 60) and none were known to recidivate sexually (Hanson, 2001).

Age is also a risk factor for violence committed by people with mental disorder. In the MacArthur Study of violence by people between 18 and 40 years old who were in psychiatric facilities, for every 1-year increase in a patient's age, the odds that the patient would commit a violent act within the first several months after discharge decreased by 20 percent (Monahan et al., 2001).

Age as a risk factor for violence is subject only to the lowest form of Fourteenth Amendment scrutiny. "States may discriminate on the basis of age without offending the Fourteenth Amendment if the age classification in question is rationally related to a legitimate state interest" (*Kimel v. Florida Board of Regents*, 2000). There being no question that preventing violence is a "legitimate" state interest, and that a person's age is "rationally" related to whether he or she will engage in it, age is never questioned as a risk factor for violence. For example, age is an explicit risk factor on the Static-99 (Anderson & Hanson, 2010) which is used in many sexually violent predator evaluations and is included in the California Static Risk Assessment Instrument (Turner at al., 2009) recently adopted to determine parole eligibility in California.

Gender

That women commit violent acts at a much lower rate than men is a staple in criminology and has been known for as long as official records have been kept. The earliest major review of this topic, by Maccoby and Jacklin (1974), concluded that "[t]he sex difference in aggression has been observed in all cultures in which the relevant behavior has been observed. Boys are more aggressive both physically and verbally.... The sex difference is found as early as social play begins—at age 2 or 2 ½" (p. 352). Another major review, by Sampson and Lauritsen (1994), concluded that "sex is one of the strongest demographic correlates of violent offending.... [M]ales are far more likely than females to be arrested for all crimes of violence including homicide, rape, robbery, and assault" (p. 19). Of the 411, 543 persons arrested for a violent crime in the United States in 2011 (the latest year for which data are available), 330,863 (80%) were men and 80,671 (20%) were women (Department of Justice, 2012). For violent offending that is explicitly sexual in nature, the gender disparity is overwhelming: of the 12,069 people arrested for forcible rape in the United States in 2011, 11,934 were men (99%) and 135 (1%) were women. Regarding violence, it is hard to gainsay the conclusion of Gottfredson and Hirschi's classic, *A General Theory of Crime* (1990): "[G]ender differences appear to be invariant over time and space" (1988, 145).

In *J.E.B. v. Alabama ex rel. T.B.* (1994), the U.S. Supreme Court noted that it consistently has subjected gender-based classifications to heightened Fourteenth Amendment scrutiny "in recognition of the real danger that government policies that professedly are based on reasonable considerations in fact may be reflective of 'archaic and overbroad' generalizations about gender... or based on 'outdated misconceptions'" (p. 135). In *U.S. v. Virginia* (1996), the Court more explicitly stated that, in reviewing classifications based on gender, the reviewing court must determine whether the proffered justification is "exceedingly persuasive" (p. 531). Justice Ginsburg wrote for the majority that the State must show "at least that the [challenged] classification serves 'important governmental objectives and that the discriminatory means employed' are 'substantially related to the achievement of those objectives.' The justification must be genuine, not hypothesized or invented post hoc in response to litigation" (p. 533).

Tested against the jurisprudential considerations articulated in cases such as *J.E.B.* and *Virginia*, using gender as a risk factor for violence should have little difficulty surviving an equal protection challenge: the government's police power objective in preventing violence in society is surely "important" (*U.S. v. Hendricks*, 1997, 357) and including gender as a risk factor on an actuarial prediction instrument is "substantially related" to the accuracy with which such an instrument can forecast violence—and therefore assist in its prevention. Gender differences in violence are genuine and not hypothesized. And while they may be archaic, they are not outdated: the same gender difference found in the earliest published crime statistics—men made up 91 percent of homicide offenders in 13th-century England (Given, 1977)—was found 800 years later in the latest published crime statistics: men made up 88 percent of homicide offenders in the United States in 2011 (Department of Justice, 2012).

Gender is a risk factor on the California Static Risk Assessment (Turner, 2009) and on the Classification of Violence Risk (Monahan, 2001). The Static-99 (Anderson & Hanson, 2010) is recommended by its developers only for use on male offenders.

Race

Most of the research on race and violence has focused on aggregate differences between whites and African Americans (Reiss & Roth, 1993). African Americans accounted for 13 percent of the American population in 2009 (U.S. Census Bureau, 2010) and for 39 percent of the people arrested for violent crime (Department of Justice, 2012).

Along these lines, LaFree, Baumer, and O'Brien (2010) have published an analysis of the black–white gap in aggregate homicide rates since 1960. They conclude that "it is somewhat discouraging to see just how resilient racial differences in homicide arrest ratios have been. In the mid-1990s, 23 of the 80 largest cities in the United States (28.8 percent) still had black homicide arrest rates that were more than 10 times higher than white rates" (p. 94).[6]

Crucially, however, Blumstein, Cohen, Roth, & Visher (1986) decomposed the aggregate crime rate into two principal components: "participation," that is, "the percentage of the population that commits crimes," and "frequency," that is, "the rate of criminal activity of those who are active [offenders]" (p. 1). The reason that this partitioning is crucial is because each component of the crime rate is relevant to different policy considerations. *Participation* is relevant to preventing people from becoming involved in crime in the first place, while the *frequency* with which active offenders commit crime is "central to the decisions of the criminal justice system," such as sentencing (p. 1).

The massive amount of data that Blumstein et al. analyzed for the National Research Council dramatically shows that "racial differences in aggregate measures of criminal behavior appear to be largely a function of differences in participation rather than offending frequencies" (p. 41), and that "the frequency rates of active white and black offenders are strikingly similar" (p. 70). Since sentencing is imposed only on individuals after they have been convicted of participation in crime, the frequency with which an offender is likely to continue in crime (i.e., the likelihood of recidivism) is the sole component of the aggregate crime rate that should bear upon forward-looking sentencing decisions:

> Thus, the demographic groups most often found to be associated with offending [e.g., African Americans] differ predominantly in the fraction of their base population who become involved in offending. To the extent that criminal justice officials use their knowledge of the demographic correlates of aggregate rates to make judgments about the future criminality of individual offenders, those judgments are likely to be incorrect (p. 94).

Legally, racial classifications are reviewed under the Fourteenth Amendment standard of strict scrutiny. As the U.S. Supreme Court has stated, racial classifications "must serve a compelling governmental interest, and must be narrowly tailored to further that interest" (*Adarand Constructors, Inc. v. Pena*, 1995). A number of circuit courts have directly addressed the issue of race as a risk factor in the context of denying parole (*White v. Bond*, 1983; *Block v. Potter*, 1980), and all have held that using race as a risk factor for violence fails the strict scrutiny test. The correlation between race and violence[7] is far from the "most exact connection" (*Adarand Constructors, Inc. v. Pena*, 1995, at 236) that the Court would require to justify the inclusion of race as a risk factor for violence in the civil commitment of people with serious mental illness, in sexually violent predator commitment, or in criminal sentencing.

Indeed, in *Buck v. Thaler* (2011), a majority of the U.S. Supreme Court for the first time explicitly took the position that the prosecution's use of race as a risk factor for violence in criminal sentencing was constitutionally improper. Duane Buck, an African American, was convicted of killing two people and injuring a third in Texas. Under Texas law, the jury then had to decide whether there was "a probability that the defendant would commit criminal acts of violence that would constitute a continuing threat to society." A positive answer to that question would require the jury to sentence Buck to death. Before making that determination, the jury has heard the testimony of a psychologist, Dr. Walter Quijano:

> Defense counsel asked Dr. Quijano, "[i]f we have an inmate such as Mr. Buck who is sentenced to life in prison [rather than to the death penalty], what are some of the factors, statistical factors or environmental factors that you've looked at in regard to this case?" [D]r. Quijano identified past crimes, age, sex, race, socioeconomic status, and substance abuse as statistical factors predictive of "whether a person will or will not constitute a continuing danger." With respect to race, he elaborated further that "[i]t's a sad commentary that minorities, Hispanics and black people, are over represented in the Criminal Justice System."

The jury sentenced Buck to death.

Buck appealed his case to the U.S. Supreme Court not on the ground that past crimes, age, sex, socioeconomic status, or substance abuse had been used as risk factors for violence, but only on the ground that race had been. The principal question he raised on appeal was "[w]hether the government may rely on the defendant's race during the sentencing phase of a capital trial as evidence that the defendant would commit criminal acts of violence that would constitute a continuing threat to society."

The U.S. Supreme Court denied certiorari in Buck's case, but in so doing, three Justices took the unusual step of explaining why they voted as they did: they voted not to review the case only because Dr. Quijano had been called as a witness *by the defense, not by the prosecution*.[8] As stated by Justice Alito (joined by Justices Scalia and Breyer):

> The petition in this case concerns bizarre and objectionable testimony given by a "defense expert" at the penalty phase of Buck's capital trial. The witness, Dr. Walter Quijano, testified that petitioner, if given a noncapital sentence, would not present a danger to society. But Dr. Quijano added that members

of petitioner's race (he is African-American) are statistically more likely than the average person to engage in crime. *Dr. Quijano's testimony would provide a basis for reversal of petitioner's sentence if the prosecution were responsible for presenting that testimony to the jury.* But Dr. Quijano was a defense witness, and it was petitioner's attorney, not the prosecutor, who first elicited Dr. Quijano's view regarding the correlation between race and future dangerousness (emphasis added).

In addition, two Justices (Justice Sotomayor, joined by Justice Kagan) dissented from the denial of certiorari. Justice Sotomayor wrote, "Today the Court denies review of a death sentence marred by racial overtones... [O]ur criminal justice system should not tolerate [this] circumstance." She went on to favorably quote the Texas Attorney General that "it is inappropriate to allow race to be considered as a factor in our criminal justice system." These two Justices would have granted certiorari in Buck's case *even though* Dr. Quijano had been called as an expert witness by the defense.

Taken together, the two statements in the Buck case indicate that a majority (five of nine Justices)[9] of the U.S. Supreme Court now find the introduction of race as a risk factor for violence in criminal sentencing—at the very least, its introduction by the government in capital sentencing—to be "bizarre," "objectionable," "a basis for reversal," "[in]toler[able]," and "inappropriate."

CONCLUSION

If biological risk factors for violence are reviewed under the Fourteenth Amendment's rational basis test, as age is, they should have no trouble passing constitutional muster. If biological risk factors for violence are reviewed under the Fourteenth Amendment's heightened scrutiny test, as gender is, they should also be admissible as evidence in court. But if biological risk factors for violence are reviewed under the Fourteenth Amendment's strict scrutiny test, as race is, they will likely share the fate of race and be inadmissible as evidence in civil commitment, sexually violent predator commitment, criminal sentencing, or any other legal proceeding predicated on a risk assessment of violence.

Which Equal Protection standard is the one most likely to be applied? If the biological risk factor is seen as merely a surrogate for race (e.g., a certain level of melanin as a surrogate for being of African descent) (Williams & Eberhardt, 2008), then I believe that courts will have little hesitation in strictly scrutinizing its admissibility in court. Yet the mere correlation of a biological risk factor with race clearly will not suffice to trigger strict scrutiny. For example, Harcourt (in press) argues that "[t]oday, risk is predominantly tied to prior criminal history, and prior criminality has become a proxy for race." Yet *every* risk assessment instrument includes prior criminal history as a major—often, *the* major—risk factor for future crime (Skeem & Monahan, 2011)—indeed, the California Static Risk Instrument (Turner et al., 2009) has 22 items, fully 20 of which (all but age and gender) are indices of prior criminal history—and, despite great racial disparities in the prevalence of having a prior criminal history (Frase, 2009; LaFree et al, 2010), no American court has ever subjected the use of prior criminal history to strict scrutiny review.

NOTES

1   The analysis in this chapter is limited to American law. Many believe that the pivotal role played by violence risk assessment in the imposition of the death penalty in a number of American states (see Cunningham, Sorensen, Vigen, & Woods, 2011; Edens, Buffington-Vollum, Keilen, Roskamp, & Anthony, 2005) raises profound ethical quandaries for the practice of risk assessment in the United States that are not present in other countries (Gunn, 2004).

2. U.S. state civil commitment statutes are compiled at http://www.treatmentadvocacy-center.org/index.php?option=com_content&task=view&id=86&Itemid=132

3. In addition, Cohen et al. (2008) operationalized "near future" in the following manner:

    "[A] reasonable interpretation of "near future" would involve a time frame, generally speaking, of up to about one week" (p. 9).

4. It should be acknowledged that there are definitions of risk more complex than the one chosen here. For example, Hart (2009, 145) states:

    The concept [of risk] is multi-faceted, referring to the nature of the hazard, the likelihood that the hazard will occur, the frequency or duration of the hazard, the seriousness of the hazard's consequences, and the imminence or duration of the hazard. The concept of risk is also inherently dynamic and contextual, as hazards arise and exist in specific circumstances.

5. I say "partially" because age, race, and gender are socially as well as biologically constructed (Ore, 2010).

6. The strongest variable that explained differences in city-level black and white homicide arrest rates was family structure:

    Cities with a smaller ratio of black to white single-parent families also had a smaller ratio of black to white homicide rates. Cities that experienced a decreasing ratio of black to white single-parent families also experienced a decreasing ratio of black to white homicide rates. These findings strongly support prior research that links single-parent families to higher rates of violent crime and that depicts this factor as one of the keys to explaining race differences in violence (p. 91, references omitted).

7. In the MacArthur study, the correlation between race and violence was 0.12 (Monahan et al., 2001, 163). As Berk (2009) noted in his large study of homicide and attempted homicide among probationers and parolees, "race does not distinguish well between those who fail and those who do not beyond what the other predictors [e.g., age, gender, prior crime] manage to accomplish" (p. 240).

8. Quijano essentially took the position that Buck was unlikely to be violent *despite* the fact that Buck was an African American and that "There is an over-representation of Blacks among violent offenders." Quijano explained that, for example, Buck "has no assaultive incidents either at [prison] or in jail," and that "that's a good sign that this person is controllable within a jail or prison setting." He also explained that Buck's "victim [was] not random" because "there [was] a preexisting relationship," and that this reduced the probability that Buck would pose a future danger. Ultimately, when the defense asked Quijano whether Buck was likely to commit violent criminal acts if he were sentenced to life imprisonment, Quijano replied, "The probability of that happening in prison would be low."

9. The remaining four justices did not express any views on the use of race as a risk factor for violence.

REFERENCES

Abraham, K. (1986). *Distributing risk: insurance, legal theory, and public policy.* New Haven: Yale University Press.

Adarand Constructors, Inc. v. Pena, 515 U.S. 200, 235 (1995).

Addington v. Texas, 441 U.S. 418 (1979).

Aharoni, E., Vincent, G., Harenski, C., Calhoun, V., Sinnott-Armstrong, W., Gazzaniga, M., & Kiehl, K. (2013). Neuroprediction of future rearrest. *PNAS, 110,* 6223–6228.

Anderson, Hanson, K. (2010). Static-99: An actuarial tool to assess risk of sexual and violent recidivism among sexual offenders. In R. Otto & K. Douglas (Eds.), *Handbook of violence risk assessment.* New York: Routledge,

Appelbaum, P. (1994). *Almost a revolution: mental health law and the limits of change.* New York: Oxford University Press.

Austin, J. (2010). Reducing America's correctional populations: A strategic plan. *Justice Research and Policy, 12,* 9–40.

Barefoot v. Estelle, 463 U.S. 880 (1983).

Beecher-Monas, E., & Garcia-Rill, E. (2009). Genetic predictions of future dangerousness: Is there a blueprint for violence? In N. Farahany (Ed.), *The impact of behavioral sciences on criminal law* (pp. 389–437). New York: Oxford University Press.

Berk, R. (2009). The role of race in forecasts of violent crime. *Race and Social Problems, 1,* 231–242.

Bergstrom, J., & Mistick, J. (2010). Danger and opportunity: Making public safety job one in Pennsylvania's indeterminate sentencing system. *Justice Research and Policy, 12,* 73–88.

Block v. Potter, 631 F.2d 233 (3d Cir. 1980).

Buck v. Thaler, 565 U.S. ___ (2011).

Bureau of Justice Statistics (2010). *Sourcebook of criminal justice statistics*, available at http://www.albany.edu/sourcebook/pdf/t482009.pdf

Cohen, B., Bonnie, R., & Monahan, J. (2008). *Understanding and applying Virginia's new statutory civil commitment criteria.* Available at http://www.dbhds.virginia.gov/OMH-MHReform/080603Criteria.pdf

Cooke, D., & Michie, C. (2010). Limitations of diagnostic precision and predictive utility in the individual case: A challenge for forensic practice. *Law and Human Behavior, 34,* 259–274.

Cunningham, M. D., Sorensen, J. R., Vigen, M. P., & Woods, S. O. (2011). Life and death in the Lone Star State: Three decades of violence predictions by capital juries. *Behavioral Sciences & the Law, 29*, 1–22.

Department of Justice (2012). *Crime in the United States.* Available at http://www.fbi. gov/about-us/cjis/ucr/crime-in-the-u.s/2011/crime-in-the-u.s.-2011

Edens, J. F., Buffington-Vollum, J. K., Keilen, A., Roskamp, P., & Anthony, C. (2005). Predictions of future dangerousness in capital murder trials: Is it time to "disinvent the wheel?" *Law and Human Behavior, 29*, 55–86.

Frase, R. (2009). What explains persistent racial disproportionality in Minnesota's prison and jail populations? *Crime and Justice, 38*, 201–280.

Given, J. (1977). *Society and homicide in thirteenth-century England.* Stanford: Stanford University Press.

Gostin, L. (2008). *Public health law: power, duty, restraint* (2nd ed.). Berkeley: University of California Press.

Gottfredson, M., & Hirschi, T. (1990). *A general theory of crime.* Stanford: Stanford University Press.

Grove, W. M. & Meehl, P. E. (1996). Comparative efficiency of informal (subjective, impressionistic) and formal (mechanical, algorithmic) prediction procedures: The clinical-statistical controversy. *Psychology, Public Policy, and Law, 2*, 293–323.

Gunn, J. (2004). The Royal College of Psychiatrists and the death penalty. *Journal of the American Academy of Psychiatry and the Law, 32*, 188–191.

Hanson, R. K. (2001). *Age and sexual recidivism: a comparison of rapists and child molesters.* Available at http://www.psepcsppcc.gc.ca/res/cor/sum/cprs200105_1-en.asp.

Hanson, R. K., & Howard, P. (2010). Individual confidence intervals do not inform decision-makers about the accuracy of risk assessment evaluations. *Law and Human Behavior, 34*, 275–281.

Harcourt, B. (in press). Risk as a proxy for race. *Criminology and Public Policy.* Available at http://ssrn.com/abstract=1677654

Hart, S. D. (2009). Evidence-based assessment of risk for sexual violence. *Chapman Journal of Criminal Justice, 1*, 143–165.

Hart, S. D., Michie, C., & Cooke, D. J. (2007) Precision of actuarial risk assessment instruments: Evaluating the 'margins of error' of group versus individual predictions of violence. *British Journal of Psychiatry, 190(Supplement 49)*, 60–65.

Heilbrun, H. (2009) Risk assessment in evidence-based sentencing: Context and promising uses. *Chapman Journal of Criminal Justice, 1*, 127–142.

J.E.B. v. Alabama ex rel. T.B, 511 U.S. 127 (1994).

Kansas v. Hendricks, 521 U.S. 346 (1977).

Kimel v. Florida Board of Regents, 528 U.S. 62 (2000).

Kraemer, H., Kazdin, A., Offord, D., Kessler, R., Jensen, P., & Kupfer, D. (1997). Coming to terms with the terms of risk. *Archives of General Psychiatry, 54*, 337–343.

Kroner, D., Mills, J., & Morgan, B. (2005). A coffee can, factor analysis, and prediction of antisocial behavior: The structure of criminal risk. *International Journal of Law & Psychiatry, 28*, 360–374.

Maccoby, E., & Jacklin, C. (1974). *The psychology of sex differences.* Stanford: Stanford University Press.

Meehl, P. (1954). *Clinical versus statistical prediction: A theoretical analysis and a review of the evidence*. Minneapolis: University of Minnesota.

Messinger, S., & Johnson, P. (1978). California's determinate sentencing statute: History and issues. In National Institute of Law Enforcement and Criminal Justice, *Determinate sentencing: reform or regression?* (pp. 13–58). Washington, DC: U.S. Department of Justice.

Monahan, J. (2006). A jurisprudence of risk assessment: Forecasting harm among prisoners, predators, and patients. *Virginia Law Review, 92*, 391–435.

Monahan, J. (2008). Structured risk assessment of violence. In R. Simon & K. Tardiff (Eds.), *Textbook of violence assessment and management* (pp. 17–33). Washington, DC: American Psychiatric Publishing.

Monahan, J., & Silver, E. (2003). Judicial decision thresholds for violence risk management. *International Journal of Forensic Mental Health, 2*, 1–6.

Monahan, J., Steadman, H., Silver, E., Appelbaum, P., Robbins, P., Mulvey, E., Roth, L., Grisso, T., & Banks, S. (2001). *Rethinking risk assessment: the MacArthur Study of Mental Disorder and Violence*. New York: Oxford University Press.

Monahan, J., & Wexler, D. (1978) A definite maybe: Proof and probability in civil commitment. *Law and Human Behavior, 2*, 37–42.

National Research Council (1989). *Improving risk communication*. Washington, DC: National Academy Press.

Ore, T. (2010). *The social construction of difference and inequality: race, class, gender and sexuality*. New York: McGraw-Hill.

Perlin, M. (2006). *Mental disability law: civil and criminal* (18th ed.). Durham: Carolina Academic Press.

Quinsey, V. L., Harris, G. T., Rice, M. E., & Cormier, C. A. (2006). *Violent offenders: Appraising and managing risk* (2nd ed.). Washington, DC: American Psychological Association.

Raine, A. (2013). *The anatomy of violence: The biological roots of crime*. New York: Random House.

Reiss, A., & Roth, J. (Eds) (1993). *Understanding and preventing violence*. Washington, DC: National Academy Press.

Rice, M., Harris, G., & Lang, C. (in press). Validation of and revision to the VRAG and SORAG: The Violence Risk Appraisal Guide-Revised (VRAG-R). *Psychological Assessment*.

Sampson, R., & Lauritsen, J. (1994). Violent victimization and offending: Individual-, situational-, and community-level risk factors. In A. Reiss & J. Roth (Eds.), *Understanding and preventing violence: social influences*. Washington, DC: National Academy Press.

Schall v. Martin, 467 U.S. 253 (1984).

Scott-Hayward, C. (2009). *The fiscal crisis in corrections: rethinking policies and practices*. New York: Vera Institute of Justice. Available at http://www.vera.org/files/The-fiscal-crisis-in-corrections_July-2009.pdf

Singh, J., Grann, M., & Fazel, S. (2011). A comparative study of violence risk assessment tools: A systematic review and metaregression analysis of 68 studies involving 25,980 participants. *Clinical Psychology Review*. DOI: 10.1016/j.cpr.2010.11.009

Skeem, J., & Monahan, J. (2011). Current directions in violence risk assessment. *Current Directions in Psychological Science, 20*, 38–40.

Sturup, J., Kristiansson, M., & Monahan, J. (in press). Gender and violent behavior in Swedish general psychiatric patients: A prospective clinical study. *Psychiatric Services.*

Tonry, M. (1999). *The fragmentation of sentencing and corrections in America. Sentencing and corrections: issues for the 21st century.* Washington, DC: National Institute of Justice. Available at http://www.ncjrs.gov/pdffiles1/nij/175721.pdf

Tonry, M. (2010). The questionable relevance of previous convictions to punishments for later crimes. In J. Roberts & A. von Hirsch (Eds.), *Previous convictions at sentencing: theoretical and applied perspectives.* Oxford: Hart.

Turner, S., Hess, J., & Jannetta, J. (2009). Development of the California Static Risk Assessment Instrument (CSRA). Available at http://ucicorrections.seweb.uci.edu/sites/ucicorrections.seweb.uci.edu/files/CSRA%20Working%20Paper_0.pdf

United States v. Virginia, 518 U.S. 515 (1996).

von Hirsch, A. (1976). *Doing justice: the choice of punishments.* New York: Hill and Wang.

Webster, C., Douglas, K., Eaves, D., & Hart, S. (1997). *HCR-20: Assessing Risk for Violence (Version 2).* Vancouver: Simon Fraser University.

White v. Bond, 720 F.2d 1002 (8th Cir. 1983).

Williams, M. J., & Eberhardt, J. L. (2008). Biological conceptions of race and the motivation to cross racial boundaries. *Journal of Personality and Social Psychology, 94*, 1033–1047.

5

Bioprediction in Criminal Cases

CHRISTOPHER SLOBOGIN

INTRODUCTION: A HYPOTHETICAL

Consider the following hypothetical, posed at a law and genetics conference at the University of Maryland:[1]

In a non-capital sentencing proceeding resulting from the defendant being found guilty of homicide, at issue is the admission of a genetic test to show the future dangerousness of the defendant. Variants of the monoamine oxidase A gene (MAOA), along with various environmental factors, are associated with violent behavior. However, it is not clear exactly what the most important environmental factors are, or exactly how they interact with the MAOA variants. Studies have shown that childhood maltreatment in combination with the MAOA variant triple the likelihood of antisocial behavior and violence as well as the likelihood of a conviction for a violent crime by age 20. (The defendant was 18 when he committed the crime.) However, other studies have shown that absent an abusive environment, the genetic variant alone does not result in any increased chance of violent behavior. In this case, the defendant has a history of childhood maltreatment. The prosecutor requests that the defendant be compelled to have a genetic test for MAOA variants. With this test result, the prosecutor wishes to show that the defendant has a proclivity toward violence ("future dangerousness"). The defendant objects to being compelled to have the test. (Assume that the background rate for violence and antisocial behavior in males aged 14 to 18 is 12 percent; assume that the background rate for conviction for a violent crime by age 18 in males is 2 percent.)

This hypothetical provides a useful springboard for discussing the legality of using genetic traits to fashion sentences. Specifically, it poses the following questions: (1) May dangerousness form the basis for a criminal sentence? If so, (2) may assessments of risk rely on genetic information? If so, (3) may the state compel genetic information from a criminal offender? Although a good case can be made for avoiding "bioprediction" in the criminal process, this chapter concludes, albeit tentatively, that all three questions should be answered in the affirmative, at least under current law in the United States.

MAY DANGEROUSNESS FORM THE BASIS FOR A CRIMINAL SENTENCE?

The essential predicate to any analysis involving facts of the type found in the hypothetical is whether "future dangerousness" or "risk" can be taken into account at sentencing and, if so, under what circumstances. Although incapacitation of dangerous individuals is often considered a legitimate purpose of punishment, there are two principal arguments against the practice, one theoretical and the other practical.

Theoretical concerns about risk assessments at sentencing

The most fundamental argument against relying on risk to enhance a person's sentence is that punishing a person for something not yet done is incoherent. This claim rests on the premise that punishment is first and foremost based on "desert"—the idea that punishment must be deserved. If that is the case, a person can only be punished for culpably choosing to harm another; some contend, further, that sentences must be proportionate to that harm (Robinson, 2001, 1442–1443). Confinement based on future actions would violate this desert principle; indeed, simply as a matter of semantics, "punishment" for future actions makes no sense. A closely related objection to punishing a person based on an assessment of risk is that it denigrates the person's humanity; it treats the individual like an automaton because it assumes the person is unable or unwilling to exercise his or her autonomy in the right direction.

One response to these concerns is that the demands of desert are met once a jury or judge has convicted an individual based on his or her previous conduct. The trial court's verdict gives autonomy its due. Disposition can therefore be aimed at achieving any other important government aim, including incapacitation of the dangerous; in other words, this argument states, indeterminate sentences of the type commonly found in the United States and many other countries are permissible. A compromise position, sometimes called "limiting retributivism," is that sentences must still adhere to desert, but that incapacitative considerations can modulate any sentence up to the maximum a desert-based approach would permit (see American Law Institute, 2007,

§ 1.02(2); Morris, 1974). For serious crimes such as the one involved in the hypothetical the maximum is often several decades and in first-degree murder cases can contemplate the death penalty, which thus provides considerable room for sentences based on relative risk in these types of cases.

Neither of these moves will appease the die-hard retributivist. But both are consistent with precedent, at least in the United States. In *Pennsylvania ex rel. Sullivan v. Ashe* (1937), the Supreme Court stated:

> [The state] may inflict a deserved penalty merely to vindicate the law or to deter or to reform the offender or for all of these purposes. For the determination of sentences, justice generally requires consideration of more than the particular acts by which the crime was committed and that there be taken into account the circumstances of the offense together with the character and propensities of the offender. His past may be taken to indicate his present purposes and tendencies and significantly to suggest the period of restraint and the kind of discipline that ought to be imposed upon him. (p. 51)

And in *Jurek v. Texas* (1976), the Court held that even death sentences may be based on dangerousness determinations, noting that "prediction of future criminal conduct is an essential element in many of the decisions rendered throughout our criminal justice system" (p. 275).

As to the alleged dehumanizing effect of incarceration based on acts yet to happen, the risk assessment in these types of cases can be thought of as, and in fact generally is, a prediction that the person will *choose* to commit crime in the future. This characterization avoids treating the individual simply as an unthinking mechanism. Furthermore, a sentence that includes rehabilitative efforts to reduce risk can be much more humanity- and autonomy-affirming than imprisonment based on desert. As I have noted, "[r]isk management, properly conducted, explores the causes of antisocial behavior and continuously stresses the offender's ability to change that behavior through cognitive restructuring, avoidance of risky behavior...and adjusting relationships" (Slobogin, 2006, 156). Compared to waiting out a period that bears no necessary relationship to one's ability to function in a law-abiding manner, the risk management response to crime is "more likely to enhance individual responsibility; time of release...is to a significant extent controlled by the offender, which should not only enhance rehabilitative success, but also energize those with the potential to be law-abiding" (p. 170).

As a theoretical matter, therefore, good arguments can be made that the prosecutor in the hypothetical should not be barred from advocating for an enhanced sentence if the genetic test indicates that the offender is at a higher-than-average risk. However, one might also make the theory-based argument that, even if reliance on dangerousness as a sentencing criterion is justifiable in the abstract, the factors that suggest risk also suggest lesser culpability, and thus should, if anything, reduce sentence. For instance, one could argue that if genetic variations are the reason the offender in the hypothetical is prone to violence, his crime is the result of a condition that is not his fault. The Supreme Court itself has intimated that even if mental illness contributes to risk it is best considered a mitigating factor, not an aggravating one (*Zant v. Stephens*, 1983, p. 885).

There are two problems with this argument as applied to genetic information. First, the case for genetic markers as a cause of reduced culpability is very weak. In the hypothetical, 64 percent of those studied committed no further antisocial act and 94 percent of those studied did not commit a violent antisocial act by age 20.[2] In other words, most people with the MAOA variant who were abused as children do not commit any type of crime. Accordingly, if they do commit such crime and the crime is intentional and rational, a defense of compulsion is very unlikely to succeed. Even in the juvenile context, where one would expect courts to be most sympathetic to neurological arguments, genetic claims of mitigation do not fare well (Maroney, 2009). Moreover, this outcome is probably correct, given the fact the genetic causes of crime are not intrinsically more powerful than other causes of crime that the legal system routinely dismisses as evidence of mitigation (see Morse, 2006).

Second, even if mitigation is warranted on this type of theory, aggravation is also warranted, if dangerousness is a legitimate sentencing criterion. A person can simultaneously both be less culpable and more dangerous. Therefore, a sentencing body that decides the latter finding outweighs the former is not acting illegitimately (Slobogin, 2009, 126–127).

Evidentiary concerns about risk assessment at sentencing

The preceding discussion suggests a significant practical argument against dangerousness as a criterion—proof of risk is hard to come by. In the hypothetical, for instance, a positive result from the genetic test would still only indicate that the offender represents an increased risk of *some* type of violence *by age 20*, not necessarily homicide (and certainly not a *second* homicide). As is true with most modern risk assessment instruments (see Litwack, 2001, 428), the outcome variable on this test is merely "violence," which the defense could argue is too vague to form the basis for a sentence increase. Furthermore, the probability of violence for an individual with a history of abuse who tests "positive" is still only in the 30 to 40 percent range, which the defense could argue is insufficiently risky to warrant an enhanced sentence.

The traditional means of evaluating a decision-maker's ability to assess risk is to ascertain the false-positive rate (the degree to which a determination that someone will be violent turns out not to be violent) and the false-negative rate (the degree to which a determination that someone will not be violent turns out to be violent). Even the best prediction methods produce false-positive rates no better than 20 or 40 percent (Monahan, 2006, 406). If decision-makers try to reduce those rates further by requiring very strong proof of dangerousness, the false-negative rate is likely to skyrocket. In short, given our present state of knowledge and the natural aversion to false negatives, a nontrivial rate of false positives is unavoidable.

Accordingly, commentators have argued that, whatever might be permissible conceptually, risk levels are so difficult to ascertain that they should never form the basis for sentence enhancement, or should do so only under very limited circumstances (see, e.g., Regnier, 2004). There are several responses to this concern. First, in the sentencing context any inaccuracy in risk assessment is mitigated by the fact that the individual will receive some type of punishment regardless of his or her risk. The risk assessment process can thus be thought of as an attempt to figure out how to allocate limited confinement capacity and treatment programs. Because that process does a good job of figuring out relative (as opposed to absolute) risk, it facilitates the most efficient allocation of these resources.

For instance, a fair number of prediction methodologies have AUC values of 0.75 or better (Slobogin, 2007, 107). AUC stands for Area Under the Curve, with the curve representing the graph produced by plotting the true-positive rate against the false-positive rate. An AUC value of 0.75 for a given prediction methodology means that there is a 75 percent chance that a recidivist will receive a higher score than a non-recidivist. Similarly, in the hypothetical an offender who tests positive for the MAOA variant and was maltreated as a child is three times as likely to be violent in the near future than offenders who do not have both of these risk factors and are otherwise comparable. This information is clearly useful in ensuring that risk management resources (including enhanced confinement and rehabilitation) are directed toward the correct individuals.

Of course, we still cannot say with a high degree of certainty that any particular offender who fits in the higher-risk category requires an enhanced sentence to prevent another offense. Note, however, that under American law proof beyond a reasonable doubt is not required for a sentencing factor unless the enhancement extends beyond the statutory maximum (*Blakely v. Washington*, 2004, 301). Furthermore, the prosecutor can still be required to prove beyond a reasonable doubt or by clear and convincing evidence that the biological test reliably measures the MAOA variant, that the offender suffered the type of child abuse that is associated with the higher degree of risk reported in the hypothesized research, and that this research meets acceptable scientific standards.

Finally, the impact of inaccuracy can be minimized by constructing a system in which only those with the highest and lowest risk levels are treated differently, while those within the midrange risk level (say, 30 to 70 percent) are sentenced based on other criteria.

To those for whom none of this is a satisfactory response, consider three other points. First, when risk rather than culpability is the issue, society is, and probably should be, willing to countenance more false positives. While a disproportionate number of false negatives might be normatively preferable when guilt is the issue (as suggested by the old adage that society should be willing to acquit ten guilty people if necessary to avoid conviction of one innocent), the calculus changes, arguably quite radically, when the released false negative will harm one or more people.

Second, a fair treatment of the accuracy issue must look at the accuracy of competing approaches to sentencing. A system based on desert, which is the primary alternative to modulating sentences based on risk, is arguably subject to at least as much error. Unless sentences in such a system are based entirely on the physical act committed, with no attempt at gauging the accompanying mental state, fact-finders can only guess at an offender's degree of culpability, because phenomena such as premeditation, "depraved indifference," recklessness, and negligence are very difficult to define and even harder to discern reliably (see Shen et al., 2011, 1347–1348).

Furthermore, even if such assessments could be made with some degree of confidence, assigning the proper desert-based sentence for a particular offense—say reckless homicide—verges on guesswork and produces wildly disparate results, even within jurisdictions, much less between them. For instance, research asking participants to assign specific punishments based on criminal offenders' perceived degree of blameworthiness routinely produces high standard deviations (see data collected in Slobogin, 2006, 310, note 18; Slobogin & Brinkley-Rubinstein, 2012, 94–96). The only reason sentences based on desert are not routinely attacked on unreliability grounds is that the unreliability of a particular culpability assessment cannot be scientifically demonstrated in the way errors concerning risk can be. The closest that litigators have come to mounting such attacks is through Eighth Amendment challenges that a particular sentence is disproportionate, but that strategy usually fails precisely because courts have great difficulty figuring out how the culpability metric can be implemented (cf. *Harmelin v. Michigan*, 1991, 1001). If concern about accuracy leads to prohibition of sentences based on risk, it should probably also bar sentences based on desert, which would leave sentencing law in a state of disarray, to say the least.

Finally, concerns about a sentencing regime based on risk assessment might be allayed by the fact that such a regime should be required, as a constitutional matter, to abide by several constraints. First, as the Supreme Court held in *Jackson v. Indiana*, the Due Process Clause requires that "the nature and duration of commitment bear some reasonable relation to the purpose for which the individual is committed" (1972, 738). Thus, incarceration even of a high-risk individual should not be automatic, given the frequent availability of less-intrusive, more-effective means of preventing harm. In the hypothetical, for instance, the offender might best be placed in a community-based "multi-systemic" program specifically aimed at rehabilitating violent juveniles; such programs have been shown to be much more successful than prison at preventing recidivism (see, e.g., Schaeffer & Borduin, 2005, 448). Second, the *Jackson* principle also requires that the duration of sentence in a preventive regime be limited by the magnitude and degree of risk posed, with progressively greater risk required for longer sentences (Slobogin, 2006, 143–150). Third, again based on the *Jackson* principle, the Supreme Court has intimated that, where prevention is the goal and treatment can help achieve that goal, treatment must be provided (*Seling v. Young*, 2001, 265–266; *Youngberg v. Romeo*, 1982, 324). Fourth, to ensure that the state is attempting to meet the prevention goal, the Court has held that periodic review of the individual's status is constitutionally mandated (*Kansas v. Hendricks*, 1997, 368–369). If mistakes in risk assessment have been made, periodic review may expose them and in any event is much better at doing so than a sentencing system based on culpability, which has no analogous post-conviction review about the culpability decision.

WHAT RISK FACTORS MAY BE CONSIDERED?

Assuming dangerousness can legitimately influence sentencing and can be predicted reliably enough, a further objection to a risk-based sentence on the specific facts of the hypothetical is that it is based on illegitimate variables—chemical imbalances and childhood maltreatment. These variables are illegitimate, the argument goes, because they are not the product of the offender's choices, but rather are phenomena over which the offender had no control. Thus, a sentence based on such factors is anathema. If sentences are to be grounded on risk, the argument concludes, risk factors should consist solely of prior criminal acts the offender has chosen to commit (Monahan, 2006, 427–428).

To put the question addressed here in its most dramatic form, is it fair to punish someone for congenital defects or for being abused by one's parents? Framed this way, the question seems to admit of only one response. But the question can also be framed another way: Is it fair to increase a person's sentence because he or she represents a significant risk? If it is theoretically and practically permissible to base sentences on dangerousness for the reasons given earlier, then the fact that some, or all, of the predictors are immutable or uncontrollable traits should not matter. Risk-based sentencing is not based on desert, it is based on risk. In such a regime, reliance on characteristics rather than conduct would be unfair only at trial, when we are determining whether the person can be held criminally responsible for committing a crime.

The related argument that risk assessments relying solely on prior bad acts are somehow more legitimate than risk assessments grounded on factors such as age, gender, or chemical imbalance is based on a false distinction between conduct and characteristics as they affect the risk assessment process at sentencing. While criminal acts are "chosen" and personality traits are not, when a prior criminal act informs a risk-based sentencing decision after a more recent offense, the resulting sentence is likely to be either much longer or shorter than is "deserved" for that choice. In other words, the prior bad act is relevant not because it was an act of free will but because it is indicative of risk.[3] Thus, its use for the latter purpose is no more (or less) legitimate than reliance on traits or characteristics.

In short, if the legislature has declared that sentences may be based on dangerousness, then the government should not be prevented from proving that an offender is at high risk simply because its evidence is based on factors over which the individual had no control. A second reason for this conclusion is purely pragmatic. Predictions based solely on chosen conduct such as prior bad acts will be less accurate (Warren, 2009, 630). Not only false negatives but false positives will increase, because the absence of certain traits and conditions can reduce risk, just as their presence can increase it.

While one can thus plausibly contend that the distinction between conduct and characteristic does not place any constraints on the government's risk-related evidence at sentencing, antidiscrimination principles may do so. For instance, given the history of racial discrimination in the United States, any decision-making process that uses race or ethnicity to formulate sentences might be considered impermissible (*Gonzalez v. Quarterman*, 2006, 389; *United States v. Taveras*, 2008, 336). Perhaps any factors that could be proxies for race should be as well.

One could also construct equal protection arguments against basing risk assessments on age, gender, and other quasi-suspect classifications that stem from immutable characteristics historically associated with outsider status. But reliance on these types of variables to make risk discriminations does not send the repugnant message that explicit use of race does. If the government can demonstrate a compelling need to use such variables in evaluating risk—which it can probably do with respect to factors such as age and gender (given the association of young males with higher risk)—then there is probably no constitutional impediment to doing so (Monahan, 2006, 429–432). Biological traits and abuse are even further removed from the politically powerless traits associated with equal protection jurisprudence.

Accordingly, basing a risk assessment on a genetic test and child abuse is not offensive in a sentencing regime that allows sentences to be based in whole or part on dangerousness. Neither factor relies on race or a proxy for race. While neither factor is the actor's "fault," risk assessments at sentencing are not based on fault.

In any event, as risk assessment becomes more sophisticated, many immutable traits are likely to be discarded as predictive variables. For instance, recent research suggests that youthfulness—an implicit risk factor in the hypothetical—is not particularly useful in predicting post-adolescent behavior, given the rapid neurological and social changes that take place in the late teen-age years (Johnston, 2011, 141). Thus, today risk assessment techniques increasingly rely on less-controversial static variables such as diagnosis, employment status, and past behavior, and also tend to focus on "dynamic" risk factors such as substance abuse, relationships, and reaction to slights, factors that are subject to some degree of control by the individual (Heilbrun, Yasuhara, & Shah, 2010, 11–14).

MAY GOVERNMENT OBTAIN GENETIC INFORMATION OVER A DEFENDANT'S OBJECTION?

Assume now that the government may base sentences on risk and that sufficient risk can be proven through legitimate means. A final issue raised by this hypothetical is whether the government can obtain the evidence of risk it needs from the offender's body, over his objection. In the United States at least two constitutional provisions are implicated by this question.

First, the U.S. Supreme Court has held that a bodily intrusion to garner evidence implicates the Fourth Amendment, which provides that searches and seizures of persons must be reasonable. Generally, a non-exigent search and seizure of a person is only reasonable if it is authorized by a warrant based on a demonstration of probable cause to believe it will produce incriminating evidence (see *Katz v. United States*, 1967, 357). In connection with very significant bodily intrusions, such as surgery requiring anesthesia, the Court has further held that the procedure must be safe, must be attentive to the person's dignity, and must produce evidence that is crucial to the state's case (*Winston v. Lee*, 1985). Perhaps the defense in the hypothetical could successfully argue that the state does not have probable cause (usually equated with a 50 percent likelihood) that a seizure of genetic material from the offender will produce evidence of risk, or that the evidence would not be essential to the prosecution.

The state might respond that sentencing is an administrative rather than policing endeavor, thereby invoking the Supreme Court's "special needs" jurisprudence that allows relaxation of the warrant and probable cause requirements when the government's goal is something other than "ordinary law enforcement" (see Whitebread & Slobogin, 2008, 337–350). A somewhat different line of Supreme Court decisions has relied on a straightforward balancing analysis in holding that, given the lessened privacy interest of offenders and the government's strong interest in prison and community safety, searches of prisoners' and probationers' belongings do not require probable cause and may not require *any* individualized suspicion (see, e.g., *Samson v. California*, 2006; *United States v. Knights*, 2001; *Hudson v. Palmer*, 1984). Most relevant to the hypothetical situation, on either special needs or balancing grounds a number of lower courts have upheld suspicionless seizure of DNA samples from prisoners and arrestees (*Maryland v. King*, 2013; *United States v. Mitchell*, 2011; *Nicholas v. Goord*, 2005). Thus, even if the state cannot demonstrate probable cause that a particular individual's chemistry will bolster a risk finding, it might be able to conduct a genetic test of a convicted felon if it can show that such a test is necessary to determine whether the offender meets the MAOA risk profile and that the test is not physically harmful to the individual.

If so, the defense could take a different tack, arguing that the Fourth Amendment prohibits seizure of genetic information because of the various sorts of personal information it can reveal. Some judges have intimated that particularly private enclaves—such as diaries—may only be accessed by the government under extraordinary circumstances (*Couch v. United States*, 1973, 350 [Marshall, J., dissenting]; see also Bradley, 1993, 208–212). Of course, a court stipulation that the only information that can be retained and used from the test is whether the offender has the MAOA variant—a step analogous to limiting orders courts have issued in computer search cases (*United States v. Comprehensive Drug Testing, Inc.*, 2009)—may moot any argument along these lines.

A second constitutional provision that could be triggered by government attempts to test for the MAOA variant over the offender's objection is the Fifth Amendment, which prevents the government from compelling incriminating testimony from a suspect. For some time, application of the Fifth Amendment to sentencing (which occurs after the offender has been "incriminated") was in doubt. But the Supreme Court has now made clear that because of the significant liberty interest at stake at sentencing, the Fifth Amendment bars prosecution use of coerced statements, as well as use of an offender's silence, to enhance a sentence (see *Estelle v. Smith*, 1981 [capital sentencing]; *Mitchell v. United States*, 1999 [non-capital sentencing]). The offender in the hypothetical might argue that the genetic material obtained by the test will constitute compelled testimony, in the sense that it will communicate the offender's relative risk. He could further argue that any prosecution mention of his refusal to take the test would constitute unconstitutional use of his silence against him.

However, these arguments are not likely to prevail. The Supreme Court has held that compelling a blood sample from an apparently intoxicated individual does not violate the Fifth Amendment prohibition against compelling testimony, because blood, like one's visage or clothing, is "non-testimonial" (*Schmerber v. California*, 1966). Thus, a Fifth Amendment argument against use of the MAOA test results—or use of any other biological predictive marker (e.g., hormones, heart rates, or brain activity)—is unlikely to be successful, unless the "statement" made by the marker ("I am a relatively greater risk") can be distinguished from the statement made by an intoxicated person's blood ("I am over the legal alcohol limit"). The Court has also held that a refusal to undergo a test aimed at obtaining evidence of intoxication can be used in evidence by the prosecution, since only non-testimonial evidence is involved (*South Dakota v. Neville*, 1983). Given these cases, the Fifth Amendment probably would not bar the government from compelling the MAOA test by threatening to introduce a refusal to submit to it.[4]

CONCLUSION

Government attempts to obtain biological evidence relevant to a risk assessment give rise to several issues. Most fundamentally, any form of risk assessment, whether based on biological or other risk factors, can be challenged on the ground that it is not a proper basis for imposing or enhancing a sentence in any system primarily based on desert. If that barrier is overcome, a second concern is that risk assessments, again whether based on biological or other risk factors, are not sufficiently accurate to permit a deprivation of liberty. Third, certain types of risk factors, including biological traits, may be off-limits if they significantly undermine the desert premise or equal protection principles. And fourth, government efforts to obtain biological information may run afoul of Fourth or Fifth Amendment guarantees.

This chapter has suggested responses to each of these concerns. If an offender is validly convicted, a sentence based on risk is a legitimate exercise of state power, certainly if the sentence stays within a retributively defined range and probably in an indeterminate sentencing regime as well. Risk assessments can provide fairly good indications of relative risk, at least as reliably as juries and judges calibrate culpability. If risk is a legitimate basis for a sentence, then any risk factor that appreciably increases or decreases risk and does not violate anti-discrimination principles can be part of the calculus, a conclusion that may at most exclude reliance on race and ethnicity as a risk factor. And the U.S.

Constitution probably does not pose an impediment to testing for biological risk factors, as long as the government obtains a court order authorizing the testing, the biological information is a crucial risk factor and is used only for that purpose, and the test process is carried out safely.

NOTES

1. The conference, entitled "Judging Genes: Implications of the Second Generation of Genetic Tests in the Courtroom," was sponsored by the Law & Health Care Program at the University of Maryland School of Law and the National Human Genome Research Institute. It took place on Jan. 31, 2008. Much of the analysis in this chapter is taken from two previous works of mine: Slobogin, 2006 (Chapters 4 and 5) and Slobogin, 2007 (Chapters 6 and 7).
2. These figures are arrived at by multiplying the base rate for crime and for violent crime (2 and 12 percent, respectively) by three (the hypothesized extent to which the MAOA variant and abuse are said to increase crime) and subtracting the quotient from 100.
3. Of course, a sentence for a second offense might also be enhanced because the offender has already committed an offense and is thus thought to be more blameworthy (see Von Hirsch, 1976, 84–85 [describing the "nose-thumbing" theory]). But such an enhancement is not based on a forward-looking risk assessment; it is bottomed on a backward-looking culpability assessment. The former type of assessment is likely to produce a sentence much different in duration than the latter.
4. For further analysis of the Fifth Amendment issue from a neuroscientific perspective, see Farahany (2012, 369–373) (arguing that the Fifth Amendment does not protect against compulsion of characteristics that do not involve conscious processing).

REFERENCES

American Law Institute (2007). *Model Penal Code: Sentencing* (Tentative Draft No. 1).
Blakely v. Washington (2004). 542 U.S. 296.
Bradley, C. M. (1993). The emerging international consensus as to criminal procedure rules. *Michigan Journal of International Law, 14,* 171–220.
Couch v. United States (1973). 409 U.S. 322.
Estelle v. Smith (1981). 451 U.S. 454.
Farahany, N. (2012). Incriminating thoughts. *Stanford Law Review, 64,* 351–408.
Gonzalez v. Quarterman (2006). 458 F.3d 384 (5th Cir.).
Harmelin v. Michigan (1991). 501 U.S. 957.
Heilbrun, K., Yasuhara, K., & Shah, S. (2010). Violence risk assessment tools: Overview and critical analysis. In R. K. Otto & K.S. Douglas (Eds.), *Handbook of violence risk assessment* (pp. 1–14). New York: Routledge.
Hudson v. Palmer (1984). 468 U.S. 517.
Jackson v. Indiana (1972). 406 U.S. 715.
Johnston, L. (2011). Assessing violence risk in children: Implications for dangerous offender provisions. In B. McSherry & P. Keyzer (Eds.), *"Dangerous" people: policy, prediction and practice* (pp. 123–145). New York: Routledge.

Kansas v. Hendricks (1997). 521 U.S. 346.

Katz v. United States (1967). 89 U.S. 347.

Litwack, T. (2001). Actuarial versus clinical assessments of dangerousness. *Psychology, Public Policy & Law, 7,* 409–443.

Maroney, T. (2009). The false promise of adolescent brain science in juvenile justice. *Notre Dame Law Review, 85,* 89–176.

Maryland v. King (2013). 133 S.Ct. 1958.

Mitchell v. United States (1999). 526 U.S. 314.

Monahan, J. (2006). A jurisprudence of risk assessment: Forecasting harm among prisoners, predators and patients. *Virginia Law Review, 92,* 391–435.

Morris, N. (1974). *The future of imprisonment.* Chicago: University of Chicago Press.

Morse, S. J. (2006). Brain overclaim syndrome and criminal responsibility: A diagnostic note. *Ohio State Journal of Criminal Law, 3,* 397–412.

Nicholas v. Goord (2005). 652 F.3d 387 (3d Cir.).

Pennsylvania ex rel. Sullivan v. Ashe (1937). 302 U.S. 51.

Regnier, T. (2004) *Barefoot* in quicksand: The future of "future dangerousness" prediction in death penalty sentencing in the world of *Daubert* and *Kumho. Akron Law Review, 37,* 469–507

Robinson, P. (2001). Punishing dangerousness: Cloaking preventive detention as criminal justice. *Harvard Law Review, 114,* 1429–1456.

Samson v. California (2006). 547 U.S. 843.

Schaeffer, C. M., & Borduin, C. M. (2005). Long-term follow-up to a randomized clinical trial of multisystemic therapy with serious and violent juvenile offenders. *Journal of Consulting & Clinical Psychology, 73,* 445–458.

Schmerber v. California (1966). 384 U.S. 757.

Seling v. Young (2001). 531 U.S. 250.

Shen, F., Hoffman, M., Jones, O., Greene, J., & Marois, R. (2011). Sorting guilty minds. *New York University Law Review, 85,* 1306–1360.

Slobogin, C. (2006). *Minding justice: laws that deprive people with mental disability of life and liberty.* Cambridge, MA: Harvard University Press.

Slobogin, C. (2007). *Proving the unprovable: the role of law, science and speculation in adjudicating culpability and dangerousness.* New York: Oxford University Press.

Slobogin, C. (2009). Capital punishment and dangerousness. In R. F. Schopp, R. L. Wiener, B. H. Bornstein, & S. L. Willborn (Eds.), *Mental disorder and criminal law: responsibility, punishment and competence* (pp. 119–133). New York: Springer Press.

Slobogin, C., & Brinkley-Rubinstein, L. (2012). Putting desert in its place. *Stanford Law Review, 65,* 77–135.

South Dakota v. Neville (1983). 459 U.S. 553.

United States v. Comprehensive Drug Testing, Inc. (2009). 579 F.3d 989 (9th Cir. en banc).

United States v. Knights (2001). 534 U.S. 112.

United States v. Mitchell (2011). 652 F.3d 387 (3d Cir.).

United States v. Taveras (2008). 585 F.Supp. 327.

Von Hirsch, A. (1976) *Doing justice: the choice of punishments.* New York: Hill & Wang.

Warren, R. K. (2009). Evidence-based sentencing: The application of principles of evidence-based practice to state sentencing practice and policy. *University of San Francisco Law Review, 43,* 585–634.

Whitebread, C., & Slobogin, C. (2008). *Criminal procedure: an analysis of cases and concepts* (5th ed.). New York: Foundation Press.

Winston v. Lee (1985). 70 U.S. 753.

Youngberg v. Romeo (1982). 457 U.S. 307.

Zant v. Stephens (1983). 462 U.S. 862.

6

The Limits of Legal Use of Neuroscience

COLIN CAMPBELL AND NIGEL EASTMAN

INTRODUCTION

Violence is increasingly recognized as a major public health problem (World Health Organization, 2002). This has resulted in an escalation of efforts to understand violence from a number of different theoretical and empirical perspectives, with the aim of reducing both the incidence of violence and the associated mortality, morbidity, and economic burden. As more sophisticated methodologies have become available over the last decade, neuroscience has contributed significantly to the understanding of aggression and violence. Such advances have not gone unnoticed by the courts, or by policymakers and lawmakers. This is unsurprising, given that both neuroscience and the law are concerned with human behavior, the former in its neural basis and the latter in its regulation. Indeed, relative to other scientific disciplines offering perspectives on violence, neuroscience may be particularly appealing to those operating within legal process, in that it is interested in aspects of human functioning that appear similar to central issues that the law also aims to address. For example, neuroscience is concerned with "thinking" and "emotion," whereas law is interested in "intention" and "guilt." Also, to the non-neuroscientist, brain science seems to offer enticing, almost easy or obvious, explanations of behavior. Yet it is this apparent, but only apparent, close relationship between the two disciplines that makes the use of neuroscientific evidence within legal proceedings not just appealing but also potentially fraught with jurisprudential danger.

In this chapter we review relevant science in relation mainly to prediction of violence, although such science may also be considered potentially relevant to higher-order concepts, such as "responsibility."

SCIENCE

Evidence regarding the neural basis of aggression and violence has come from a range of neuroscientific disciplines employing a wide range of technologies and methodologies. This has resulted in the development of increasingly complex models of aggression and violence, from which testable hypotheses can be derived. Studies have employed multiple methods, allowing for cross-validation of findings with convergent data, thereby offering a robust basis for testing such models and hypotheses. For example, a single hypothesis may be open to interrogation using both functional neuroimaging studies and electrophysiological techniques, such as electroencephalography and event-related potentials.

Psychophysiology

Psychophysiological studies have identified a number of ways in which antisocial populations differ from controls in how they psychologically process particular stimuli. These differences may confer increased risk of aggressive behavior. For example, lower resting autonomic activity levels, as manifested in reduced heart rate and skin conductance, and reduced cortical arousal, with enhanced slow wave activity in frontal and temporal regions, have been described in antisocial populations, particularly children and adolescents (Ortiz & Raine, 2004; Raine, 1996). Although data regarding the reactivity of the autonomic nervous system are less consistent in suggesting differences between antisocial and other individuals (Babcock et al., 2004), they do suggest possible differences between specific subpopulations of antisocial individuals. Hence, autonomic reactivity to stressors has been shown to be enhanced in antisocial individuals with high trait aggression (Peters et al., 2003) but reduced in response to aversive cues in psychopaths (Frick, 2002).[1] Various components of event-related potentials, brain responses that result directly from a thought or perception, have been investigated in aggressive subjects. The most consistent association is that of reduction in the amplitude of the P300 response to intermittent target stimuli in aggressive individuals (Gerstle et al., 1998). This abnormality is also associated with other impulse control problems and may be an endophenotypic marker of externalizing behavior more broadly (Krueger et al., 2002). Significantly, prospective studies have demonstrated that some of the electrophysiological abnormalities described above are evident prior to the onset of criminal behavior. Raine et al. (1990) described evidence of electrodermal, cardiovascular, and cortical under-arousal in 15-year-olds who went on to commit an offense by the age of 24 years. That is, the abnormalities were present in adolescents who went on to offend, compared to control subjects who did not, at a stage when neither had yet engaged in criminal behavior.

Neuroendocrinology

The possible role of hormones in aggression has been the subject of much investigation, not least because of the observation that males have higher levels of androgens and demonstrate higher levels of physical aggression than females (van Goozen & Fairchild, 2009). Although the roles of other hormones have been investigated, androgens remain the main focus of neuroendocrinology research in aggression.

Androgens have two types of effects on the brain, activational and organizational effects. The former are acute and temporary effects; the latter result from actions on the brain, during brief developmental windows, that permanently alter the structure or functional potential of the brain (Rubinow & Schmidt, 1996). Evidence of the organizational effects of androgens is seen in rodents: if castrated within 6 days postnatally, they display little inter-male aggression when stimulated with testosterone as adults (an activational effect). However, neonatal androgen replacement restores normal adult aggressive behavior in these rodents (Brain, 1979).

The association between androgens and aggression in humans is less clear. This may be because, in humans, testosterone is more closely linked to social dominance than aggressive behavior, or because the effect of testosterone on aggression is moderated by interaction with specific genetic factors.

Glucocorticoids and the hypothalamic-pituitary-adrenal axis more generally have been implicated in aggression, due to the observed association between trauma, stress response, and aggressive behavior. Studies in both animal models and humans have suggested an inverse relationship between plasma glucocorticoid levels and aggression. It has been proposed that the interaction of early trauma with other developmental factors may blunt the adrenocortical response, resulting in inappropriate aggression in response to relatively minor subsequent stressors (van Goozen & Fairchild, 2009). The relationship between insulin, hypoglycemia, and aggression is less clear. There is some evidence that the glucose nadir seen during the glucose tolerance test is significantly lower in offenders with intermittent explosive personality disorder (Virkkunen et al., 1994), and attempts have been made to use postprandial hyperglycemia as a defense against murder, the so-called "Twinkie defense" (Pogash, 2003).

Despite the promise of the emerging evidence base from psychophysiology and neuroendocrinology, however, it is developments in neuroimaging and behavior genetics that have perhaps most strongly captured the legal and policy imagination. While this preference must, in part, reflect the relative extent of the various bodies of evidence, it is undoubtedly also due to the perceived potential utility in legal proceedings of neuroimaging and genetics. This may be due to greater congruence, or lesser incongruence, of these scientific models and law, or it may be due to neuroimaging and genetics being easier for the non-scientist to "get hold of" or understand. More worryingly, it may result from a "folk science" effect; that is, neuroimaging and genetics appear to offer "obvious answers," but not necessarily validly so. Indeed, all that is obvious may not be true.

Neuroimaging

Neuroimaging studies have sought to determine whether there are differences in both brain structure and function between various antisocial and control populations. Specifically, structural neuroimaging studies, using computed tomography and magnetic resonance imaging, have identified abnormalities in a range of antisocial populations, most commonly in psychopaths and individuals with antisocial personality disorder.[2] The most consistent findings are a reduction in prefrontal gray matter (Raine et al., 2000; Yang et al., 2005b), particularly within the dorsolateral prefrontal cortex (DLPFC) and the orbitofrontal cortex (OFC) (Yang & Raine, 2009), and a reduction in the total volume of the temporal lobe (Barkataki et al., 2006; Dolan et al., 2002), more specifically the hippocampus (Laakso et al., 2001) and amygdala (Yang et al., 2009). Structural abnormalities have also been reported in the corpus callosum (Raine et al., 2003).

Functional imaging studies use tasks that tap into cognitive processes that have been shown, by other psychological means, to be abnormal in antisocial populations, in order to determine whether the relevant brain activation patterns differ significantly between antisocial and control subjects—that is, whether brain activation abnormality can be mapped onto psychologically measured abnormality. Two commonly used tasks are aversive (or fear) conditioning and response inhibition (or perseveration) tasks. The former tests the capacity to learn associations between aversive or fearful stimuli and previously neutral contexts or stimuli and underpins the ability to predict (and avoid) aversive events. The latter assesses the ability to suppress actions that are no longer appropriate, or that are no longer associated with reward, and is important in relation to both responding to environmental changes and to initiating goal-directed behavior. In functional neuroimaging studies using such tasks, altered brain activity in variously defined antisocial populations has been identified in the frontal lobe, particularly the DLPFC (Hirono et al., 2000; Schneider et al., 2000; Vollm et al., 2004) and OFC (Birbaumer et al., 2005; Horn et al., 2003; Siever et al., 1999), and in the medial temporal lobe, including the hippocampus (Kiehl et al., 2001) and amygdala (Birbaumer et al., 2005; Muller et al., 2003; Raine & Yang, 2006; Schneider et al., 2000). Other regions, including the cingulate cortex (Birbaumer et al., 2005; Kiehl et al., 2001; Kumari et al., 2006;

New et al., 2002), have been implicated, but these findings have been less well replicated.

Although some of the findings in neuroimaging studies of antisocial behavior are mutually inconsistent, or are yet to be replicated, it is clear that some have been described in a wide range of antisocial populations, using a variety of imaging methodologies, and are consistent across both structural and functional imaging studies. It is likely therefore that the most consistently implicated structures form part of a functional neural circuit underpinning specific types of aggression (Raine & Yang, 2006; Yang & Raine, 2009), and several sophisticated neuropsychological models have been proposed to test this hypothesis and further to delineate these functional circuits.

Some neuroimaging studies have focused on the processes implicated in antisocial behavior that are potentially relevant to legal questions. Using structural MRI, individuals defined as being "pathological liars" have been shown to have abnormalities of the prefrontal cortex not seen in either antisocial or normal controls (Yang et al., 2005a). Raine and Yang have proposed a neuro-moral model of antisocial behavior based on imaging findings in both antisocial behavior and moral reasoning (Raine & Yang, 2006). They propose that the emotional component of "morality," centered on the prefrontal cortex and amygdala, is impaired in psychopaths, rather than moral reasoning itself. Thus psychopaths may *know* an action to be immoral, but the lack of *feeling* that it is immoral prevents this cognitive recognition from being translated into behavioral inhibition. The dissociation of components of moral reasoning, *knowing* what is wrong and *feeling* what is wrong, may have significant implications for legal definitions of responsibility *per se*, as we will discuss later. However, lack of moral inhibition also has potentially profound significance for prediction, since an individual who lacks "moral capacity" may likely represent a higher future risk of violence than someone who does not suffer such a lack. Also, lack of a normal capacity for moral responsibility may bear upon the ethics of preventive detention, based upon prediction of future violence.

Behavioral genetics

Meta-analyses of twin and adoption studies have indicated that approximately 40 percent of the variation in adolescent and adult antisocial behavior is attributable to genetic factors. The remainder is attributable to nonshared environmental factors and, to a lesser extent, to shared environmental factors (Rhee & Waldman, 2002). However, some types of antisocial behavior appear to be more heritable than others. This has been demonstrated particularly well in studies of children and adolescents, where antisocial behavior in children with callous-unemotional traits,[3] antisocial behavior with comorbid hyperactivity, and aggressive antisocial behavior are more heritable than other subtypes. Studies using increasingly sophisticated quantitative genetic designs have begun to describe the extent to which genetic and environmental factors interact with each other; for example, the extent to which genetic factors influence the likelihood of exposure, and sensitivity, to specific environmental factors. This relationship has been further disentangled by way of studies investigating whether environmental factors are themselves causal of behavior or whether their influence in determining antisocial behavior in adulthood can, to some degree, be explained by genetic factors (Moffitt, 2005). A number of specific gene–environment interactions have described in relation to antisocial behavior. Perhaps the best replicated is the interaction demonstrated between the monoamine oxidase A (*MAOA*) gene and early childhood adversity (Caspi et al., 2002). (See the discussion in Chapter 8.) Several studies have shown that a functional polymorphism in the MAOA gene moderates the impact of early childhood maltreatment on the development of antisocial behavior. In a meta-analysis based on eight studies looking at the interaction between the *MAOA* gene and childhood maltreatment on the risk of later conduct problems and criminality, the authors reported a significant pooled interaction effect size of 0.17 (Taylor & Kim-Cohen, 2007).

In parallel with quantitative genetic studies, molecular genetic studies have identified a large number of specific genes that are associated with aggression (McGuffin et al., 2002; Nelson & Chiavegatto, 2001). Many of these genes have a role in the neurotransmitter systems that have been implicated in aggression, such as the serotonergic and noradrenergic systems, and many also have a role in neurodevelopment.

Both quantitative and molecular genetic approaches indicate that multiple genes influence the overall antisocial phenotype, each with a relatively small effect, and that these genes interact both with each other and with multiple environmental factors (Craig & Halton 2009; McGuffin et al., 2002). Thus, as the role of genetic factors in the etiology of antisocial behavior becomes better understood, it seems clear that the impact of individual genes is limited, and that their interaction with other genes, and with environmental factors, is extremely complex.

LIMITATIONS OF THE SCIENCE

We turn now to the limitations of neuroscience viewed within its own paradigm. Recent developments in the understanding of the neurobiological basis of antisocial behavior appear promising and have generated a range of hypotheses for future work. This promise has undoubtedly been a factor in stimulating the interest of the lawyers and policymakers in the possible relevance of neuroscience to legal questions, and in the subsequent modest increase in cases within which neuroscientific evidence has been introduced into legal proceedings. However, the neuroscientific findings reviewed above are at best preliminary. This in itself is reason to exercise caution in using such evidence in legal proceedings or in policymaking. In addition, there are significant, identifiable methodological limitations that pose a further obstacle to the responsible use of neuroscientific evidence in courts, and more broadly within the criminal justice system. At a minimum, these limitations should determine that the use of neuroscientific evidence within legal process is pursued with great, and explicitly stated, caution.

Who (and what) is being described neuroscientifically?

Defining antisocial phenotypes is a problematic endeavor. Experimental populations vary considerably between studies, from those scoring above a particular cutoff on a relevant psychometric instrument, to individuals convicted of murder, to those with an ill-defined lifetime history of violence. Control samples are equally varied and often fail to achieve control for even the most well-established confounders, such as substance use and medication (Silva, 2009). The validity of using convenience samples, such as students, as controls is also questionable, given the limited extent to which they can be thought of as representative of those likely to be involved in legal proceedings. Many neuroimaging studies also have small sample sizes, which limit their power to detect real differences between antisocial and control populations. However, even if a sufficiently large sample is used, the outcome is expressed in terms of averages based on group data. This is in itself problematic as the law is concerned with evidence regarding a specific individual. And it is not the case that specific inferences, or predictions, regarding the individual can validly be drawn on the basis of observed statistically significant differences between a group to which the individual belongs and a relevant control group. Indeed, differences with regard to the variable in question may be greater within groups than between experimental and control groups.

Further, the statistical analyses used in studies are often based on questionable assumptions. For example, it is often assumed that the risk for each variable under investigation is independent, rather than due to, say, a third factor; and the probability for the co-occurrence of the two events is rarely compared with the probability of an alternative possibility. Assumptions are also often made about the statistical context or conditionals of the observation, and this can lead to confusion between achieving an understanding of the probability of the observed co-occurrence of the specific events and the probability of guilt or innocence (the so-called "prosecutor's fallacy"[4]). The vast majority of studies identify a statistical association between two variables. Thus, they do not determine causality, much less its direction. Yet this is so often of interest to courts, even though the law does not define causation in ways necessarily congruent with science.

A related concern lies in the interpretation of neuroscientific findings and, in particular, the interpretation of brain scan data. It is frequently assumed that activity in a particular brain region means that a particular mental process is or was taking place (the "fallacy of inverse inference"). However, mental processes involve many brain regions and, similarly, particular brain regions are involved in many mental processes. Thus activity in any one region may be the result of numerous mental processes and not just of the one of interest. Further, the relationship between neuronal activity and mental processes is inferential at best and relies on assumptions that may not be valid. Neuronal activity is measured by blood flow; increases in blood flow are assumed to reflect increased neuronal activity, and neuronal activity suggests a "mental process" is taking place. However, even the baseline assumption in this inferential stream has been questioned, in that studies have shown that it is possible for there to be increased blood flow in brain regions without an increase in neuronal activity (Sirotin & Das, 2009).

Neuroimaging as statistics

The fallacy of inverse inference is of particular relevance to neuroimaging studies. However, there are many other methodological limitations to studies using neuroimaging to investigate the neurobiological basis of antisocial behavior. Neuroimaging studies rely on a statistical comparison between the experimental image and a normative template. However, there is no "gold standard" template, or consensus concerning which measures should form the basis of such a template (Canli & Amin, 2002). Thus any given experimental image may be considered normal using one measure and statistically abnormal using another. A threshold for statistical significance, which is set by convention and is not an absolute standard, is used to define the observed activation pattern (Canli & Amin, 2002). The interpretation of the data is thus dependent on the subjective selection of a particular threshold and may vary between studies. The interpretation of data in functional neuroimaging is also dependent on the choice of control condition. "Rest" is commonly used as a control condition, although the notion that it is a zero-activity condition has been challenged. Brain regions that appear to be activated during a task when rest is used as a control condition may not appear activated when an alternative baseline is used (Stark & Squire, 2001).

Even if, despite these methodological difficulties, it is possible to conclude that activation is abnormal, it cannot necessarily be inferred that function is abnormal, as there may be an undetected alternative neural strategy subserving the same function (Martell, 2009).

The dynamic nature of functional neuroimages and difficulties with replication also limit their potential relevance for legal questions that are essentially historical or predictive. Images are context-specific, and images produced at different times and under different circumstances may have little or no relevance to the brain state of a defendant, for example, at the time of a previous offense (Martell, 2009). Indeed, related to this, there is evidence that countermeasures can be employed to produce misleading or uninterpretable results, and this further undermines the potential utility of neuroimaging evidence in legal proceedings.

Despite these methodological limitations, the potential for neuroimaging being appealing as a potential source of evidence in court is obvious. Yet it is precisely the apparently visually compelling nature of brain images that undermines their usefulness and should alert the uninformed user to danger. Simplicity in science either (rarely) reflects real underlying truth or (more commonly) hides a complexity that currently evades identified truth. This danger of "reading too much into an image," or other scientific description, has been attributed to a failure to recognize "inferential distance." That is, non-experts, such as jury members, may assume that neuroimages are photographs of brain activity, when in fact there are a number of necessary inferential steps, often based on provisional theories, between the images observed and the brain activity data upon which they are based. Thus a non-scientist may believe that the visually appealing subjective components of the image correspond to objective findings, based upon little or no inferential distance (Roskies, 2008; Silva, 2009). This may result in the illusion that there are significant differences in relevant aspects of brain activity between individuals, or brain states in an individual, where little actually exists. The dangers of this illusion are evident if lack of inferential steps goes unnoticed, or is even deliberately ignored, by policymakers, or courts, in designing sentencing law, and in deciding sentencing of individuals. The risk that the illusion of significant differences is taken as fact is enhanced within a political culture, and social and media discourse, within which risk aversion is predominant.

Methodological problems in behavior genetic studies

Studies investigating the role of genetic factors in antisocial behavior encounter many of the same methodological limitations that restrict the utility of neuroimaging data in court. Definition of phenotype and applying generalizations from group studies to individuals are particularly relevant within this particular approach. Each genetic factor must be understood in the context of the individual's entire genome, including genetic factors that may confer protection or resilience. Gene expression is also a dynamic process influenced by a large number of genetic and environmental factors that cannot be assumed to have been operating at both the time of an offense and at the time of testing for the purposes of legal proceedings. These limitations all have major significance in properly restricting the utility of such science for the prediction of violent behavior by the individual.

NEUROSCIENCE VERSUS SOCIAL FACTORS

We have addressed some of the limitations of the types of, particularly brain imaging and genetic, studies we have described in terms of science. However, might not the application *per se* of natural science to what is ultimately a social phenomenon, or problem, risk "political denial" of relevant social factors determining of antisocial behavior, including aggregate social factors that go beyond the experience of the individual? As Bostock and Adshead observe, "In a culture of social fear, in which public protection tops the political agenda, good quality legal and moral reasoning might come under threat" (Bostock & Adshead, 2003).

There is little room in a chapter devoted to "how good is the neuroscience of violence and how relevant is it to law?" also to consider whether neuroscience might not simply miss the point. Yet by limiting our view to "how good so far is the science?" might we not risk applying, or at least wrongly privileging, the wrong paradigm? And is such a risk not particularly pertinent where the purpose of reviewing the neuroscience of violence is to form a view of its proper utility in legal process, given that law and legal process themselves bear a far more natural relation to social and political science than to natural science?

We shall return to this point later when we consider whether there are, or can ever be, congruence, or even "translational possibility," between scientific and legal domains. However, in passing we seek here simply to make the point that it may be not just that "law often asks science questions that science cannot answer," but also that a social or political response to law's questions might well be both possible and more appropriate than one originating in natural science.

NEUROSCIENCE AND POLITICAL SCIENCE

It is clear that current evidence supporting a neurobiological basis to antisocial behavior is promising, yet tentative, and that there are many methodological limitations, both general and specific to particular approaches, that limit the extent to which such evidence can be used, validly and responsibly, to inform legal proceedings in relation to prediction of future violence by individuals.

However, even if the evidence available to date were to be well replicated in further studies and the major methodological difficulties addressed in those studies, its interpretation and application would continue to be subject to the influence of the prevailing social and political climate. Evidence can be interpreted, within a particular political context, for example, to limit the extent to which the state is seen to be responsible for antisocial behavior, or the social inequalities or other factors that contribute to it (Bostock & Adshead, 2003). For example, emphasis on, or overstating, the role of genetic factors in predicting antisocial behavior, by comparison with social factors, can locate the problem in the individual and create a sense of nihilism within efforts to address the problem at the societal level.

Moreover, the current ambiguity inherent in the scientific evidence makes the risk of deliberate misinterpretation of the evidence for "whatever purpose," be it social, political, or economic, far greater (Rose, 2001).

CURRENT LEGAL USE OF NEUROSCIENTIFIC EVIDENCE

The courts *should* be less subject to any political or social agenda in their adoption and use of ambiguous neuroscientific evidence than other social and state institutions. Hence the obstacles to the proper use of neuroimaging and genetic evidence in courts are perhaps reflected in the small number of cases within which such evidence has been invoked. This is particularly the case in UK jurisdictions, compared with other jurisdictions, notably the United States. However, even in jurisdictions where such evidence has been admitted, its use has been limited to specific legal and medical contexts. In the United States, neuroimages have been used in evidence in relation to acquired brain injury, damage, or atrophy, and to brain development, in order to mitigate culpability, even though reduced culpability may also suggest enhanced predicted risk, with custodial implications flowing from this in order to manage such enhanced risk (Moriarty, 2008). However, neuroimages have not been used in relation to "non-acquired" abnormalities that are inherent to the individual, and their use has largely been confined to civil cases.

One context, however, within which neuroimages have been used in criminal proceedings has been within the penalty phase of some capital cases, where courts have been relatively more flexible, perhaps lenient, in admitting such evidence (Moriarty, 2008). This is of interest in relation to adherence, or not, to the rules of expert evidence. Where, within a trial to verdict, the court applies strict evidential rules, such that neuroimages unrelated to damage or deterioration are largely deemed inadmissible, within the sentencing phase, a much looser approach to admissibility is sometimes adopted. This appears, on its face, to reflect what, in the United Kingdom, has been termed "the benign medico-legal conspiracy."[5] Hence, in all UK jurisdictions there is a mandatory life sentence applicable on conviction of murder, but not on a finding of manslaughter, based, for example, on a finding of "diminished responsibility." Yet even prosecutors at times recognize that such a sentencing requirement can give rise to injustice in the individual case. Thus lawyers from both sides of the case may search for a psychiatrist prepared to "stretch his discipline" so as to support a plea of diminished responsibility where, in true reflection of the medical evidence, none properly lies. That is, there is obvious values incursion into the behavior of both doctors and lawyers, which supports poor use of science aimed at mollifying the effects of law properly administered, in its own terms. In death penalty sentencing, it seems likely that a similar values incursion can sometimes operate, in order to avoid killing the defendant.[6] Using science in this way reflects poorly on both doctors and the justice system. The fault lies in rules relating to imposition of the death penalty, and it should not be "put right" by misuse of science within law. Of course, again, winning on the "reduced culpability" swings can be matched by losing on the "preventive detention" roundabout.[7]

Put simply, science should be represented as it really is within legal proceedings and law should accept the consequences, or law should alter its rules (and not its rules about the admissibility and acceptance of expert evidence). In terms of jurisprudence, lack of consistent application of legal rules, including in relation to expert evidence, lays the foundation for "arbitrary (non) justice."[8] We shall return to this point in relation to "risk-based sentencing" and "preventive detention."

The use of neuroimaging evidence has indeed been more limited in the United Kingdom, perhaps because of the absence of the death penalty. In these jurisdictions, neuroimages have been used as evidence that a defendant had a mental condition that rendered him unfit to plead[9]; to support claims of personality change as a result of brain damage[10]; and as evidence in relation to the capacity to make a will.[11] However, such evidence has not been used in the United Kingdom to argue for mitigation of culpability in criminal proceedings, or in relation to diminished responsibility or insanity at trial, other than in support of other medical evidence suggesting acquired brain damage or deterioration.

Recently, neuroimaging evidence has been admitted in court in combination with relevant genetic information and neuropsychological assessment (Rigoni et al., 2010). By demonstrating consistency of findings among diagnostic approaches, such cross-validation of particular "views" of the brain can help corroborate a clinical opinion considered to be relevant to the legal question.

As such the neuroscientific evidence is used to improve the accuracy and objectivity of a particular diagnosis or clinical formulation, which may itself then form the basis of an "offense narrative," developed by lawyers, where particular symptoms may be argued to be legally (not scientifically) causally related to the offense in question. Here the use of neuroscientific evidence is in an entirely different mode. It is the clinical opinion, albeit with all of *its* ambiguities and uncertainties, supported partly by neuroscientific evidence, that the court adopts in direct relation to a legal question; there is no leap from neuroscience to legal question and answer. And, in considering clinically based evidence, the court is more likely to take account of clinically based ambiguities, which may themselves be obvious, by comparison with erroneously adopting only apparently "obvious" valid neuroscientific evidence.

The possibility that neuroscientific evidence may be used in a similar mode in relation to violence risk prediction has also been proposed (Royal Society, 2011). While individual neurobiological markers may not have sufficient predictive validity, or may not be used responsibly in legal proceedings for the reasons already discussed, they may be used in combination with well-established risk factors to enhance the predictive validity of existing risk assessment instruments. If it proved possible to establish that specific neurobiological markers incrementally improved the accuracy of risk predications based on standard risk assessment instruments, such information could, in theory, be used to inform a number of risk management decisions, including those relating to treatment, sentencing, parole, and supervision in the community.

FUNDAMENTAL REASONS WHY NEUROSCIENTIFIC EVIDENCE SHOULD BE USED WITH GREAT CARE IN CRIMINAL LEGAL PROCEEDINGS AND POLICY

Legal and medical constructs, and their differences

Aside from all of the scientific reasons for exercising extreme caution in considering possible use of neuroscientific evidence within legal proceedings, there are more profound reasons for caution, originating from the very different purposes and modes of operation of law and science.

The constructs of law and science are derived from the purposes of each. In simple terms, law pursues justice, an abstract notion, and science pursues understanding and explanation of "things in being." Specifically, medical science pursues welfare, even if via understanding and explanation; that is, the purpose of medical science is ultimately intervention in pursuit of increased welfare. Since the purposes of each, law and science, are fundamentally different from those of the other, law often asks questions that science cannot answer, and science often answers questions the law does not ask (Eastman & Campbell 2006a, 2006b).[12] Clearly this is so where the law adopts "high-order" constructs" such as "responsibility," which has no equivalence in science. Even where science pursues understanding and explanation, or prediction, it does so not toward justice, even though understanding derived from science may then be used within a given justice process and calculus (e.g., a given understanding or explanation of a set of events and their apparent determination may then be "translated" into a "justice solution"). And even where the law adopts an apparently ordinary and "lower-order" construct, for example that of "risk," in relation to sentencing, it is not clear that this concept means the same thing in law as it might in the clinic, or that "risk" calculations follow the same process in these different contexts.[13]

Even though this proposition of ultimate inherent incongruence is "necessarily" true in relation to higher-order constructs, and may sometimes be true in relation to more mundane constructs, courts often ignore such truth by asking science for answers to some of its questions—and scientists frequently agree to answer those questions. So what seems practically at issue, therefore, is the following question: How can the construct disparity between each law and science be made evident to both sides, so that the law's use of science is both insightful into the disparity, and properly cautious? Or, stated differently: How can the questions asked of science by law be limited to those where the answer can be congruent with scientific answers?

The dangers of mismatch and miscommunication

Although law always tends to find a way to "use" (real) science toward its own (abstract) justice purposes, if such differences of meaning and discourse between law and science are not explicitly recognized, then the relevance of science to law may be assumed when it is not present, or not directly or strongly so. Taken to its logical and perhaps rather extreme conclusion, "loose thought costs lives," or "wrongly" saves them (in some jurisdictions that retain the death penalty[14]), or at least may impact "wrongly" on liberty.

At the heart of the problem of the relation of law and science is both incongruities of substance, in terms of the varying constructs and processes of each, *and* the risk of failure of each to *recognize* such incongruity; or even if there is recognition, the danger is of miscommunication between scientists giving expert evidence and courts hearing it. Neuroscience is almost certainly at particular risk of both unobserved incongruity with law and miscommunication within legal process, given the frequently apparent, but not real, similarity of their constructs. Although such risk of intrusion of both mismatch and miscommunication is likely to be particularly emphasized in jury decision making concerning verdict, it would be unwise to assume that judges are immune from misunderstanding scientific evidence in the context of risk-based sentencing that adopts evidence of prediction of future behavior.

Hence, the presence of structural or functional brain "abnormalities" in some individuals who are violent, or who represent a phenotype prone to violence, seems on its face to suggest causation relevant both to criminal responsibility ("it wasn't me, it was my brain") and to public protection ("it's his brain, and so there is justification for preventive detention"). However, leaving aside all the scientific weaknesses of such findings, as we have indicated this is not just to ignore the incongruence between "brain observation" and, for example, "responsibility," or "intent," or "specific intent," but also to presume that brain state when tested reflects brain state at the time of a previous violent act; or at some specified time, and in some specified circumstance, in the future, in regard to future risk. And even that is to ignore the real scientific "meaning" of the observed brain abnormality, which we have already described at length.

Even more fundamentally, all the brain data only have meaning in terms of comparing a population with violent or violence-related phenotypes with "normals," with no necessary implication for the individual (Silva, 2009). And yet justice is dispensed essentially within an individual model, not, for example, on the basis that an individual is a member of a class of individuals more likely to offend than others.

Perhaps the point is best made by posing the question: If particular brain regions and neural circuits are (or soon may prove to be) strongly implicated in violence across populations of offenders, or particular relevant phenotypes, would that justify genetic or pharmacological manipulation of the implicated regions and circuits in any individual showing such a brain pattern? Surely not, and this intuitively negative answer tends perhaps to draw one away from such an (un)ethical transposition from populations to the individual. This may be particularly the case when such neurobiological markers are identified in a child or adolescent who is "asymptomatic"—that is, has not yet engaged in offending behavior or has yet to enter the developmental stage during which such behavior is most likely to occur.

MISMATCHES OF PROCESS

Turning more directly to process, a further problem occurs in presenting science into legal proceedings in that the proper paradigm for testing a scientific hypothesis is unlikely always to be capable of adequate challenge within a legal process that is adversarial rather than (as it is in science) investigative, whatever the evidential rules of admissibility. This applies even to evidence relevant to "lower-order" legal constructs (Law Commission, 2011). Questions put within legal process may be "incapable" of adequately testing the evidence, because it is evidence susceptible only to scientific challenge and not legal challenge; that is, because it is not fully possible to ask questions from one paradigm inquiring of another.

Moreover, the legal context may determine different degrees of stringency in exposing the incongruence of any scientific evidence in relation to its legal use, or indeed even its scientific weakness—hence the example described above of greater leniency being shown in capital appeal cases than elsewhere legally.

As we have emphasized, the law determines its constructs and rules, including setting the rules concerning which pieces of scientific evidence should be "admissible" (leaving aside their reliability), not by reference to scientific paradigms, or standards, but according to paradigms and standards required in terms of a particular setting of the scales of justice. What drives the rules and process through which the law uses such constructs is not "what could be investigatively helpful in determining the truth" but "what would it be fair to admit as evidence," reflected in the current rules of admissibility of evidence. Also the standards in regard to admissibility are often different between different legal contexts, usually reflecting particular policy goals. As a result, scientific evidence is open to being used to provide a rationale for *various* particular goals, as represented in law. And scientifically *weak* evidence is open to being used spuriously, so as apparently to justify a particular social goal—for example, "preventive detention."

RULES FOR ADMISSIBILITY OF EXPERT EVIDENCE, AND REFORM IN THE UNITED KINGDOM

The Law Commission for England and Wales, in its recent proposal for reform of the legal basis for the admission of expert evidence,[15] observed "the common law approach to the admissibility of expert opinion evidence is one of *laissez-faire*, with such evidence being admitted without sufficient regard to whether or not it is sufficiently reliable to be considered by a jury." The Commission opined this to be "unsatisfactory" and proposed that "the common law approach should be replaced by a new admissibility test set out in primary legislation... [with] particular concern about expert opinion evidence which is presented as scientific... [where] there is a danger that juries will abdicate their duty to ascertain and weigh the facts and simply accept the experts' own opinion evidence, particularly if the evidence is complex and difficult for a non-specialist to understand and evaluate."

The Commission recommended specifically that "expert evidence [be] admissible in criminal proceedings only if (1) the court is likely to require the help of an expert witness (the *Turner* test[16]) and (2) it is proved on the balance of probabilities that the individual claiming expertise is qualified to give such evidence," with the latter being based upon "study, training, experience or any other appropriate means."

Under the Commission's proposal, evidence would be sufficiently reliable to be admitted if (a) the opinion is *soundly based* and (b) the strength of the opinion is warranted *having regard to the grounds on which it is based*. Examples of reasons why an expert's opinion evidence would *not* be sufficiently reliable to be admitted would be that the opinion (a) "is based on a *hypothesis which has not been subjected to sufficient scrutiny*" (including, where appropriate, experimental or other testing), or which has "*failed to stand up to scrutiny*"; (b) it "is *based on an unjustifiable assumption*"; (c) it "is *based on flawed data*"; (d) it "*relies on an examination, technique, method or process which was not properly carried out or applied, or was not appropriate* for use in the particular case"; and (e) "*relies on an inference or conclusion which has not been properly reached*" (emphases added).[17]

The description of features of evidence that would make a given piece of evidence legally *un*reliable is potentially applicable to neuroscience evidence relevant to violence.[18] Indeed, it is arguable that the proposals, if enacted, would go a long way toward ensuring that expert evidence specifically relating to neuroscience and violence would be the subject of proper scrutiny. This includes particular protection within the proposals that "unfounded inference" would rule expert evidence inadmissible. By contrast, there is *currently* a risk of lack of such scrutiny.

In summary, current law in England and Wales is not such as to ensure adequate safeguards against misuse or miscommunication of expert evidence relating to the neurobiology of violence, while the proposed reform would go a long way toward doing so.

RISK-BASED SENTENCING AND PREVENTIVE DETENTION

There are clearly two sides to the neuroscience and violence coin, in that whereas evidence might be used purportedly to demonstrate "reduction" of a high-order construct, such as culpability, it might also be used to validate preventive detention directed at public protection ("you are less responsible because of the nature of your brain, but also more dangerous").[19] Hence, again the defendant might win on the responsibility swings only to lose on the preventive detention roundabout.

All of the arguments concerning "scientific weakness" we have deployed above apply to sentencing, as well as to subsequent assessment of "risk of violence" by parole boards hearing applications for release on license of prisoners serving indeterminate sentences. They do not require repetition.

However, sentencing, and certainly parole hearings and mental health tribunal hearings, are determined within a looser model, in terms of admissible evidence, rules of evidence, and mode of decision making, than that which applies within a trial to verdict. This might offer comfort that neuroscientific evidence is unlikely to be misused, in that it is being applied to legal constructs that are not usually *inherently* incongruous with scientific ones. However, lack of incongruence between the science and law may harbor a different danger, which is that the absence of strict rules of admissibility (such as those now proposed by the Law Commission) may allow loose thought and judgment on suspect scientific evidence. There is some reason already to be concerned about this in terms of judicial adoption, or at least use, of "clinical risk assessment" evidence, with very limited reliability and validity foundations, and based largely upon population data. Faced with a concept that, to a judge, appears "clinical," the judge is likely to turn to clinical or scientific evidence. This is an almost inevitable result of legislating for sentencing based not only on what the defendant has done, either recently or in the past, but also on "who he is" (and what is his personal riskiness is).[20]

Hence, there is a risk that the weaknesses and ambiguities of neuroscientific evidence relating to violence will be less than fully acknowledged by courts, and even less so by parole boards and mental health tribunals, in determining risk-based sentencing and risk-based release decisions than in determining verdict.

The risk of improper use of any "science of risk assessment" is enhanced where there are no interventions offered to offenders, or available and effective, to allow them to modify their risk. And, in the context of mental health legislation in England and Wales, as recently reformed, there is effectively no "treatability" requirement for detention to be lawful, only that "appropriate medical treatment is available," wherein there is the "intention" to reduce disorder and risk, with no likelihood of patient benefit required.[21] And such a basis for preventive detention can be applied either where the individual has committed no offense, or where a determinate sentence given for commission of an offense has expired, with continued detention achieved by way of transfer to the hospital of a sentenced prisoner under S. 47 of the Mental Health Act 1983, as amended by the 2007 Act, lapsing into a "notional S. 37" on the prisoner/patient reaching what would have been his or her prison release date.[22]

What should be sought is merely "neuroscientifically informed" sentencing and parole or mental health tribunal decision making, where the evidence is used, if used at all, alongside other "ordinary" evidence (see above in relation to "triangulation" and "cross-validation").

There is some emerging evidence that suggests further investigation of whether some children who go on to offend violently are neurobiologically different from those who do not (see the discussion in Chapter 9). If further validated, such early evidence of "predisposition" would imply possibly early preventive intervention, if the brain abnormality was reflective of experience, which experience could be reversed. But such evidence might also support a charter for early abandonment to preventive detention. These are heady waters.

In broad terms preventive detention is justified in law only if it is "proportionate" to the risk posed by the individual to others. However, any "proportionality" calculus needs to be operated with full inclusion of reference to not only the strengths but also the weaknesses of the basis, including neuroscientific basis, of the risk assessment conducted. Predictive accuracy (the "receiver operator characteristic") of any risk assessment must be included within a weighing process that sets individual liberty, or its deprivation, against public protection.

PRIVACY AND CONSENT TO ASSESSMENT

The foregoing has been concerned with the potential for use, and misuse, of neuroscience in predicting violence by individuals. We turn, finally, however, to matters concerning ownership of the right to acquire and use neuroscientific data concerning an individual, where the state may have an interest in its collection and use, for reasons of public protection, and the subject of such data might have an interest in risk-related data on him or her not being acquired or used.

Unlike some psychological investigations of brain and mind function, which require necessarily that the subject both consent to the investigation and participate in it, some, though by no means all, neuroimaging investigations can be carried out nonconsensually if sedation is applied. Genetic testing can be achieved with minimal or even no cooperation. What does this imply in terms of balancing the right of a defendant still to refuse investigation, and for that to be respected, against the right of society to be protected from the risks posed by that individual, such that the requirement of consent can be waived? (In the case of a defendant wishing to rely on neuroscientific evidence to reduce his culpability, or sentence, then of course he would wish to, and would consent; although, if the information that might thereby be collected has relevance for other members of his family, especially in relation to genetic information, there is a question as to whether he can validly consent alone.)

Where a subject does consent, clearly he should do so only with maximum knowledge of both the potential outcomes of the investigation and their scientific weaknesses, but also in full knowledge of the uses to which it is intended they be put. However, uses currently envisaged might not be the only uses to which, over time, the data might be put, as his circumstances change. Or the uses to which such data can be put, or the inferences that can be drawn from the data, may develop, so that any consent gained could amount to at least partially blind consent. Indeed, arguably "informed consent" is frequently "blind to the future," across a wide range of human interventions.

Finally, are the results of investigations potentially available only to that branch of the state in relation to which they were originally gained, or are there no boundaries between state agencies? And what are, or should be, the boundaries between state and private agencies—for example, insurance companies?

These are huge questions that go beyond the scope of this chapter, but it is important at least to acknowledge them here.

CONCLUSIONS AND FUTURE PROSPECTS

Responsibility and public protection represent two sides of an ethical and policy coin, and any biological markers of violence are potentially relevant to each. However, it is clear that, aside from all the scientific weaknesses of relevant studies of imaging in particular, given the "high-order" nature of responsibility, science is still very far from answering, and perhaps ever answering, legal questions concerning culpability. That may not serve to exclude neuroscience from such legal process but to restrict its role to informing decisions by way of providing information additional to other types of medical, and nonmedical, information, in terms of corroboration. Even science that offers a contribution to "explaining" violence cannot be used to "determine" such a high-order construct as responsibility, and brain scanning offers evidence that is statistical and correlational in nature in any event.

Aside from the neurosciences having methodological weaknesses within themselves, they also offer a "weak" paradigm, compared with philosophical and legal notions of responsibility, and social variables and explanations of violence sit more easily with law, since law is itself a social discipline, perhaps informed by philosophy and even logic, far removed from science.

As regards risk, by comparison with brain or genetic markers, markers such as race, age, and gender, which all amount to "phenotypic" markers, are very limited in their "risk aspirations," in that they are "status" markers. Brain imaging addresses, in some measure, process information, as in another sense do genetics. They are therefore far more adventurous in that they seek not only to "correlate" factors with violence but to explain it, and therefore even better to predict it.

Yet, it may well be inappropriate to legal process to determine individual case disposal based upon the defendant's membership of a class of individuals. Mere consideration of the possibility of execution "because of membership of a class of individuals actuarially at high risk of future violence, or even homicide" surely makes the justice point. It may be justified to punish someone for an accumulation of offending, on a "just deserts" basis, but that is different from placing an individual within a class of "apparently similar" individuals with similar offending records and "disabling" him, by imprisonment or execution, because of the risk of future violence associated, within a group, with such a past history. And the point holds even more strongly in relation to neurobiological markers, with all their attendant inherent scientific methodological problems. In any event, whether by reference to group statistics or individual data, punishing offenders "for what they have done" is a very different exercise from "disabling them for who they are," and the more justifiable.

Where science is admitted, or in future is to be admitted, into the legal process, the legal rules of admissibility must serve to inhibit the inappropriate use of science, both in terms of "relevance" (to what may sometimes be high-order questions) and "reliability." The former addresses a fundamental question, the latter a more functional and mundane one. However, where the issue at legal hand is a "lower-order concept," such as risk of future violence, and where that is considered either within the legally looser framework within court of sentencing, or by a parole board or mental health tribunal, certainly in the latter two contexts strict rules of evidence do not apply. And it is here, therefore, where the danger is not one of "mismatch" between science and law (as with determination of responsibility) but of law adopting scientific techniques and results the weaknesses of which are unlikely to be fully apparent to the court, if apparent at all. And here the risk of misuse in future is indeed high, given the increasing sophistication of neurobiology and its "folk appeal." In a related fashion, therefore, we would be far more cautious than Monahan (see Chapter 4 in this volume) even in relation to "static" markers. Moreover, we would urge consideration of whether it is ethical at all to use "clinicians" to inform what amount to "punishment" decisions.

It is doubtful that even the most robust findings regarding brain abnormalities in antisocial individuals meet the Law Commission criteria in relation to their application to either "high-order" or "low-order" constructs. The significant lack of replication, and largely unaddressed methodological limitations, in neuroimaging studies are such that the findings cannot be considered to have been subjected to sufficient scrutiny. We have suggested that the data may be fundamentally flawed. The assumption that such group data could have any relevance to the individual, or have any predictive validity within individuals across situations, is not justified. Further, the techniques used have only been validated for experimental use, and in specific experimental contexts. As such the data are far from conclusive; there then remains the fundamental issue of whether the cognitive processes under investigation have any relevance to the constructs that courts adopt.

In *Barefoot v. Estelle* it was held "the suggestion that no psychiatrists' testimony may be presented with respect to a defendant's future dangerousness is somewhat like asking us to disinvest in the wheel." Justifying the use of psychiatrists, or psychologists, within sentencing hearings addressing future risk by way of suggesting that risk assessment "is done, has always been done, and so must be capable of being done, and surely better done by a professional than by a lay person" (paraphrased, also from *Schall v. Martin*) (see Chapter 4) is to suggest that the "something pretending to be round is a wheel." As regards neuroscientific evidence which purports to "explain" or "predict" human violence, this amounts not to pretense at being a wheel, but a wheel that is both wobbly, in terms of its connection with the vehicle it purports to serve, and also is more square than round. It hardly serves its purpose as does even the crudest cartwheel.

NOTES

1. The term *psychopath* refers in modern psychiatric terms to those individuals with personality disorder who show particular characteristics likely to be associated with offending in terms of the Hare Psychopathy Checklist (PCL-R) (Hare, 2003). The classification *antisocial personality disorder* (ASPD) is an accepted diagnostic term within the *Diagnostic and Statistical Manual of the American Psychiatric Association*, 4th ed. (DSM IV). It is much broader than the concept of *psychopathy* and is essentially behavioral in its foundations (psychopathy by contrast is both behavioral *and* psychological). In terms of comparison of populations, most "Hare psychopaths" would satisfy the diagnostic criteria for ASPD, but many with the latter "condition" would not count as "psychopaths." In terms of research findings relating to violence, as many as 70 percent of the prison population satisfy the diagnostic criteria for ASPD, which makes it more difficult to demonstrate an association with violence.
2. See Footnote 1.
3. A core aspect of "psychopathy."
4. A famous example of this in England and Wales in recent years relates not to neuroscience but to statistical implications in a different context. Professor Roy Meadow, a pediatrician, commonly gave evidence in "cot death murder trial" and would often describe "the rule of three" of sudden infant death syndrome (SIDS), which he had published: "one death is a tragedy, two is suspicious and three is murder." Famously, in one trial, *Regina v. Clarke*, he opined that the chances of three such sequential deaths arising validly from SIDS was "one in seven million," based on cubing the chance of one such death and ignoring the fact that each death alters the chance of the next occurring. Although the defendant's conviction was subsequently overturned by the Court of Appeal not on the basis of this evidence but based upon cerebrospinal fluid bacteriological evidence, the case became a *cause celebre* in regard to both avoiding the misuse at trial of statistics *per se* and the risk that, based upon false statistical inferences, a jury might conclude in favor of a guilty verdict based upon such statistics and not upon the evidence in the particular case at hand.
5. See, for example, the unpublished paper by D. Ormerod (2010). *Coroners and Justice Act 2009—Homicide and Partial Defences*, for the Judicial Studies Board.

6. This contrasts with adoption of "status" variables within risk assessment schedules, which, as described by Monahan (see Chapter 4), have been approved by courts as potentially founding the basis for imposition of the death penalty. In the conclusion to this chapter we address the analogy that Monahan draws between legal use toward "risk-based sentencing" of "partially biological" variables, from within actuarial risk assessment schedules, *with* biological variables described in the chapter.

7. Reform of the partial defense to murder of "diminished responsibility," through S. 52 Coroners and Justice Act 2009 amendment of Section 2 of the Homicide Act 1957, was designed to bring the defense "up to date" and congruent modern psychiatric thinking. And predictably (see Eastman, N., "New versus Old Diminished Responsibility" [2010], unpublished paper for the Judicial Studies Board), and anecdotally in practice, reform appears to have made achieving "diminished responsibility" easier for defendants with "psychopathy," or ASPD. However, the Court of Appeal has "responded" effectively by lengthened tariffs for diminished responsibility manslaughter in such cases within use of the "discretionary life sentence."

8. An example of perhaps an overly flexible approach to the administration of justice in the United Kingdom relates to *Regina v. Sutcliffe* the trial of the "Yorkshire Ripper." All psychiatrists, for both the Crown and defense, diagnosed severe schizophrenia and laid the foundation for a finding of diminished responsibility manslaughter. Despite the Crown's acceptance of the plea, the judge directed that there should be a trial. Subsequently, in an editorial, the *Times* opined (paraphrased) that "it was absolutely right that there was a trial, public catharsis required it … of course if we had had the death penalty in England then that would have been different matter." It is, of course, jurisprudential nonsense to suggest that whether or not there should be a trial in a case depends upon the penalty that would apply on a finding of guilt. The admission of ambiguous scientific evidence at sentencing that courts would not admit at trial represents a similar "arbitrary" approach to justice.

9. *Regina v. Mohammed Sharif* [2010] EWCA Crim 1709.

10. *Meah v Mcreamer* [1985] 1 All ER 367.

11. *Carr and another v. Thomas* [2008] EWHC 2859.

12. It is clearly the case that, "on the way" to achieving justice, law poses factual questions, and here there may be no disparity between what law asks of science and what science can offer. However, where the constructs adopted by law in translating facts into justice are "high-order" constructs (e.g., "responsibility"), law and science fundamentally part company.

13. Monahan describes (in Chapter 4) how, in the U.S. case of *Schall v. Martin*, it was determined that any argument that inherent difficulties in achieving any scientifically acceptable level of reliability and prediction of future violence by a defendant did not make any sentencing decision based upon the exercise "intrinsically arbitrary." Rather, the court determined "from a legal point of view there is nothing *inherently unattainable* about a prediction of future criminal conduct... such a judgment forms an important element of many decisions" (emphasis added). What this amounts to is the law's assumption that "it must be doable"; or rather, the assertion that "courts do it so it must be doable." This is suggested by the assertion that there is "nothing intrinsically unattainable" in assessing risk. But it is a nonsense statement in any real rather than abstract sense and means that "it will be done however

unreliably." This poses an interesting justice question: while it may be justifiable to "punish" a defendant for what he has done, what is the justice basis for preventively detaining him based upon risk assessment where there is no adequately reliable basis for assessing that risk?

14. Those who oppose the death penalty in any circumstance (such as the authors) may wish there to be lives saved by whatever means, even via spurious use of science (not the authors). However, in terms of justice as defined by the relevant jurisdiction, such saving of life may be "wrong," and the authors would not wish to see science "abused" in order to save lives where the "right" route to doing so would be in abolition of the death penalty.

15. See above.

16. *Regina v. Turner* [1975] QB 834.

17. These criteria bear close resemblance to the *Daubert* criteria adopted in some of the United States, but see *Schall v. Martin* referred to by Monahan, and also above.

18. Some of the text that immediately follows also occurs in Campbell C. and Eastman N. (2012). The Neurobiology of violence: science and law. In Richmond S., Rees G. and Edwards S. J. L. (Eds.), *I know what you're thinking: brain imaging and mental privacy (pp. 139-153).* Oxford: Oxford University Press.

19. Infamously, one psychiatrist in a Southern state was renowned for giving evidence in capital sentencing hearings in terms of "he is a psychopath, will therefore kill again," with the direct inference that the man be subjected by the jury to the death penalty.

20. Notably, the Justice Secretary, the Rt. Hon. Kenneth Clark, has recently described "imprisonment for public protection" (IPPs), a form of indeterminate sentence not passed as or justified on the same stringent basis as a discretionary "life sentence," as "a stain on our justice system" and intends to repeal the relevant legislation.

21. Judicial interpretation of the "availability of appropriate treatment" test has been so loose and wide as to effectively remove it as a real legal protection of "detention for treatment of patients obviously untreatable."

22. If a prisoner is transferred to hospital under the Mental Health Act while serving a prison sentence, if that sentence was a "determinate" one then, at the prison/patient's date of release (from prison) he becomes detained as if he had been made the subject of a "hospital order" by the original sentencing court, with no power residing in the Ministry of Justice over the patient (who is no longer a prisoner), but the detention continues until either the patient's "responsible clinician" or a Mental Health Tribunal, determines his discharge.

REFERENCES

American Psychiatric Association (1994). *Diagnostic and statistical manual* (4th ed.). Washington DC: American Psychiatric Association.

Babcock, J. C., Green, C. E., et al. (2004). A second failure to replicate the Gottman et al. (1995) typology of men who abuse intimate partners…and possible reasons why. *Journal of Family Psychology, 18*(2), 396–400.

Barkataki, I., Kumari, V., et al. (2006). Volumetric structural brain abnormalities in men with schizophrenia or antisocial personality disorder. *Behavioural Brain Research, 169*(2), 239–247.

Birbaumer, N., Veit, R., et al. (2005). Deficient fear conditioning in psychopathy: a functional magnetic resonance imaging study. *Archives of General Psychiatry, 62*(7), 799–805.

Bostock, J., & Adshead, G. (2003). Criminal responsibility and genetics. In: *Encyclopedia of the human genome*. D. Cooper (Ed). London: Nature.

Brain, P. (1979). Effects of the hormones of the pituitary-gonadal axis on behavior. *Chemical influence on behavior*. K. Brown and S. Cooper. New York: Academic Press, pp. 255–329.

Canli, T., & Amin, Z. (2002). Neuroimaging of emotion and personality: scientific evidence and ethical considerations." *Brain and Cognition, 50*(3), 414–431.

Caspi, A., McClay, J., et al. (2002). Role of genotype in the cycle of violence in maltreated children. *Science, 297*(5582), 851–854.

Craig, I. W., & Halton, K. E. (2009). Genetics of human aggressive behavior. *Human Genetics, 126*(1), 101–113.

Dolan, M. C., Deakin, J. F., et al. (2002). Quantitative frontal and temporal structural MRI studies in personality-disordered offenders and control subjects. *Psychiatry Res, 116*(3), 133–149.

Eastman, N., & Campbell, C. (2006a). Crime, biologie et chatiment. *Grands Articles, 4,* 62–71.

Eastman, N., & Campbell, C. (2006b). Neuroscience and legal determination of criminal responsibility. *Nature Reviews Neuroscience, 7*(4), 311–318.

Frick, P. J. (2002). Juvenile psychopathy from a developmental perspective: implications for construct development and use in forensic assessments. *Law Hum Behav, 26*(2), 247–253.

Gerstle, J. E., Mathias, C. W., et al. (1998). Auditory P300 and self-reported impulsive aggression. *Progress in Neuropsychopharmacology and Biological Psychiatry, 22*(4), 575–583.

Hare, R. D. (2003). *Manual for the Revised Psychopathy Checklist* (2nd ed.). Toronto, ON, Canada: Multi-Health Systems.

Hirono, N., Mega, M. S., et al. (2000). Left frontotemporal hypoperfusion is associated with aggression in patients with dementia. *Archives of Neurology, 57*(6), 861–866.

Horn, N. R., Dolan, M., et al. (2003). Response inhibition and impulsivity: an fMRI study. *Neuropsychologia, 41*(14), 1959–1966.

Kiehl, K. A., Smith, A. M., et al. (2001). Limbic abnormalities in affective processing by criminal psychopaths as revealed by functional magnetic resonance imaging. *Biological Psychiatry, 50*(9), 677–684.

Krueger, R. F., Hicks, B. M., et al. (2002). Etiologic connections among substance dependence, antisocial behavior, and personality: modeling the externalizing spectrum. *Journal of Abnormal Psychology, 111*(3), 411–424.

Kumari, V., Aasen, I., et al. (2006). Neural dysfunction and violence in schizophrenia: an fMRI investigation. *Schizophrenia Research, 84*(1), 144–164.

Laakso, M. P., Vaurio, O., et al. (2001). Psychopathy and the posterior hippocampus. *Behavioural Brain Research, 118*(2), 187–193.

Law Commission for England and Wales, (2011) Expert Evidence in Criminal Proceedings (Report 325), London, The Stationary Office.

Martell, D. A. (2009). Neuroscience and the law: philosophical differences and practical constraints." *Behavioral Sciences and the Law, 27*(2), 123–136.

McGuffin, P., Moffitt, T. E., et al. (2002). Personality disorders. In *Psychiatric genetics and genomics*. P. McGuffin, M. J. Owen and I. Gottesman. New York: Oxford University Press, pp. 183–210.

Moffitt, T. E. (2005). The new look of behavioral genetics in developmental psychopathology: gene-environment interplay in antisocial behaviors. *Psychological Bulletin, 131*(4), 533–554.

Moriarty, J. C. (2008). Flickering admissibility: neuroimaging evidence in the U.S. courts. *Behavioral Sciences and the Law, 26*(1), 29–49.

Muller, J. L., Sommer, M., et al. (2003). Abnormalities in emotion processing within cortical and subcortical regions in criminal psychopaths: evidence from a functional magnetic resonance imaging study using pictures with emotional content. *Biological Psychiatry, 54*(2), 152–162.

Nelson, R. J., & Chiavegatto, S. (2001). Molecular basis of aggression. *Trends in Neurosciences, 24*(12), 713–719.

New, A. S., Hazlett, E. A., et al. (2002). Blunted prefrontal cortical 18fluorodeoxyglucose positron emission tomography response to meta-chlorophenylpiperazine in impulsive aggression. *Archives of General Psychiatry, 59*(7), 621–629.

Ortiz, J., & Raine, A. (2004). Heart rate level and antisocial behavior in children and adolescents: a meta-analysis. *Journal of the American Academy of Child and Adolescent Psychiatry, 43*(2), 154–162.

Peters, M. L., Godaert, G. L., et al. (2003). Moderation of physiological stress responses by personality traits and daily hassles: less flexibility of immune system responses. *Biological Psychology, 65*(1), 21–48.

Pogash, C. (2003). Myth of the "Twinkie defense." *San Francisco Chronicle*. Available at: http://www.sfgate.com/cgi-bin/article.cgi?f=/c/a/2003/11/23/INGRE343501.DTL.

Raine, A. (1996). Autnomic nervous system factors underlying disinhibited, antisocial, and violent behavior. Biosocial perspectives and treatment implications." *Annals of the New York Academy of Sciences, 794*, 46–59.

Raine, A., Lencz, T., et al. (2000). Reduced prefrontal gray matter volume and reduced autonomic activity in antisocial personality disorder. *Archives of General Psychiatry, 57*(2), 119–127.

Raine, A., Lencz, T., et al. (2003). Corpus callosum abnormalities in psychopathic antisocial individuals. *Archives of General Psychiatry, 60*(11), 1134–1142.

Raine, A., Venables, P. H., et al. (1990). Relationships between central and autonomic measures of arousal at age 15 years and criminality at age 24 years. *Archives of General Psychiatry, 47*(11), 1003–1007.

Raine, A., & Yang, Y. (2006). Neural foundations to moral reasoning and antisocial behavior. *Social Cognitive and Affective Neuroscience, 1*(3), 203–213.

Rhee, S. H., & Waldman, I. D. (2002). Genetic and environmental influences on antisocial behavior: a meta-analysis of twin and adoption studies. *Psychology Bulletin, 128*(3), 490–529.

Rigoni, D., Pellegrini, S., et al. (2010). How neuroscience and behavioral genetics improve psychiatric assessment: report on a violent murder case. *Frontiers in Behavioral Neuroscience, 4*, 160.

Rose, N. (2001). At risk of madness. *Embracing risk* (pp. 209–237). T. Baker and J. Simon. Chicago: University of Chicago Press.

Roskies, A. L. (2008). Neuroimaging and inferential distance. *Neuroethics, 1*(1), 19–30.

Royal Society (2011). *Brain waves module 4: Neuroscience and the law.* London: The Royal Society.

Rubinow, D. R., & Schmidt, P. J. (1996). Androgens, brain, and behavior. *American Journal of Psychiatry, 153*(8), 974–984.

Schneider, F., Habel, U., et al. (2000). Functional imaging of conditioned aversive emotional responses in antisocial personality disorder. *Neuropsychobiology, 42*(4), 192–201.

Siever, L. J., Buchsbaum, M. S. et al. (1999). d,l-fenfluramine response in impulsive personality disorder assessed with [18F]fluorodeoxyglucose positron emission tomography. *Neuropsychopharmacology, 20*(5), 413–423.

Silva, J. A. (2009). Forensic psychiatry, neuroscience, and the law. *Journal of the American Academy of Psychiatry and the Law, 37*(4), 489–502.

Sirotin, Y., & Das, A. (2009). Anticipatory haemodynamic signals in sensory cortex not predicted by local neuronal activity. *Nature, 457,* 475–480.

Stark, C. E., & Squire, L. R. (2001). When zero is not zero: the problem of ambiguous baseline conditions in fMRI. *Proceedings of the National Academy of Sciences of the United States of America, 98*(22), 12760–12766.

Taylor, A., & Kim-Cohen, J. (2007). Meta-analysis of gene-environment interactions in developmental psychopathology. *Development and Psychopathology, 19,* 1029–1037.

van Goozen, S., & Fairchild, G. (2009). The neuroendocrinology of antisocial behavior. *The neurobiological basis of aggression: science and rehabilitation.* S. Hodgins, V. E and P. A. Oxford: Oxford University Press, pp. 201–221.

Virkkunen, M., Rawlings, R., et al. (1994). CSF biochemistries, glucose metabolism, and diurnal activity rhythms in alcoholic, violent offenders, fire setters, and healthy volunteers. *Archives of General Psychiatry, 51*(1), 20–27.

Vollm, B., Richardson, P., et al. (2004). Neurobiological substrates of antisocial and borderline personality disorder: preliminary results of a functional fMRI study. *Criminal Behaviour and Mental Health, 14*(1), 39–54.

World Health Organization (2002). *World report on violence and health.* Geneva: World Health Organization.

Yang, Y., & Raine, A. (2009). Prefrontal structural and functional brain imaging findings in antisocial, violent, and psychopathic individuals: a meta-analysis. *Psychiatry Research, 174*(2), 81–88.

Yang, Y., Raine, A., et al. (2005a). Prefrontal white matter in pathological liars. *British Journal of Psychiatry, 187,* 320–325.

Yang, Y., Raine, A., et al. (2005b). Volume reduction in prefrontal gray matter in unsuccessful criminal psychopaths. *Biological Psychiatry, 57*(10), 1103–1108.

Yang, Y., Raine, A., et al. (2009). Localization of deformations within the amygdala in individuals with psychopathy." *Archives of General Psychiatry, 66*(9), 986–994.

7

Rethinking the Implications of Discovering Biomarkers for Biologically Based Criminality

PAUL ROOT WOLPE

INTRODUCTION

For over a century and a half, scientists have turned their latest and most sophisticated technologies toward finding a biological basis for criminal behavior. The results have been, at best, mixed. Over the first century of the endeavor, much misery befell the unfortunate individuals whose bodies happened to conform in some way to the latest theoretical model of inherited criminality. The cautionary tale has been written and rewritten, and the question that confronts our modern, more sophisticated attempts to achieve the same ends is this: Given the repeated failures and suffering that have resulted from this pursuit, can we ensure that this time the findings of our science result in an enlightened, considered, and appropriate set of criminal justice policies?

The argument that certain physiological traits increase the likelihood of anti-social behavior in some people is strong, especially among certain narrow categories of violent offenders. The evidence for this claim is reviewed in other chapters of this volume and so need not be reviewed here. However, the *extent* of the biological predisposition toward criminal behavior—both in terms of incidence and prevalence, to use epidemiological terminology—is much more controversial. People with certain biomarkers may be more likely to engage in certain behaviors that are currently illegal, but it is also true that the majority of offenders do not have such biomarkers. It may turn out that the predictive value of biological markers for criminal activity is so weak as to be of little use in policy, or is so complexly mediated by environmental factors as to be difficult if not impossible to untangle. Criminal biomarkers may be applicable to only a small range of criminal activity, perhaps among the most violent offenders, or to only a small number of people no matter what the crime, and that most criminal activity will not be predictable by those markers.

Given the history of the pursuit of a physiological basis for crime and its relation to racism, eugenics, and economic oppression, the search for such biomarkers has often been criticized as a dangerous pursuit in and of itself. However, the scientific enterprise to determine biological predictors of various kinds of antisocial behaviors may have many positive outcomes. For example, Adrian Raine et al. (2010), drawing from the 40-year longitudinal Mauritius Child Health Project, found that malnutrition seems to predispose people to later criminal behavior because of its impact on brain development. Such research adds another compelling argument for ending hunger. Even seemingly pernicious claims, such as claims of genetic predispositions to violence or antisocial behavior, can prove valuable if used to understand the relation of physiology or brain development to behavior.

Science is an eminently social activity, embedded in the fabric and sharing the assumptions of its host society. The questions science asks, its definitions and assumptions, and the framing of the problems science explores are all products of the culture in which science is embedded. Before scientists can explore the question of a biological basis to crime, they must, of course, define what crime is. As an even cursory glance at the history and sociology of criminal behavior shows, the definition of criminal activity varies greatly from time to time and society to society. What is obviously criminal to one society is not to another. The same is true of other kinds of social behaviors and categories. For example, as I have argued elsewhere (Wolpe, 2004), sexuality researchers often contrast "homosexuals" and "heterosexuals" in searching for a biological basis of sexuality. The concept of homosexuality itself, however, is an invention of the late 19th century, when the gender of one's sexual partner became a defining characteristic of individual identity, rather than a behavior alone. Even today, many societies do not conceptualize sexual behavior in terms of homosexuality and heterosexuality, but rather "masculinity" and "femininity." "Masculine" activity, for example, is defined as engaging in an act of penetration, no matter the gender of the person being penetrated. "Homosexual" is thus a cultural, not biological, category, and much of the biological research being done on human sexuality may be flawed because the fundamental definitional predicates on which it is based are misguided.

Criminal activity is similarly culturally defined. Engaging in homosexual behavior was a serious crime in many societies but part of the formal mentorship system in ancient Athens, where philosophers such as Plato and Plutarch considered it fundamental to a civilized society. Societies can also have similar definitions of criminality but accommodate them differently. For example, imagine one could show a genetic or physiological propensity to "violence" in a group of men. One society might provide appropriate outlets for violent tendencies by having a culture of warfare and soldiering, or perhaps by fighting environmental threats (like wild animals), and see those men as vital or even heroic. A more peaceful or agrarian society that does not have legitimate outlets for the expression of that level of aggression may view the same types of behavior as criminal, and see those men as deviant and biologically flawed. Modern Western societies have both legitimate and illegitimate outlets for violent behaviors, so that the difference between the criminal and the noncriminal may not be any innate propensity for violence but instead culturally situated access to legitimate outlets for that tendency.

Similarly, it is important to note early on that the research examining the biological basis of crime does not actually look at the genetics of criminal behavior itself. There is no gene that codes for criminality, as criminality itself is a legal and social category, not a behavioral one. In a society where everything is legal there is no biological criminal. Rather, what is claimed to be genetic is other kinds of traits associated with criminality—aggression, antisocial affect, low impulse control, psychiatric syndromes such as conduct disorders and borderline personality disorder, and so on.[1] It is postulated that possessing such traits makes one more likely to engage in behaviors that most societies consider crimes, but it is not criminality itself that is in the genes.

For the purposes of this discussion, the key question is not about the truth of the claim that there are genetic or neuropsychological biomarkers that increase the likelihood of future arrest for criminal behavior (and most of the research is on the incarcerated or others formally labeled "criminal"). While the validity of the scientific claim is quite important, ultimately the policy question is not whether the science is accurate, but whether it is *believed* to be accurate. The impact of policies on people is independent of the truth of the claim that informs those policies. For example, as this chapter is being written, there is a hearing going on in front of a panel of legislators in the state of North Carolina (http://articles.cnn.com/2011-06-22/us/raleigh.eugenics. hearing_1_sterilization-program-task-force-eugenics-law?_s=PM:US), where victims of the state's involuntary sterilization law are expressing their grief and anger. The law, which resulted in the sterilization over 7,600 citizens, few of whom were convicted of any crime and the majority of whom were coerced or given no consent at all, was predicated on the belief that the victims were genetically more likely to give birth to criminals or the mentally ill. While the scientific basis of that claim is clearly spurious—being poor and illiterate was considered a sufficient condition to invoke the law—would the injustice of that law be any less evident if we could prove that the group sterilized *was* somehow more likely to have criminal or mentally ill offspring?

For these and other reasons, the scientific inquiry into the biological basis of criminal behavior is problematic. However, our intent in this chapter is not to provide a critique of the science of biological criminology, but of the ethical implications of that pursuit for public policy. What are the potential pitfalls of a biologically based approach to criminal justice? What are the ethical challenges to criminal, penal, and jurisprudential policy based on the notion that we can predict which individuals, families, or ethnic or racial groups might have a predisposition to criminal behavior?

Before continuing, one important comment: Modern scholars who study and comment on the nature of biomarkers for criminal behavior are not naïve. They understand many of the ethical challenges and caveats discussed below, and this chapter is in no sense meant to suggest that those who study these problems are uninterested or uninformed about the potential pitfalls of too strong a policy emphasis on biomarkers. In fact, it is often those most immersed in the research who are the first to caution against the misuse of these data. The purpose of the chapter is to caution against the mistranslation of the science of biological criminality into policy, a process that often happens outside of, or in spite of, the influence of scientists.

POLICY AND ETHICS

History has shown us the repeated policy failures of a biologically based approach to criminal justice. Whether the approach was the 19th-century Lombrosian belief in atavists and stigmata, the phrenologists' belief in detecting criminal tendencies through brain region analysis, the early 20th-century American theory of genetically based central nervous system defects, the midcentury European extension to physiologically inferior ethnic, religious, medical, and socioeconomic groups, or psychosurgical intervention such as lobotomies for violence and "moral degeneracy," the historical legacy is cautionary and deeply disturbing. It would not be an exaggeration to suggest that the historical belief in a physiological basis of crime has almost always resulted in deeply misguided public policy. Whether a more sophisticated approach to the scientific question can counteract the tendency to translate the science into bad, even tragic public policy is an open question.

Nevertheless, physiological explanations for crime are attractive to policymakers for a number of reasons. First, they identify potential offenders with (the illusion of?) accuracy, allowing preventive measures to be targeted to specified subgroups. While the social and economic factors that contribute to crime are complex, and the solutions require strong political will and often significant investments of money, reducing that complexity to a biological flaw allows for more directed social policy. Similarly, reforming social institutions to try to mitigate environmental causes of crime is difficult and expensive, but proposed "medical" solutions to crime can be implemented by existing medical institutions without major social engineering. The claim that criminals are biologically flawed also plays generally well to the public and is an easy rhetorical resource for politicians to differentiate the "good citizen" from the criminal element. Finally, if criminals are biologically identifiable, policymakers may believe, a clear path exists for separating those with predispositions for crime from those without, even at an early age, allowing for remedial programs and tracking. For these and other reasons, governments are very attracted to the idea that criminal behavior is physiologically caused. However, the dangers of this attraction are many.

The most obvious danger occurred repeatedly in the examples above: despite the caveats and conditions scientists put on their conclusions, governments and their agents are apt to reduce that science to simple concepts and to uncritically accept theories that make policy easier or reinforce existing prejudices. It is difficult to detect the flaws that later generations see so clearly. That is why policy must always be conservative and with a bias toward doing no harm; there is no clear standard to determine when a scientific claim about the biological basis of criminality passes a threshold that warrants defining and targeting one group of people over others. While one can argue that claims about social criminogenic factors also suffer from a lack of scientific proof, the solutions—alleviating poverty, supporting communities, finding activities for idle juveniles, dismantling gangs, and so on—*are defensible on their own*. The solutions proposed for trying to identify and target biological criminals are only defensible if the science itself is unassailable.

Even if the science was reliable, the crimes for which there may be a biological cause are only a fraction of the crimes committed in any society. No theorist has yet suggested a biological cause for cheating on your taxes, or insider trading, or casual use of drugs (though one study suggests white collar criminals have *higher* cortical functioning than controls, Raine et al., 2011). In fact, very little research has been done on white collar crime and biomarkers, reflecting society's disproportionate concern with lower-class crime, even though it is established that white collar crime is far more costly in money and in lives lost (Friedrichs, 2004). The belief in biomarkers for crime could easily and disproportionately refocus efforts on the people and crimes for which we believe we have such markers, and skew our system of criminal justice.

It is difficult to know how to shape policy for an individual or group identified as potential offenders through biomarkers. Do we track them in school? Create prophylactic or remedial programs for them? Monitor them more closely for potential offense? Add their gene profiles to marital or preconception genetic counseling? Subject them to coercive medical interventions? And should offenders with such biomarkers receive different penal or rehabilitative strategies? Should jurisprudence consider them more—or less—culpable for their crimes?

In the final analysis, many kinds of public policies that use biomarkers for criminal behaviors would be problematic, given that so many of them threaten individual liberty, discriminate against individuals still innocent of wrongdoing, or misidentify those at risk. It is even debatable whether using such biomarkers on convicted criminals, to track them or create different remedial programs for them, is a proper use of biomarkers. Such programs must first be proven to be differentially effective on those with such biomarkers. At the very least, it is crucial that policies be restricted to people already guilty of crimes, and only for purposes that do not inappropriately discriminate against them.

SCIENTIFICALLY SUPPORTED STEREOTYPING

The risk of genetic stereotyping leading to ethnic, racial, and other subgroup discrimination is the one that is most recognized and discussed in the literature of the history of biological criminology. On the basis of that fear, the National Institutes of Health abruptly withdrew funds for a conference on genetics and crime in 1992 after complaints that its intent was fundamentally eugenic. The president of the Association of Black Psychologists at the time declared that such research was in itself "a blatant form of stereotyping and racism" (*New York Times*, June 19, 2011). The conference was eventually rescheduled and held at the University of Maryland, amid protesters who swarmed the conference room (Roush, 1995).

Empirical studies have found that a sizable percentage of Americans endorse lay genetic theories to explain perceived race differences (Jayaratne et al., 2006). In a racialized society, genetic explanations for behavior exert a powerful influence, so genetic explanations of crime will be interpreted as innate characteristics of the groups from which those individuals might disproportionately come.

The belief in the importance of genetics for individual differences in behavior has a substantial effect on a person's attitudes toward genetics-related policies in general, independent of his or her political orientation or other measures (Shostak et al., 2009). Therefore, restricting genetic or neuropsychological evaluations to individuals will not prevent generalization to groups. And of course, scientifically speaking, such generalization is inevitable. If one believes in a genetic basis for crime, then one must also believe in the heritability of criminal tendencies, and therefore the increased likelihood of crime in specific gene pools. Science must therefore use population genetics to understand, and prevent, biologically based criminal activity. Once biomarkers are tied to crime it becomes virtually impossible to avoid the problem of stereotyping.

BIOLOGICAL REDUCTIONISM

In an editorial in a 2008 issue of the journal *Medical Hypothesis* entitled "Genetic evidence that Darwin was right about criminality: Nature, not nurture," Ricardo Baschetti writes that violent criminal behavior is almost entirely genetically determined, that social factors are trivial, and that the medicalization of it, especially under rubrics like "psychopathy," is misguided:

> The term "psychopathy"...is clearly inappropriate because its suffix "-pathy", which derives from the ancient Greek word pathos (suffering) and is properly used to define afflictively impairing diseases...does not reasonably apply to healthy and unimpaired individuals who are often "successful" criminals.... these socially destructive individuals...should more aptly be defined "inhuman mutants", a definition that captures both their genetically determined monstrous deviance and their socially revolting inhumanity. The adjective "inhuman" is not inappropriate, because most humans, unlike those selfish antisocial mutants, still conserve genes for unselfishness, cooperation, and even altruistic self-sacrifice for the common good, all of which enabled the typically small groups of our ancestors to survive in their harshly savage habitats. (Baschetti, 2008, 1096)

Aside from the astonishing tone of the paragraph, which reads almost identically to eugenic tracts of the early 20th century,[2] the claim reduces complex human behavior to that of "selfish antisocial mutants" and underscores a biological reductionism that can characterize genetic approaches to crime. The article itself demonstrates that such perspectives are neither obsolete nor restricted to those outside the scientific community. Most modern biological criminologists are far more nuanced; in a recent review, three well-known advocates of the study of biological criminology take great pains to emphasize the mediating influence of environmental factors, with the now-common claim that biological factors explain 50 percent of the variance in violent criminal behavior, leaving the other 50 percent to environmental causes (Moffit, Ross, & Raine, 2011).

Reductionist explanations of criminal behavior too easily bypass environmental mediators. While the quote from Baschetti above is extreme, and it is frankly astonishing that a respected medical journal would publish it in that form, it reflects a belief that ignores the overwhelming evidence of the contribution of context in the definitions and conduct of violent crime. Baschetti *is* correct in his distrust of psychopathology as an explanatory framework for these kinds of crimes, as there is a lack of consensus among psychiatrists and psychologists about what psychopathology is, precisely, and which individuals fit that diagnosis (Bergner, 1997; Stanghellini, 2009). A psychiatric dysfunction undoubtedly underlies at least some percentage of violent crime. However, even in those cases, the idea that the behavior is completely physiological and is not modified or exacerbated by environmental factors ignores much of what we know about psychiatric illness in general and the behaviors considered psychopathological in general (Moffitt, Caspi, & Rutter, 2006; Moffit, Ross, & Raine, 2011).

It may well be determined that there is a strong biological contribution to some percentage of the most extreme offenders, and a weaker one to some other range of offenders. However, the political and, as we see above, scientific temptation to reduce crime in general, or even most violent crime, primarily or solely to biology is to make a crucial jurisdictional mistake that will likely result in misplaced emphasis in crime policy and further suffering among the guilty and innocent alike.

STIGMA

Recently, there has been renewed interest in the effects of labeling on offenders and people designated as potential offenders (e.g., Bernburg et al., 2006; Chiricos et al., 2007; Grattet, 2011). Labeling theory has long demonstrated that both formal (regulatory) and informal (social) mechanisms restrict options among offenders to rehabilitate, find employment, and integrate into social spaces other than those occupied by other offenders. Formal mechanisms include withdrawing social privileges, which then further separates the offender, structurally or culturally, from others in society. Felons, for example, lose the right to vote, serve on juries, own firearms, or hold public office in the United States. Informal mechanisms include social shunning, difficulty finding employment, housing discrimination, and so on (Leavitt, 2002; Olphen et al, 2009).

In one study, researchers examined a cohort in Florida of over 95,000 people who had encounters with the criminal justice system (Chiricos et al., 2007). Florida allows judges the option of "withholding adjudication" of guilt for convicted felons who are being sentenced to probation. This natural experiment allowed the researchers to compare those found similar in factual guilt but who had the label of felon withheld versus those who did not. While the decision to use that option is not purely random, it is used in almost half of factually identical felony cases, and the researchers compensated for this possible "selection bias" statistically. The result was that those who were labeled felons had a recidivism rate more than twice that of those who were not burdened with that label.

The Florida study is simply one example of decades of research that have conclusively demonstrated the negative effects of being labeled as an offender or potential offender (Grattet, 2011). Being designated as having a biological propensity to offend will certainly involve its own social stigma and the associated negative effects. There is a profound ethical challenge in knowingly burdening an individual with the label of "potential offender" or even "more likely to reoffend" because of some assumed innate characteristic. In addition, it is clear that the best that science can do is to find general tendencies. Rarely will science be able to use biomarkers to predict that any specific individual will offend or reoffend without some intervention.

Being labeled a biological criminal can stigmatize differently from other forms of criminal labeling. Such labeling can impede the possibility of rehabilitation or reform. Also, most young males, who commit the majority of crimes, eventually outgrow or lessen their criminal behavior. However, if people believe that criminality is innate, that one is born with those tendencies and they are part of the fabric of one's makeup, they may assume that they cannot be changed by rehabilitation, or that people cannot outgrow them. Stigma due to a belief in the innateness of a behavior is well illustrated by current attitudes toward sexual offenders in the United States. Americans retain a deep suspicion of past sexual offenders no matter how much they seem to have rehabilitated themselves (Levenson et al., 2007), based on their belief that the impulse is innate and unchangeable and the best that the offender can do is to try and control it.

JUVENILE TRACKING

One advantage to being able to identify genetic or neuropsychological predictors of criminality is early intervention. A primary objective of such research is identifying the potential of juvenile offenders to reoffend (see, e.g., Arsenault et al., 2003; Moffit, Ross, & Raine, 2011). However, using genetic, biopsychological, or other physiological measures to identify juveniles with a greater likelihood to reoffend poses a number of ethical and social challenges.

The risks of labeling juveniles as biologically predisposed to reoffend seem clear. Labeling is particularly powerful in children, influencing their scholastic careers in addition to future employment (Sampson & Laub, 1997). The impact of biological labeling on children can be greater than that of behavioral labeling. We know, for example, that a finding of "low IQ" influences how children are treated beyond the impact of the intelligence level itself (Sternberg, Grigorenko, & Bundy, 2001). While most teachers and others who work with children understand that children go through developmental phases, so that the misbehaving child today may mature into a well-behaved adolescent later, what kind of developmental benefit-of-the-doubt would a teacher give a student who is believed to be biologically predisposed to bad behavior?

The impulse, should we believe we have biological predictors for delinquent behavior, would be to track or intervene early in selected juveniles. Yet research shows that there are significant risks in separating juveniles out of the mainstream, even to administer justice. For example, juveniles who offend similarly are much more likely to end up in the adult penal system later in their lives if they get involved in the juvenile justice system in the first place—in other words, those that get caught, or those caught who are not released with a warning but arrested or turned in, are far more likely to reoffend than those who get away or are let go (e.g., Bernburg & Krohn, 2003; Gatti, Tremblay, & Vitaro, 2009; Sampson & Laub, 1997). So it is worrisome that "potential" juvenile offenders might be placed in a preventive program, or that "biological" offenders might be given more intense or different involvement in the juvenile justice system. The entire enterprise could become a self-fulfilling prophecy.

If we did find reliable biomarkers for greater likelihood for delinquency in juveniles, it is difficult to know how to make best use of them. First, any biomarker of this type indicates a tendency, not a certainty, so any program would suffer from a number of false positives (i.e., children identified as potential reoffenders who might never reoffend).

Even more problematic is the temptation to try and use such biomarkers to prescreen juveniles before they engage in a first offense. While a widespread screening program may seem unlikely, it is important to remember that juveniles engage in a spectrum of behaviors that are not serious enough to be considered offenses—acting out in class, minor schoolyard skirmishes and fights, minor vandalism, and a variety of teen foolishnesses. If biomarkers are seen as reliable indicators of which teens might go on to more serious offenses, it is clear that there can be a temptation to use such biomarkers to separate the mischief-makers from the serious offenders.

For reasons already described, the risks of such identification are particularly problematic in juvenile populations. It is also difficult to imagine what kinds of post-offense treatment or punishment might be more appropriate for "biological" offenders: Do we treat them more leniently, knowing that it is perhaps not as free a behavioral choice, or more harshly, knowing that behavioral rehabilitation is less likely to have an impact?

GENETIC COMPLEXITIES

The simple view of genetics that characterized the 1990s and early 2000s has given way to a much more complex picture, with a greater understanding of epigenetics, transcription factors, multi-gene traits and multi-trait genes, and so on. Single genes can encode for multiple proteins, and sometimes what seems to be an aberrant or maladaptive gene may have unrecognized adaptive traits as well. It is well known that certain genetic diseases were adaptive in their original environments. For example, in the case of the sickle cell disease gene, heterozygosity protects against malaria (Aidoo et al., 2002), which is why the gene persisted as a recessive trait. The same may be true for genes for traits now associated with criminal activity.

The behaviors genes encode for may themselves have adaptive elements. As mentioned earlier, research on biological criminality detects genes associated with violence, or poor impulse control, or antisocial behavior—not "criminality" *per se*, which is a social category. Some of these traits, such as aggression, are quite adaptive in other social contexts. Evolutionary perspectives on attention-deficit/hyperactivity disorder (ADHD), for example, claim that such traits were an adaptive response in a hunter-gatherer culture (Baydala et al., 2006; Jensen et al., 1997). A society that does not provide outlets for such traits, or that insists that children sit still for hours at a time in school, can precipitate the expression of these behavioral tendencies in ways seen as disruptive. Similarly, certain forms of aggression may be adaptive in a setting threatened by animal predators or war, and become maladaptive in societies without accepted social structures or spaces to express those traits. That would also explain why groups with fewer life and occupational options more often express aggressive traits through criminal behavior.

Of course, that is not necessarily an argument against selecting against, or mitigating the effects of, genetic traits that are no longer adaptive. We medicate our children with ADHD whether or not that trait was adaptive when we were hunter-gatherers. Still, it changes our perspective on the claim for "biological criminality." Now the claim must be tempered to something more akin to "biological propensity toward forms of aggression or other behaviors that have no legitimate outlet given the environmental niche of the individual and thus is likely to be expressed through activity defined as criminal." Not quite as pithy as biological criminality, but probably much more accurate.

CONCLUSION

Scholarly interest in biological criminality is not itself racist or unethical, as some critics have claimed. The evidence that there is a biological basis to certain forms of behaviors that increase the likelihood of criminal behavior in people with those biomarkers is compelling. The racist history of the enterprise still haunts modern scholars, unfortunately, so that major criminology journals still tend to shy away from this kind of biological research (*New York Times*, 2011). The real challenge is in the ways the science is understood, translated, and implemented into policy by society.

Credit should be given to the many scientists who pursue this research carefully, who insist on the importance of the environment in mediating behavior, and who caution against misapplication of the research in criminal justice policy. Still, the temptations of using the results of their inquiry as an excuse to create simpler, cheaper solutions to the complex problem of crime is always present. Given the historical track record, it is important that both the critics and advocates of the research enterprise remain vigilant and advocate for an informed, nuanced, and humane application of this research to public policy.

NOTES

1. A perusal of the references at the end of the most thorough recent review, by Moffit, Ross, and Raine (2011), demonstrates this fact: more of the articles referenced are about the genetics of psychiatric disorders than the genetics of crime.
2. In fact, Baschetti accepts the rubric of eugenics, arguing that modern geneticists largely accept eugenics, even as conceptualized in the early 20th century (Baschetti, 1999).

REFERENCES

Aidoo, M., Terlouw, D. J., Kolczak, M. S., McElroy. P. D., ter Kuile, F. O., Kariuki, S., Nahlen, B. L., Lal, A. A., & Udhayakumar, V. (2002). Protective effects of the sickle cell gene against malaria morbidity and mortality. *The Lancet, 359*(9314), 1311–1312

Arsenault, L., Moffit, T. E., Caspi, A., Taylor, A., Rijsdiijk, F. V., Jaffee, S. R., Ablow, J. C., & Measelle, J. R. (2003). Strong genetic effects on cross-situational antisocial behavior among 5-year-old children according to mothers, teachers, examiner-observers, and twins' self-reports. *Journal of Child Psychology and Psychiatry, 44*, 832–848.

Baschetti, R. (1999). People who condemn eugenics may be in minority now. *BMJ, 319*, 1196.

Baschetti, R. (2008). Genetic evidence that Darwin was right about criminality: Nature, nto nurture. *Medical Hypothesis, 70*(6), 1092–1102.

Baydala, L., Sherman, J., Rasmussen, R., Wikman, E., & Janzen, H. (2006). ADHD characteristics in Canadian Aboriginal children. *Journal of Attention Disorders, 9*(4), 642–647.

Bergner, R. M. (1997) What is psychopathology? And so what? *Psychology: Science and Practice, 4*(3), 235–248.

Bernburg, J. G., & Krohn, M. D. (2003). Labeling, life chances, and adult crime: The direct and indirect effects of official intervention in adolescence on crime in early adulthood. *Criminology, 41*, 1287–1318.

Bernburg, J. G., Krohn, M. D., & Rivera, C. J. (2006). Official labeling, criminal embeddedness, and subsequent delinquency: A longitudinal test of labeling theory. *Journal of Research in Crime and Delinquency, 43*, 67–88.

Chiricos, T., Barrick, K., Bales, W., & Bontrager, S. (2007). The labeling of convicted felons and its consequences for recidivism. *Criminology, 45*(3), 547–581.

Friedrichs, D. O. (2004). Trusted Criminals: White Collar Crime in Contemporary Society. Belmont, CA: Wadsworth.

Gatti, U., Tremblay, R. E., & Viraro, F. (2009). Iatrogenic effect of juvenile justice. *Journal of Child Psychology and Psychiatry, 50*(8), 991–998.

Grattet, R. (2011). Societal reactions to deviance. *Annual Review of Sociology, 37,* 9.1–9.20.

Jayaratne, T. E., Ybarra, O., Sheldon, J. P., Brown, T. N., Feldbaum, M., Pfeffer, C. A., & Petty, E. M. (2006). White Americans' genetic lay theories of race differences and sexual orientation: Their relationship with prejudice toward blacks, and gay men and lesbians. *Group Processes Intergroup Relations, 9*(1), 77–94.

Jensen, P. S., Mrazek, D., Knapp, P. K., Steinberg, L., Pfeffer, C., Schowalter, J., & Shapiro, T. (1997). Evolution and revolution in child psychiatry: ADHD as a disorder of adaptation. *Child and Adolescent Psychiatry, 36*(12), 1672–1681.

Leavitt, J. (2002). Walking a tightrope: Balancing competing public interests in the employment of criminal offenders. *Connecticut Law Review, 34,* 1281.

Levenson, J., Brannon, Y., Fortney, T., & Baker, J. (2007). Public perceptions about sex offenders and community protection policies. *Analyses of Social Issues and Public Policy, 7*(1), 137–161.

Moffitt, T. E., Caspi, A., & Rutter, M. (2006). Measured gene–environment interactions in psychopathology: Concepts, research strategies, and implications for research, intervention, and public understanding of genetics. *Perspectives on Psychological Science, 1,* 5–27.

Moffitt, T. E., Ross, S., & Raine, A. (2011). Crime and biology. In J. Q. Wilson & J. Petersilla (Eds.), *Crime and Public Policy* (pp. 5–52). New York: Oxford University Press.

New York Times (2011). Genetic basis for crime: A new look. June 19, 2011, C1.

Raine, A., Liu, J., Venables, P. H., Mednick, S. A., & Dalais, C. (2010). Cohort profile: The Mauritius Child Health Project. *International Journal of Epidemiology,39*(6), 1441–1451.

Raine, A., Laufer, W. S., Yang, Y., Narr, K. L., Thompson, P., & Toga, A. W. (2011). Increased executive functioning, attention, and cortical thickness in white-collar criminals. *Human Brain Mapping,33*(12), 2932–2940.

Roush, W. (1995) Conflict marks crime conference. *Science, 269,* 1808–1809.

Sampson, R. J., & Laub, J. H. (1997). A life course theory of cumulative disadvantage and the stability of delinquency. In T. P. Thornberry (Ed.), *Development Theories of Crimes and Delinquency* (pp. 133–161). New Brunswick, NJ: Transaction.

Shostak, S., Freese, J., Link, B. G., & Phelan, J. C. (2009) The politics of the gene: Social status and beliefs about genetics for individual outcomes. *Social Psychology Quarterly, 72*(1), 77–93.

Sternberg, R. J., Grigorenko, E., & Bundy, D. A. (2001). The predictive value of IQ. *Merrill-Palmer Quarterly, 47*(1), 1–41.

Stanghellini, G., (2009). The meanings of psychopathology. *Current Opinion in Psychiatry, 22*(6), 559–564.

Van Olphen, J., Eliason, M. J., Freudenberg, N., & Barnes, M. (2009). Nowhere to go: How stigma limits the options of female drug users after release from jail. *Substance Abuse Treatment, Prevention, and Policy, 4,* 10.

Wolpe, P. R. (2004) Ethics and social policy in research on the neuroscience of human sexuality. *Nature Neuroscience, 7*(10), 1031–1033.

8

MAOA and the Bioprediction of Antisocial Behavior: Science Fact and Science Fiction

JOSHUA W. BUCKHOLTZ AND ANDREAS MEYER-LINDENBERG

In the next year, nearly 17,000 individuals will be murdered in the United States alone (Corso et al., 2007). An additional 2.2 million Americans will require medical treatment for a violence-related injury that is not self-inflicted (Corso et al., 2007). While the emotional and psychological consequences of violence for victims and their families are clearly monumental, society as a whole bears an astounding economic burden as well. Each violent fatality costs approximately $1.3 million in combined medical costs and lost productivity, and each nonfatal violent assault leads to over $80,000 in total costs (Corso et al., 2007; UK Home Office, 2007). In aggregate, it is estimated that the total cost of violence is equal to approximately 3.3 percent of the United States' annual gross domestic product (GDP), and economic assessments for other countries reveal similarly astounding statistics (Corso et al., 2007; Waters et al., 2004).

Given these numbers, directing public and private sector spending toward preventing antisocial behavior would seem likely to provide a significant return on investment. However, with limited resources at their disposal, governments and philanthropic foundations alike need guidance on 'how' and 'where' to invest. By 'how,' we mean deciding how to select the most effective and empirically supported interventions for reducing aggression and antisocial conduct (Caldwell, 2011; Fossum et al., 2008; Gibbon et al., 2010; Khalifa et al., 2010). The 'where' component refers to identifying those who would most likely benefit from such interventions (i.e., individuals who are most at risk for engaging in antisocial acts) in order to target prevention- and treatment-related spending toward this group (Brooks-Crozier, 2011). Given the need to evaluate the future dangerousness of convicted offenders both at sentencing and at parole, the ability to identify individuals predisposed toward violence and antisocial behavior clearly has great relevance for forensic science and law. This chapter is chiefly addressed toward the use of genetics to answer the 'where' question in these contexts.

THE NEUROPREDICTION OF VIOLENCE AND ANTISOCIAL BEHAVIOR

Traditionally, the determination of future dangerousness involved clinical evaluations that were unstructured, subjective, and of dubious reliability or predictive validity (Monahan, 1981). Actuarial methods of violence risk addressed many of these issues, but this approach faces limited acceptance by mental health professionals and the courts (Corso et al., 2007; Monahan, 2006; Skeem & Monahan, 2011; Waters et al., 2004). More recently, advances in brain imaging and genomic science have begun to shed light on the genetic and neurobiological architecture of violence and antisocial behavior (Buckholtz & Meyer-Lindenberg, 2008), spurring intense discussion and debate about their potential use as predictive tools (Nadelhoffer et al., 2010; Nadelhoffer and Sinnott-Armstrong, 2012). Some have embraced this potential with particular avidity, heralding the coming age of neuroprediction with an enthusiasm that we argue is premature and incautious. We believe that such enthusiasm is particularly unwarranted as it pertains to putative genetic biomarkers for violence and antisocial behavior, such as monoamine oxidase A (MAOA), the erroneously nicknamed "warrior gene."

The purpose of this chapter is to ascertain precisely what manner of predictive inference, if any, is permissible based on the current state of the science. We will review what is currently known about the role that MAOA plays in risk for violence and antisocial behavior and evaluate the suitability of genetic variability in MAOA as a predictive biomarker. We will discuss findings from brain imaging studies of MAOA that shed light on the neurobiology of human aggression. Finally, we will discuss the genetic architecture of individual differences in human behavior and complex traits generally and the broad implications of this for the 'genoprediction' enterprise. We argue that fundamental challenges severely constrain our ability to use genetic data for prediction now and in the foreseeable future; owing to these limits, efforts toward genoprediction should move forward only with due caution and humility.

VIOLENT DISPOSITION IS PARTLY INHERITED

All prediction efforts assume that the variable one wishes to predict—be it preference for dark chocolate over milk, susceptibility to cardiovascular disease, or individual propensity for violence—is not randomly distributed in the population. With respect to antisocial behavior, this non-randomess is clearly evident. One of the most striking aspects of the costs of antisocial conduct is that they are attributable to a relatively small number of individuals. In the United Kingdom, 50 percent of the total crimes committed, including violent crime, are committed by roughly 10 percent of the population (UK Home Office, 2007). This clustering of criminal behavior in the country as a whole closely mirrors what we know about the familial aggregation of crime within individual communities. Within any given community, roughly 50 percent of the crime is committed by 10 percent of the families in that community. The familial nature of crime in communities is consistent with the known inter-generational transmission of antisocial traits and behavior; both point to an inherited predisposition to criminal behavior and violence (Farrington et al., 2001). In fact, there is unambiguous evidence from over 30 years of twin stud-ies showing that antisocial behavior has a heritable component (Moffitt, 2005). Two words of caution are appropriate, however. First, partitioning risk into heritable and nongenetic factors is not as neat as one might assume; in par-ticular, interactions between genes and the environment may lead to inflated heritability estimates. Second, environmental risk factors such as traumatic brain injury, alcohol dependence, or childhood abuse have also been clearly identified (Tuvblad & Baker, 2011) that could show exactly that kind of gene–environment interplay.

MAOA: HISTORY AND BIOLOGY OF A "WARRIOR GENE"

Merely knowing that antisociality is heritable is not especially useful from a pre-diction standpoint. In practice, heritability metrics tell us nothing about how much (or even whether) genetic factors influence the expression of violent or antisocial behavior in any one individual. However, demonstrating heritability answers the fundamental threshold question for any genetic prediction effort. Given heritability, it would next be necessary to identify specific inherited genetic variants or mutations that are responsible for the intergenerational transmission of violence and antisocial behavior. As with any putative biomarker, one would need to demonstrate both high sensitivity and high specificity to claim validity. In other words, the genetic marker or markers linked to violence should be pres-ent in most people who commit violent acts and absent in most people who do not engage in violent behavior. In the section that follows, we discuss a genetic variant in the MAOA gene that has garnered considerable interest as a potential genetic biomarker for aggression and violence. We will recount its history, biol-ogy, and record of association to psychiatric illness. In so doing, we will show that this variant has neither the sensitivity and specificity nor the phenotypic selectivity that would be required to support any claims about prediction.

MAOA was first highlighted as a violence risk gene through genetic analysis of a violent Dutch family. In a seminal series of papers, Han Brunner and his colleagues sequenced members of a large and notorious kindred (Brunner et al., 1993a, 1993b). A sizeable proportion of males in this clan exhibited such bizarre behavior that they were feared both by townsfolk and by other members of the family. These men showed evidence of mild mental retardation that was coupled with a propensity toward violent outbursts, often in response to minor frustrations and typically massively out of proportion to the inciting event. They were severely impulsive, with behaviors ranging from assault and arson to rape and murder. Brunner found that affected males also exhibited altered monoamine metabolism, including reduced urine 5-hydroxy indoleacetic acid (5-HIAA) levels compared to unaffected males. 5-HIAA is produced via oxidative degradation of serotonin by the catabolic enzyme monoamine oxidase A (MAOA); the gene encoding this enzyme is located on the X chromosome.

Remarkably, an examination of town records revealed that this pattern of behavior had been evident in the family for many generations; however, only men were ever affected. It thus appeared that aberrant behavior and monoamine metabolism in this family were highly heritable and followed an X-linked mode of transmission, leading Brunner to focus on the X chromosome as a source of causal genetic mutations. Subsequent linkage analysis in this family highlighted the MAOA locus on Xp11.23-11.4, confirming this suspicion, and later sequencing of the MAOA gene in probands revealed a point mutation (C936T) in exon 8. The C936T substitution results in a premature stop codon, producing a functional MAOA knockout in males (who have only one X chromosome). Consistent with this, MAOA activity was essentially undetectable in fibroblasts cultured from probands. This finding was the first clear demonstration that a specific genetic variant could account for the intergenerational transmission of antisocial and criminal behavior through Mendelian inheritance. It also gave MAOA an unfortunate and inaccurate nickname by which many still know it today—"the warrior gene."

In the ensuing decade, mouse transgenic techniques permitted further and more granular investigation of the role that MAOA plays in the heritability of violence. Murine MAOA knockout studies largely recapitulated (in analogy) the effects described by Brunner. Transgenic mice with deletions of the MAOA gene show much higher levels of reactive aggression, coupled with markedly increased monoamine levels. The strongest neurochemical effects are seen for serotonin, and these changes are strongest in youth and adolescence (Cases et al., 1995; Kim et al., 1997; Popova et al., 2001). Emotional (fear) learning is enhanced in the MAOA knockouts, even though other forms of learning (e.g., motor learning) are not affected (Kim et al., 1997). Behavioral pharmacology studies showed that blocking postsynaptic serotonin signaling or depleting serotonin levels rescues the hyperaggressive phenotype, implying that the behavioral effects of disrupting MAOA function are specifically due to the excessive serotonin levels that result from diminished serotonin metabolism (Shih et al., 1999). Of note, a similar phenotype has been observed more recently in a line of mice with a spontaneous point mutation in exon 8 of the murine MAOA gene. In contrast to the transgenic knockout mice described above, this mutation produces a direct murine analog (A863T) to the human sequence variant (C936T) identified by Brunner. These mice show heightened reactive aggression, with undetectable MAOA activity in the brain and periphery, further suggesting that genetically mediated reductions in serotonin catabolism could be involved in susceptibility to violence (Scott et al., 2008).

THE MAOA U-VNTR: DISCOVERY AND ASSOCIATIONS

The MAOA C936T mutation generated considerable excitement in psychiatry and psychiatric genetics, as it gave investigators interested in violence and aggression a gene on which to concentrate their efforts (this being an era before inexpensive genome-wide genotyping methods were available). But it must be noted that MAOA C936T is a private mutation, held only by members of that Dutch kindred. In fact, monogenic patterns of inheritance for violence and aggression are typically exclusive to such private mutations (but see Bevilacqua et al., 2010, for a counter-example). However, in contrast to these rare sequence alterations, a number of common polymorphic variants have been identified in the MAOA gene region (Balciuniene et al., 2002). The best studied of these, by far, is a variable number of tandem repeats (VNTR) polymorphism located in the promoter region of the gene, 1.2 kilobase pairs upstream of its start site. Originally characterized by Sabol and colleagues, the MAOA u-VNTR (so named because it is upstream of the gene itself) is a 30bp repeat. In the original report by Sabol, the u-VNTR was shown to affect transcription in an *in vitro* heterologous expression system and MAOA activity in fibroblast cultures (Sabol et al., 1998). The presence of 3.5 or 4 repeats was linked to relatively higher MAOA expression and activity (these are thus referred to as MAOA-H alleles), while the presence of 3 repeats results in relatively lower expression and activity (MAOA-L alleles) (Deckert et al., 1999; Denney et al., 1999; Sabol et al., 1998; Zhang et al., 2010). However, the precise functional effect of the MAOA u-VNTR is not entirely settled, as several *in vivo* studies (including one positron emission tomography study in humans) have since contradicted the original report (Balciuniene et al., 2002; Cirulli & Goldstein, 2007; Fowler et al., 2006).

In light of Brunner's finding and the preclinical data linking MAOA to aggression, discovery of the u-VNTR sparked widespread interest in this variant as a biomarker for violence and aggression. To date, a broad array of clinical diagnostic measures, personality assessments, and behavioral assays have been tested for association to antisocial phenotypes. However, on balance, evidence favoring association is largely inconsistent. Supporting the notion that the MAOA u-VNTR increases aggression and violence, several studies have linked the MAOA-L allele to antisocial behavior in adult substance abusers (Contini et al., 2006; Guindalini et al., 2005; Moffitt, 2005; Parsian et al., 2003; Saito et al., 2002) and in adolescents with behavioral problems (Brunner et al., 1993a, 1993b; Lee, 2011). Further, MAOA-L individuals show higher levels of antisocial traits (Reti et al., 2011; Williams et al., 2009), are more likely to be involved in gangs and to report past use of a weapon (Beaver et al., 2010), and behave more aggressively (McDermott et al., 2009) and less cooperatively (Mertins et al., 2011) in laboratory-based experimental paradigms.

THE MAOA U-VNTR: ASSESSMENT OF SENSITIVITY AND SPECIFICITY

Although the associations outlined above are suggestive, the picture is considerably complicated by the fact that many have failed to replicate these findings (Barnett et al., 2011; Garpenstrand et al., 2002; Koller et al., 2003; Lee et al., 2008; Syagailo et al., 2001; Tochigi et al., 2006; Vanyukov et al., 2007; Yu et al., 2005; Zalsman et al., 2005). In addition, a significant fraction of studies that do show positive associations to MAOA u-VNTR genotype report an allelic directionality that is counter to what one might expect from prior clinical and animal data. Several investigators have demonstrated increased impulsive aggression (Manuck et al., 2000), higher retrospectively reported childhood aggression (Beitchman et al., 2004), elevated risk for Cluster B personality disorders (Jacob et al., 2005), lower cerebrospinal fluid 5-HIAA levels (Jönsson et al., 2000), and blunted PRL-fen in MAOA-H allele carriers (Manuck et al., 2000). Moreover, even for the studies that do report significant associations in the 'right' direction (i.e.. higher risk associated with MAOA-L), effect sizes are quite small.

Given that the MAOA u-VNTR accounts for such a small proportion of the population variance in antisocial behavior and violence, possessing an MAOA-L allele provides little useful information about whether a given individual is more or less likely to commit violent acts. Considered in isolation from other risk factors, it is likely that a nontrivial proportion of individuals carrying an MAOA-L allele are not at increased risk of violence compared to MAOA-H carriers (constituting a false positive). Likewise, it is likely that a nontrivial proportion of individuals carrying an MAOA-H allele are more predisposed to violence compared to MAOA-L individuals (constituting a false negative). To recap: Effect sizes for the MAOA u-VNTR are small in published positive reports; there is significant directional heterogeneity among the published positive findings; and there are a large number of published negative findings. Together, these indicate poor sensitivity and specificity; we therefore conclude that MAOA u-VNTR cannot be considered a valid biomarker for antisociality and violence.

THE MAOA U-VNTR: ASSESSMENT OF PHENOTYPIC SELECTIVITY

While inconsistent findings of small effect size imply that the MAOA u-VNTR has poor sensitivity and specificity, findings of association to other psychiatric disorders and symptoms speak to poor phenotypic selectivity as well. By phenotypic selectivity, we mean the likelihood that a susceptibility factor selectively affects risk for a target phenotype. First, variability at this locus has been linked to disorders that, while possibly linked to antisocial behavior on a conceptual or epidemiological level, are not themselves directly characterized by violence. For example, positive associations to polymorphic variability in MAOA have been reported for alcohol dependence (Contini et al., 2006), self-injury (Lung et al., 2011), and attention-deficit/hyperactivity disorder (ADHD) (Wargelius et al., 2012). Furthermore, MAOA has been linked to disorders that would appear to have only oblique relationships to violence or aggression, including autism (Cohen et al., 2011) schizophrenia (Sun et al., 2012), major depressive disorder (Fan et al., 2010; Zhang et al., 2010), bipolar disorder (Müller et al., 2007), and panic disorder (Reif et al., 2012). This broad pattern of association belies the notion that MAOA is in any meaningful way a "warrior gene," in the sense that variability at this genetic locus deterministically and selectively induces violence and aggression. Germane to the present discussion, apparent pleiotropic effects of the MAOA u-VNTR weaken the plausibility of claims that the gene is a specific predictor of violence and aggression.

GENE–ENVIRONMENT INTERACTIONS

The impact of MAOA genetic variation on antisocial behavior and violence is much more robust in individuals (particularly males) who have been exposed to childhood maltreatment. Caspi et al. (2002) were the first to report a gene-by-environment interaction between MAOA u-VNTR genotype and early life maltreatment. In that prospective study, the authors found no main effect of genotype on risk for aggression in men; however, MAOA-L men who had been exposed to abuse early in life were more likely to commit violent criminal acts than MAOA-H men (Caspi et al., 2002). Although some groups have reported negative findings for an MAOA gene–environment interaction, the effect has been independently replicated several times over (Derringer et al., 2010;

Ducci et al., 2006; Edwards et al., 2010; Enoch et al., 2010; Fergusson et al., 2011; Foley et al., 2004; Frazzetto et al., 2007; Huang et al., 2004; Kim-Cohen et al., 2006; Kinnally et al., 2009; Nilsson et al., 2006, 2007; Reif et al., 2007; Widom and Brzustowicz, 2006). It has meta-analytic support (Kim-Cohen et al., 2006) and has been partially replicated in at least one nonhuman primate study (Newman et al., 2005). Sex appears to play an important moderating role in this interaction, as some studies suggest that MAOA-H women are actually at greater risk following early life stress (Aslund et al., 2011; Nilsson et al., 2011; Sjöberg et al., 2007). Available data support the idea that the impact of MAOA u-VNTR genotype is more penetrant on a background of early life maltreatment. However, the true predictive value of this interaction for violence and antisocial behavior remains highly ambiguous. More work is needed to determine the formal sensitivity, specificity, and phenotypic selectivity of this effect; its robustness to variability in the measurement of maltreatment; the impact of maltreatment exposure duration and timing; and effects of ethnic background, among other factors. These are crucial gaps in our understanding of the MAOA–environment interaction.

IMAGING GENETICS OF MAOA

While we argue that the value of the MAOA u-VNTR for forensic prediction is highly dubious, studies of the variant have provided key insights into the neurobiology of antisocial behavior. Studying quantitative biological phenotypes that are closer to the direct impact of the genetic variant under study than the corresponding clinical or behavioral phenotype increases our ability to detect subtle genetic effects that may not penetrate to the level of behavior (Meyer-Lindenberg & Weinberger, 2006). The use of neuroimaging in concert with genetic analysis allows investigators to probe the brain at the systems level, providing a functional readout of the impact of a genetic variant on brain function, structure, and connectivity. Across studies, this "intermediate phenotype" strategy has produced a compelling picture that implicates dysfunction within corticolimbic circuitry for affective arousal, emotion regulation, inhibitory control, and social cognition in genetic risk for violence.

BRAIN STRUCTURE

One of the first studies of genetic effects on brain morphometry examined women with Turner syndrome (45,X) and those with partial deletions of the X chromosome encompassing the MAOA gene (Good et al., 2003). These women showed structural changes in the orbitofrontal cortex and amygdala; they were also relatively impaired at facial expression recognition, an amygdala-dependent function (Adolphs et al., 1994). Since then, several studies have found that MAOA-L allele carriers show characteristic changes within a corticolimbic circuit involved in social and emotional processing. We have shown that MAOA-L allele carriers have pronounced gray matter volume deficits (relative to MAOA-H carriers) in the amygdala and insula and throughout the cingulate gyrus (Meyer-Lindenberg et al., 2006). Using measurements of cortical surface thickness, other groups have independently replicated the cingulate and orbitofrontal cortex findings (Cerasa et al., 2008).

BRAIN FUNCTION

Functional imaging studies support the idea that the genetically determined structural alterations in corticolimbic circuitry detailed above are linked to functional consequences for brain information processing. In several early studies using experimental tasks that require inhibitory control, MAOA-L carriers showed decreased engagement of anterior cingulate and ventral prefrontal cortex, the degree of which predicted scores on a measure of trait impulsivity (Fan et al., 2003; Passamonti et al., 2005, 2008). We found significant genotype-related differences in other domains of cognitive function that are linked to aggression and violence. During aversive facial emotion processing (angry and fearful faces), MAOA-L subjects showed exaggerated amygdala and insula activation, with diminished recruitment of regulatory regions of prefrontal cortex (orbitofrontal and anterior cingulate cortices). Using an emotional memory paradigm, we found a specific effect on aversive memory retrieval, with MAOA-L allele carriers showing greater activation in amygdala and hippocampus during the recall of negatively valenced visual scenes. Finally, MAOA-L males, but not females, showed reduced activation in dorsal cingulate during a go/no-go task, replicating earlier studies in a significantly larger sample (Meyer-Lindenberg et al., 2006). Other groups have replicated the finding of enhanced amygdala activation in MAOA-L carriers (Lee & Ham, 2008) and extended it by showing that increased amygdala activation in MAOA-L individuals is associated with higher levels of self-reported anger reactivity (Alia-Klein et al., 2009). Notably, two studies suggest that MAOA-L carriers show enhanced responsivity in corticolimbic circuitry to social rejection, and this exaggerated reactivity is associated with trait aggression and interpersonal hypersensitivity (Eisenberger et al., 2007).

BRAIN CONNECTIVITY

Using functional connectivity analyses, we found that MAOA-L men showed stronger coupling between amygdala and ventromedial prefrontal cortex (vmPFC). The degree of functional connectivity was correlated with the magnitude of amygdala hyperactivity in MAOA-L men ($R^2 > 0.3$), suggesting regulation, and positively correlated with a trait measure of emotional reactivity (Buckholtz et al., 2008). In a subsequent analysis, we (Buckholtz et al., 2008) found that activity in perigenual anterior cingulate—robustly interconnected with both amygdala (Carmichael & Price, 1995; 1996) and vmPFC (Ongur & Price, 2000)—strongly tracked the magnitude of amygdala–vmPFC coupling. These findings suggested that vmPFC is brought online to provide compensatory support to perigenual cingulate, the structure and function of which is compromised in MAOA-L males. To test this model, we used path analysis to parse the directional connections within this network. This analysis suggested that vmPFC regulates amygdala activation indirectly, via an input to perigenual cingulate, which sends a direct inhibitory projection to amygdala (Buckholtz et al., 2008). To date, one other study has found similar MAOA u-VNTR genotype-dependent alterations in corticolimbic connectivity (Dannlowski et al., 2009).

Taken together, these data are consistent with the idea that genetic variability in MAOA is associated with distinct patterns of change in brain structure, function, and connectivity. Relative to MAOA-H individuals, MAOA-L allele carriers show reduced gray matter volume in amygdala and medial prefrontal cortex (mPFC), exaggerated reactivity to aversive stimuli in amygdala in concert with compromised engagement of regulatory control by mPFC, and degraded functional and structural connectivity within this same amygdala–mPFC circuit for affective arousal and regulation. Such findings accord with available data suggesting that this circuit is dysregulated in disorders that are characterized by high levels of impulsive aggression. A wealth of data highlight mPFC as critical in providing inhibitory cortical feedback to amygdala (Quirk et al., 2003; Rosenkranz & Grace, 1999), underlying its essential role in fear extinction (Quirk et al., 2003; Sotres-Bayon et al., 2006), emotion regulation, and temperamental variation (Pezawas et al., 2005). This region is highly sensitive to modulation by serotonin, as it has the greatest density of serotonin receptors in human cortex (Varnäs et al., 2004). Thus, available data suggest that heritable variability in MAOA may alter serotonin levels during ontogeny to disrupt the development of corticolimbic circuitry.

In considering the implications of these imaging genetic findings, it must be noted that all of the results from our group, and the majority of data from other groups, were obtained in healthy controls who were screened for major psychopathology. In other words, even though we and others have reported statistically significant differences in brain structure, function, and connectivity between groups of MAOA-L and MAOA-H individuals, these differences are largely compatible with psychiatric health. The value of this approach, then, is not in supporting the claim that the MAOA u-VNTR is a specific risk factor that by itself deterministically predicts psychopathology, but rather in using this variant as a tool to uncover neural systems that that may be disrupted in violent or antisocial individuals. The combination of genetic and neuroimaging methodologies to study violence improves our ability to build tractable neurobiological models of violence, furthering our biological understanding of this complex and relevant phenomenon. However, the fact that these findings are important from a scientific standpoint does not make them forensically or legally relevant. While the intermediate phenotype approach provides insight into the pathomechanisms through which heritable risk factors affect behavior and psychopathology, this approach *per se* is forensically and legally inert. In other words, knowledge of how inter-individual genetic variability maps onto inter-individual differences in neural information processing does not improve one's ability to use a given genetic marker to predict behavior in a given individual.

THE GENETIC ARCHITECTURE OF PSYCHOPATHOLOGY: IMPLICATIONS FOR PREDICTION

Two untenable assumptions about the genetics of psychopathology color much of the current thinking about forensic "genoprediction." First is the notion that specific genetic variants are selectively linked to specific disorders or behaviors. This belief is particularly evident in discussions of violence prediction, where MAOA is often considered as a "violence gene," an "antisocial gene," or a "warrior gene." However, as discussed earlier, clinical associations of MAOA u-VNTR span multiple diagnostic categories, encompassing such 'unwarriorlike' syndromes as depression and panic disorder. The current portrait of the MAOA u-VNTR would therefore suggest that what it predisposes to is not a specific behavior (violence) or set of behaviors (antisocial conduct), but rather a broader pattern of emotional dysregulation that can, but does not necessarily, overlap with these. In fact, this would be consistent with what we know about the genetic architecture of psychopathology more generally. On the whole, genetic risk for psychiatric disorders and behavioral dispositions is pleiotropic, meaning that heritable factors confer liability to broad dimensions of symptomatically related disorders, such as schizophrenia and bipolar disorder, rather than discrete syndromes (Gejman et al., 2011; International Schizophrenia Consortium et al., 2009). This fact would seem to seriously complicate genetic prediction of antisocial behavior and violence, as no individual marker would ever come close to the phenotypic selectivity that would be desired of a genetic biomarker. This fact significantly constrains the value of any putative genetic marker for violence, as (in the case of MAOA) possessing that marker would be equally likely to signify mood or anxiety psychopathology as antisocial behavior.

The second flawed assumption is that individual common genetic markers are discrete causal entities, accounting for a significant enough proportion of the variance in a target behavior to provide adequate sensitivity and specificity. However, it is increasingly recognized that most major forms of psychopathology and complex traits are characterized by polygenic inheritance (Gejman et al., 2011), meaning that many small-effect risk alleles produce a continuous distribution of genetic liability (Buckholtz and Meyer-Lindenberg, 2012; Plomin et al., 2009). Susceptibility to complex behaviors like violence and aggression likely follows a similar mode of inheritance. Polygenicity implies that an individual's aggregate genetic profile will determine where he or she falls on a continuous population distribution of traits. The extremes of some of these genetically influenced trait distributions are associated with social impairment and dysfunctional behaviors like violence. However, even assuming that we would be able to construct a reliable and valid polygenic profile for 'violence' (see above comment), setting forensically relevant thresholds or cutpoints for forensic prediction would be a challenging and controversial enterprise.

We are less bearish if the focus were shifted from the genes themselves to the neural circuits on which they act: as we have recently proposed, these brain circuits may in fact turn out to be optimal descriptors of biological factors underlying psychopathology (Buckholtz & Meyer-Lindenberg, 2012). They may therefore be better suited to understand violence. Certainly, information of this kind would be a necessary evidence base for designing individualized therapies of violent offenders that takes causal risk profiles and neural circuit abnormalities into account, in a field where currently no accepted and proven effective therapies exist. Whether, however, such circuits would be useful for forensic prediction is again subject to similar caveats as outlined for genes above. Currently, we believe overlap between normal and forensic populations is too great and the variance explained too small for that to be a near-term possibility.

META-CHALLENGE FOR PREDICTION: THE GROUP TO INDIVIDUAL PROBLEM

In the preceding sections, we raised several key limitations for forensic genoprediction, using the specific example of the MAOA u-VNTR. However, there is a larger challenge that should be considered in any attempt at biologically based prediction of individual behavior. This challenge has its roots in a key difference between the aim and methods of science and the goals of the legal system. Science is focused on understanding general phenomena, aggregating data across groups of individuals to enable inferences about the population as a whole. By contrast, law (and psychiatric practice, for that matter) is solely concerned with making determinations about individuals (Treadway & Buckholtz, 2011). Group- or population-level scientific data are relevant to law only to the extent that the data bolster or weaken the evidence provided in an individual case. To give one example, the relationship between MAOA and violence (a population-level inference obtained by averaging across many individuals) would be of interest to the law only insofar as it speaks to the probative value of any given individual's MAOA genotype. As Faigman (1999) has put it, "science attempts to discover the universals hiding among the particulars, trial courts attempt to discover the particulars hiding among the universals."

We raise this issue because implicit in much of the discussion of bioprediction is an assumption that scientific inferences about population-level phenomena, obtained by averaging data across large numbers of individuals, can straightforwardly form a basis for making determinations about specific individuals. However, this assumption is, as a general proposition, untenable (Faigman, 2010; Treadway & Buckholtz, 2011). While the difficulty inherent in attempting to "individualize" group-level scientific data (the so-called "group to individual" or "G2I" problem) has been recognized in other domains of science, it has not received the attention it warrants in the area of forensic bioprediction. For example, if a study (or set of scientific studies) found that allele X in gene Y is statistically associated with violence risk, one might assume that finding out whether Mr. Q has allele X in gene Y would provide important information for determining whether Mr. Q was likely to become violent. In this chapter we have sought to explain why this assumption is terminally flawed. Similar issues obtain for cognitive neuroscience. If a study found that on average, people with relatively lower fMRI signal in region A during task B were more likely to commit crime C (relative to people with higher fMRI signal in region A during task B), it does not follow that any one individual's fMRI signal level in region A during task B will have any meaningful predictive power. Accordingly, we argue that it is extremely premature to speculate about specific potential biomarkers for violence and antisocial behavior based on neuroimaging and genetic studies in antisocial populations.

CONCLUSION

Neuroscience and genetics continue to shed new light on the factors and mechanisms that contribute to human variability, with a precision that was unthinkable even a decade ago. These advances bring with them an array of ethical, legal, and social implications. While scientists are steeped in the concept of inductive logic and make an intuitive distinction between group-level inferences and individual datapoints, this distinction is too often not made when science 'escapes' from the lab into society at large. In some areas, such as law, this transmission has already occurred; individual brain images and genotypes are beginning to be introduced as evidence in trial courts (Farahany & Bernet, 2006; Farisco & Petrini, 2012; Nadelhoffer & Sinnott-Armstrong, 2012). Science may yet progress to the point where neuroscientific data may be individualized to permit valid person-level inferences of a sort that would be relevant to law. Without consensus standards for evaluating the validity of such inferences, we fear that the potential harms associated with the misapplication of scientific data for prediction may far outweigh any potential benefits.

At the same time, there is a dire need to advance our understanding of the neurobiology of violence—not to predict violence in individuals, but to create an evidence base for treatment and ultimately prevention in an area of unquestionable societal relevance. We must vigilantly guard against the impulse to rush scientific findings to the courtroom where they do not belong. The justifiable concern that science can be misused in the courtroom can, regrettably, lead to an unwarranted fear of (and restrictions on) any biological research with legal implications. There is an unquestionable need for better data on the pathobiology of violence and antisocial behavior. This can only be promoted by the voluntary participation of severely violent incarcerated individuals in ethical neuroscientific research. However, some societies restrict research of this kind due to the fears highlighted above. We believe that such restrictions are misguided and ultimately damaging. Careful neuroscientific research that heeds the limitations outlined above will benefit the perpetrators of violence, their victims, and society as a whole.

REFERENCES

Adolphs, R., Tranel, D., Damasio, H., & Damasio, A. (1994). Impaired recognition of emotion in facial expressions following bilateral damage to the human amygdala. *Nature, 372,* 669–672.

Alia-Klein, N., Goldstein, R. Z., Tomasi, D., Woicik, P. A., Moeller, S. J., Williams, B., Craig, I. W., Telang, F., Biegon, A., Wang, G.-J., et al. (2009). Neural mechanisms of anger regulation as a function of genetic risk for violence. *Emotion, 9,* 385–396.

Aslund, C., Nordquist, N., Comasco, E., Leppert, J., Oreland, L., & Nilsson, K. W. (2011). Maltreatment, MAOA, and delinquency: sex differences in gene-environment interaction in a large population-based cohort of adolescents. *Behavior Genetics, 41,* 262–272.

Balciuniene, J., Emilsson, L., Oreland, L., Pettersson, U., & Jazin, E. (2002). Investigation of the functional effect of monoamine oxidase polymorphisms in human brain. *Human Genetics, 110,* 1–7.

Barnett, J. H., Xu, K., Heron, J., Goldman, D., & Jones, P. B. (2011). Cognitive effects of genetic variation in monoamine neurotransmitter systems: a population-based study of COMT, MAOA, and 5HTTLPR. *American Journal of Medical Genetics B Neuropsychiatric Genet, 156*, 158–167.

Beaver, K. M., DeLisi, M., Vaughn, M. G., & Barnes, J.C. (2010). Monoamine oxidase A genotype is associated with gang membership and weapon use. *Comprehensive Psychiatry, 51*, 130–134.

Beitchman, J. H., Mik, H. M., Ehtesham, S., Douglas, L., & Kennedy, J. L. (2004). MAOA and persistent, pervasive childhood aggression. *Molecular Psychiatry, 9*, 546–547.

Bevilacqua, L., Doly, S., Kaprio, J., Yuan, Q., Tikkanen, R., Paunio, T., Zhou, Z., Wedenoja, J., Maroteaux, L., Diaz, S., et al. (2010). A population-specific HTR2B stop codon predisposes to severe impulsivity. *Nature, 468*, 1061–1066.

Brooks-Crozier, J. (2011). The Nature and Nurture of Violence: Early Intervention Services for the Families of MAOA-Low Children as a Means to Reduce Violent Crime and the Costs of Violent Crime *Conn L Rev.*

Brunner, H. G., Nelen, M., Breakefield, X. O., Ropers, H. H., & van Oost, B. A. (1993a). Abnormal behavior associated with a point mutation in the structural gene for monoamine oxidase A. *Science, 262*, 578–580.

Brunner, H. G., Nelen, M. R., van Zandvoort, P., Abeling, N. G., van Gennip, A. H., Wolters, E. C., Kuiper, M. A., Ropers, H. H., & van Oost, B. A. (1993b). X-linked borderline mental retardation with prominent behavioral disturbance: phenotype, genetic localization, and evidence for disturbed monoamine metabolism. *American Journal of Human Genetics, 52*, 1032–1039.

Buckholtz, J. W., & Meyer-Lindenberg, A. (2008). MAOA and the neurogenetic architecture of human aggression. *Trends in Neuroscience, 31*, 120–129.

Buckholtz, J. W., & Meyer-Lindenberg, A. (2012). Psychopathology and the human connectome: toward a transdiagnostic model of risk for mental illness. *Neuron, 74*, 990–1004.

Buckholtz, J. W., Callicott, J. H., Kolachana, B., Hariri, A. R., Goldberg, T. E., Genderson, M., Egan, M. F., Mattay, V. S., Weinberger, D. R., & Meyer-Lindenberg, A. (2008). Genetic variation in MAOA modulates ventromedial prefrontal circuitry mediating individual differences in human personality. *Molecular Psychiatry, 13*, 313–324.

Caldwell, M. F. (2011). Treatment-related changes in behavioral outcomes of psychopathy facets in adolescent offenders. *Law and Human Behavior, 35*, 275–287.

Carmichael, S. T., & Price, J. L. (1995). Limbic connections of the orbital and medial prefrontal cortex in macaque monkeys. *J Comp Neurol, 363*, 615–641.

Carmichael, S. T., & Price, J. L. (1996). Connectional networks within the orbital and medial prefrontal cortex of macaque monkeys. *J Comp Neurol, 371*, 179–207.

Cases, O., Seif, I., Grimsby, J., Gaspar, P., Chen, K., Pournin, S., Müller, U., Aguet, M., Babinet, C., & Shih, J.C. (1995). Aggressive behavior and altered amounts of brain serotonin and norepinephrine in mice lacking MAOA. *Science, 268*, 1763–1766.

Caspi, A., McClay, J., Moffitt, T. E., Mill, J., Martin, J., Craig, I. W., Taylor, A., & Poulton, R. (2002). Role of genotype in the cycle of violence in maltreated children. *Science, 297*, 851–854.

Cerasa, A., Gioia, M. C., Labate, A., Lanza, P., Magariello, A., Muglia, M., & Quattrone, A. (2008). MAO A VNTR polymorphism and variation in human morphology: a VBM study. *Neuroreport, 19*, 1107–1110.

Cirulli, E. T., & Goldstein, D. B. (2007). In vitro assays fail to predict in vivo effects of regulatory polymorphisms. *Human Molecular Genetics, 16*, 1931–1939.

Cohen, I. L., Liu, X., Lewis, M. E. S., Chudley, A., Forster-Gibson, C., Gonzalez, M., Jenkins, E. C., Brown, W. T., & Holden, J. J. A. (2011). Autism severity is associated with child and maternal MAOA genotypes. *Clinical Genetics, 79*, 355–362.

Contini, V., Marques, F. Z. C., Garcia, C. E. D., Hutz, M. H., & Bau, C. H. D. (2006). MAOA-uVNTR polymorphism in a Brazilian sample: further support for the association with impulsive behaviors and alcohol dependence. *Am J Med Genet B Neuropsychiatr Genet, 141B*, 305–308.

Corso, P., Mercy, J., Simon, T., Finkelstein, E., & Miller, T. (2007). Medical costs and productivity losses due to interpersonal and self-directed violence in the United States. *American Journal of Preventive Medicine, 32*, 474–482.e2.

Dannlowski, U., Ohrmann, P., Konrad, C., Domschke, K., Bauer, J., Kugel, H., Hohoff, C., Schöning, S., Kersting, A., Baune, B. T., et al. (2009). Reduced amygdala-prefrontal coupling in major depression: association with MAOA genotype and illness severity. *Int J Neuropsychopharmacol, 12*, 11–22.

Deckert, J., Catalano, M., Syagailo, Y. V., Bosi, M., Okladnova, O., Di Bella, D., Nöthen, M. M., Maffei, P., Franke, P., Fritze, J., et al. (1999). Excess of high activity monoamine oxidase A gene promoter alleles in female patients with panic disorder. *Human Molecular Genetics, 8*, 621–624.

Denney, R.M., Koch, H., & Craig, I.W. (1999). Association between monoamine oxidase A activity in human male skin fibroblasts and genotype of the MAOA promoter-associated variable number tandem repeat. *Human Genetics, 105*, 542–551.

Derringer, J., Krueger, R. F., Irons, D. E., & Iacono, W. G. (2010). Harsh discipline, childhood sexual assault, and MAOA genotype: an investigation of main and interactive effects on diverse clinical externalizing outcomes. *Behavioral Genetics, 40*, 639–648.

Ducci, F., Newman, T. K., Funt, S., Brown, G. L., Virkkunen, M., & Goldman, D. (2006). A functional polymorphism in the MAOA gene promoter (MAOA-LPR) predicts central dopamine function and body mass index. *Mol Psychiatry, 11*, 858–866.

Edwards, A. C., Dodge, K. A., Latendresse, S. J., Lansford, J. E., Bates, J. E., Pettit, G. S., Budde, J. P., Goate, A. M., & Dick, D. M. (2010). MAOA-uVNTR and early physical discipline interact to influence delinquent behavior. *J Child Psychol Psychiatry, 51*, 679–687.

Eisenberger, N. I., Way, B. M., Taylor, S. E., Welch, W. T., & Lieberman, M. D. (2007). Understanding genetic risk for aggression: clues from the brain's response to social exclusion. *Bps, 61*, 1100–1108.

Enoch, M.-A., Steer, C. D., Newman, T. K., Gibson, N., & Goldman, D. (2010). Early life stress, MAOA, and gene-environment interactions predict behavioral disinhibition in children. *Genes Brain Behav, 9*, 65–74.

Faigman, D. L. (1999). *Legal alchemy: the use and misuse of science in the law.* New York: W. H. Freeman and Company.

Faigman, D. L. (2010). Evidentiary incommensurability: a preliminary exploration of the problem of reasoning from general scientific data to individualized legal decision-making. *Brooklyn L Rev, 75*(4), 1115–1136.

Fan, J., Fossella, J., Sommer, T., Wu, Y., & Posner, M.I. (2003). Mapping the genetic variation of executive attention onto brain activity. *Proc Natl Acad Sci USA, 100*, 7406–7411.

Fan, M., Liu, B., Jiang, T., Jiang, X., Zhao, H., & Zhang, J. (2010). Meta-analysis of the association between the monoamine oxidase-A gene and mood disorders. *Psychiatr Genet, 20,* 1–7.

Farahany, N., & Bernet, W. (2006). Behavioural genetics in criminal cases: past, present and future. *Genomics, Society and Policy, 2*(1), 72–79.

Farisco, M., & Petrini, C. (2012). The impact of neuroscience and genetics on the law: a recent Italian case. *Neuroethics.*

Farrington, D. P., Jolliffe, D., Loeber, R., Stouthamer-Loeber, M., & Kalb, L. M. (2001). The concentration of offenders in families, and family criminality in the prediction of boys' delinquency. *J Adolesc, 24,* 579–596.

Fergusson, D. M., Boden, J. M., Horwood, L. J., Miller, A. L., & Kennedy, M. A. (2011). MAOA, abuse exposure and antisocial behaviour: 30-year longitudinal study. *British Journal of Psychiatry, 198,* 457–463.

Foley, D. L., Eaves, L. J., Wormley, B., Silberg, J. L., Maes, H. H., Kuhn, J., & Riley, B. (2004). Childhood adversity, monoamine oxidase a genotype, and risk for conduct disorder. *Arch Gen Psychiatry, 61,* 738–744.

Fossum, S., Handegård, B. H., Martinussen, M., & Mørch, W. T. (2008). Psychosocial interventions for disruptive and aggressive behaviour in children and adolescents: a meta-analysis. *Eur Child Adolesc Psychiatry, 17,* 438–451.

Fowler, J. S., Alia-Klein, N., Kriplani, A., Logan, J., Williams, B., Zhu, W., Craig, I. W., Telang, F., Goldstein, R., Volkow, N. D., et al. (2006). Evidence that brain MAO A activity does not correspond to MAO A genotype in healthy male subjects. *Biological Psychiatry 62,* 355–358.

Frazzetto, G., Di Lorenzo, G., Carola, V., Proietti, L., Sokolowska, E., Siracusano, A., Gross, C., & Troisi, A. (2007). Early trauma and increased risk for physical aggression during adulthood: the moderating role of MAOA genotype. *PLoS ONE, 2,* e486.

Garpenstrand, H., Norton, N., Damberg, M., Rylander, G., Forslund, K., Mattila-Evenden, M., Gustavsson, J. P., Ekblom, J., Oreland, L., Bergman, H., et al. (2002). A regulatory monoamine oxidase a promoter polymorphism and personality traits. *Neuropsychobiology, 46,* 190–193.

Gejman, P. V., Sanders, A. R., & Kendler, K. S. (2011). Genetics of schizophrenia: new findings and challenges. *Annual Review of Genomics and Human Genetics, 12,* 121–144.

Gibbon, S., Duggan, C., Stoffers, J., Huband, N., Völlm, B. A., Ferriter, M., & Lieb, K. (2010). Psychological interventions for antisocial personality disorder. *Cochrane Database Syst Rev* CD007668.

Good, C. D., Lawrence, K., Thomas, N. S., Price, C. J., Ashburner, J., Friston, K. J., Frackowiak, R. S. J., Oreland, L., & Skuse, D. H. (2003). Dosage-sensitive X-linked locus influences the development of amygdala and orbitofrontal cortex, and fear recognition in humans. *Brain, 126,* 2431–2446.

Guindalini, C., Scivoletto, S., Ferreira, R. G. M., Nishimura, A., Zilberman, M. L., Peluso, M. M., & Zatz, M. (2005). Association of MAO A polymorphism and alcoholism in Brazilian females. *Psychiatr Genet, 15,* 141–144.

Huang, Y.-Y., Cate, S. P., Battistuzzi, C., Oquendo, M. A., Brent, D., & Mann, J. J. (2004). An association between a functional polymorphism in the monoamine oxidase a gene promoter, impulsive traits and early abuse experiences. *Neuropsychopharmacology, 29*, 1498–1505.

International Schizophrenia Consortium, Purcell, S. M., Wray, N. R., Stone, J. L., Visscher, P. M., O'Donovan, M. C., Sullivan, P. F., & Sklar, P. (2009). Common polygenic variation contributes to risk of schizophrenia and bipolar disorder. *Nature, 460*, 748–752.

Jacob, C. P., Müller, J., Schmidt, M., Hohenberger, K., Gutknecht, L., Reif, A., Schmidtke, A., Mössner, R., & Lesch, K. P. (2005). Cluster B personality disorders are associated with allelic variation of monoamine oxidase A activity. *Neuropsychopharmacology, 30*, 1711–1718.

Jönsson, E. G., Norton, N., Gustavsson, J. P., Oreland, L., Owen, M. J., & Sedvall, G. C. (2000). A promoter polymorphism in the monoamine oxidase A gene and its relationships to monoamine metabolite concentrations in CSF of healthy volunteers. *J Psychiatr Res, 34*, 239–244.

Müller, D. J., Serretti, A., Sicard, T., Tharmalingam, S., King, N., Artioli, P., Mandelli, L., Lorenzi, C., & Kennedy, J. L. (2007). Further evidence of MAO-A gene variants associated with bipolar disorder. *Am J Med Genet B Neuropsychiatr Genet, 144B*, 37–40.

Khalifa, N., Duggan, C., Stoffers, J., Huband, N., Völlm, B. A., Ferriter, M., & Lieb, K. (2010). Pharmacological interventions for antisocial personality disorder. *Cochrane Database Syst Rev*, CD007667.

Kim, J. J., Shih, J. C., Chen, K., Chen, L., Bao, S., Maren, S., Anagnostaras, S. G., Fanselow, M. S., De Maeyer, E., Seif, I., et al. (1997). Selective enhancement of emotional, but not motor, learning in monoamine oxidase A-deficient mice. *Proc Natl Acad Sci USA, 94*, 5929–5933.

Kim-Cohen, J., Caspi, A., Taylor, A., Williams, B., Newcombe, R., Craig, I. W., & Moffitt, T. E. (2006). MAOA, maltreatment, and gene-environment interaction predicting children's mental health: new evidence and a meta-analysis. *Mol Psychiatry, 11*, 903–913.

Kinnally, E. L., Huang, Y.-Y., Haverly, R., Burke, A. K., Galfalvy, H., Brent, D. P., Oquendo, M. A., & Mann, J. J. (2009). Parental care moderates the influence of MAOA-uVNTR genotype and childhood stressors on trait impulsivity and aggression in adult women. *Psychiatr Genet, 19*, 126–133.

Koller, G., Bondy, B., Preuss, U. W., Bottlender, M., & Soyka, M. (2003). No association between a polymorphism in the promoter region of the MAOA gene with antisocial personality traits in alcoholics. *Alcohol Alcohol, 38*, 31–34.

Lee, B.-C., Yang, J.-W., Lee, S.-H., Kim, S.-H., Joe, S.-H., Jung, I.-K., Choi, I.-G., & Ham, B.-J. (2008). An interaction between the norepinephrine transporter and monoamine oxidase A polymorphisms, and novelty-seeking personality traits in Korean females. *Prog Neuropsychopharmacol Biol Psychiatry, 32*, 238–242.

Lee, B.-T., & Ham, B.-J. (2008). Monoamine oxidase A-uVNTR genotype affects limbic brain activity in response to affective facial stimuli. *Neuroreport, 19*, 515–519.

Lee, S. S. (2011). Deviant peer affiliation and antisocial behavior: interaction with monoamine oxidase A (MAOA) genotype. *Journal of Abnormal Child Psychology, 39*, 321–332.

Lung, F.-W., Tzeng, D.-S., Huang, M.-F., & Lee, M.-B. (2011). Association of the MAOA promoter uVNTR polymorphism with suicide attempts in patients with major depressive disorder. *BMC Med Genet, 12*, 74.

Manuck, S. B., Flory, J. D., Ferrell, R. E., Mann, J. J., & Muldoon, M. F. (2000). A regulatory polymorphism of the monoamine oxidase-A gene may be associated with variability in aggression, impulsivity, and central nervous system serotonergic responsivity. *Psychiatry Res, 95*, 9–23.

McDermott, R., Tingley, D., Cowden, J., Frazzetto, G., & Johnson, D. D. P. (2009). Monoamine oxidase A gene (MAOA) predicts behavioral aggression following provocation. *Proceedings of the National Academy of Sciences USA, 106*, 2118–2123.

Mertins, V., Schote, A. B., Hoffeld, W., Griessmair, M., & Meyer, J. (2011). Genetic susceptibility for individual cooperation preferences: the role of monoamine oxidase A gene (MAOA) in the voluntary provision of public goods. *PLoS ONE, 6*, e20959.

Meyer-Lindenberg, A., & Weinberger, D. R. (2006). Intermediate phenotypes and genetic mechanisms of psychiatric disorders. *Nat Rev Neurosci, 7*, 818–827.

Meyer-Lindenberg, A., Buckholtz, J. W., Kolachana, B., R Hariri, A., Pezawas, L., Blasi, G., Wabnitz, A., Honea, R., Verchinski, B., Callicott, J. H., et al. (2006). Neural mechanisms of genetic risk for impulsivity and violence in humans. *Proc Natl Acad Sci USA, 103*, 6269–6274.

Moffitt, T. E. (2005). Genetic and environmental influences on antisocial behaviors: evidence from behavioral-genetic research. *Adv Genet, 55*, 41–104.

Monahan, J. (1981). *Predicting violent behavior: an assessment of clinical techniques.* Beverly Hills, CA: Sage Publications.

Monahan, J. (2006). The MacArthur studies of violence risk. *Criminal Behav Ment Health, 12*, S67–S72.

Nadelhoffer, T., & Sinnott-Armstrong, W. (2012). Neurolaw and neuroprediction: potential promises and perils. *Philosophy Compass, 7*, 631–642.

Nadelhoffer, T., Bibas, S., Grafton, S., Kiehl, K. A., Mansfield, A., Sinnott-Armstrong, W., & Gazzaniga, M. (2010). Neuroprediction, violence, and the law: setting the stage. *Neuroethics, 5*, 67–99.

Newman, T. K., Syagailo, Y. V., Barr, C. S., Wendland, J. R., Champoux, M., Graessle, M., Suomi, S. J., Higley, J. D., & Lesch, K. P. (2005). Monoamine oxidase A gene promoter variation and rearing experience influences aggressive behavior in rhesus monkeys. *Biological Psychiatry, 57*, 167–172.

Nilsson, K. W., Comasco, E., Åslund, C., Nordquist, N., Leppert, J., & Oreland, L. (2011). MAOA genotype, family relations and sexual abuse in relation to adolescent alcohol consumption. *Addict Biol, 16*, 347–355.

Nilsson, K. W., Sjöberg, R. L., Damberg, M., Leppert, J., Ohrvik, J., Alm, P. O., Lindström, L., & Oreland, L. (2006). Role of monoamine oxidase A genotype and psychosocial factors in male adolescent criminal activity. *Biological Psychiatry, 59*, 121–127.

Nilsson, K. W., Sjöberg, R.L., Wargelius, H.-L., Leppert, J., Lindström, L., & Oreland, L. (2007). The monoamine oxidase A (MAO-A) gene, family function and maltreatment as predictors of destructive behaviour during male adolescent alcohol consumption. *Addiction, 102*, 389–398.

Ongur, D., & Price, J.L. (2000). The organization of networks within the orbital and medial prefrontal cortex of rats, monkeys and humans. *Cereb Cortex, 10*, 206–219.

Parsian, A., Cloninger, C. R., Sinha, R., & Zhang, Z. H. (2003). Functional variation in promoter region of monoamine oxidase A and subtypes of alcoholism: haplotype analysis. *Am J Med Genet B Neuropsychiatr Genet, 117B*, 46–50.

Passamonti, L., Cerasa, A., Gioia, M. C., Magariello, A., Muglia, M., Quattrone, A., & Fera, F. (2008). Genetically dependent modulation of serotonergic inactivation in the human prefrontal cortex. *NeuroImage, 40*, 1264–1273.

Pezawas, L., Meyer-Lindenberg, A., Drabant, E. M., Verchinski, B. A., Munoz, K. E., Kolachana, B. S., Egan, M. F., Mattay, V. S., Hariri, A. R., & Weinberger, D. R. (2005). 5-HTTLPR polymorphism impacts human cingulate-amygdala interactions: a genetic susceptibility mechanism for depression. *Nat Neurosci, 8*, 828–834.

Passamonti, L., Fera, F., Magariello, A., Cerasa, A., Gioia, M.C., Muglia, M., Nicoletti, G., Gallo, O., Provinciali, L., and Quattrone, A. (2006). Monoamine oxidase-a genetic variations influence brain activity associated with inhibitory control: new insight into the neural correlates of impulsivity. *Bps 59*, 334–340.

Plomin, R., Haworth, C. M. A., & Davis, O. S. P. (2009). Common disorders are quantitative traits. *Nat Rev Genet, 10*, 872–878.

Popova, N. K., Skrinskaya, Y. A., Amstislavskaya, T. G., Vishnivetskaya, G. B., Seif, I., & de Meier, E. (2001). Behavioral characteristics of mice with genetic knockout of monoamine oxidase type A. *Neurosci Behav Physiol, 31*, 597–602.

Quirk, G. J., Likhtik, E., Pelletier, J. G., & Pare, D. (2003). Stimulation of medial prefrontal cortex decreases the responsiveness of central amygdala output neurons. *J Neurosci, 23*, 8800–8807.

Reif, A., Rösler, M., Freitag, C. M., Schneider, M., Eujen, A., Kissling, C., Wenzler, D., Jacob, C. P., Retz-Junginger, P., Thome, J., et al. (2007). Nature and nurture predispose to violent behavior: serotonergic genes and adverse childhood environment. *Neuropsychopharmacology, 32*, 2375–2383.

Reif, A., Weber, H., Domschke, K., Klauke, B., Baumann, C., Jacob, C. P., Ströhle, A., Gerlach, A. L., Alpers, G. W., Pauli, P., et al. (2012). Meta-analysis argues for a female-specific role of MAOA-uVNTR in panic disorder in four European populations. *Am J Med Genet B Neuropsychiatr Genet, 159B*, 786–793.

Reti, I. M., Xu, J. Z., Yanofski, J., McKibben, J., Uhart, M., Cheng, Y.-J., Zandi, P., Bienvenu, O. J., Samuels, J., Willour, V., et al. (2011). Monoamine oxidase A regulates antisocial personality in whites with no history of physical abuse. *Compr Psychiatry, 52*, 188–194.

Rosenkranz, J. A., & Grace, A. A. (1999). Modulation of basolateral amygdala neuronal firing and afferent drive by dopamine receptor activation in vivo. *J Neurosci, 19*, 11027–11039.

Sabol, S. Z., Hu, S., & Hamer, D. (1998). A functional polymorphism in the monoamine oxidase A gene promoter. *Hum Genet, 103*, 273–279.

Saito, T., Lachman, H. M., Diaz, L., Hallikainen, T., Kauhanen, J., Salonen, J. T., Ryynänen, O.-P., Karvonen, M. K., Syvälahti, E., Pohjalainen, T., et al. (2002). Analysis of monoamine oxidase A (MAOA) promoter polymorphism in Finnish male alcoholics. *Psychiatry Res, 109*, 113–119.

Scott, A. L., Bortolato, M., Chen, K., & Shih, J.C. (2008). Novel monoamine oxidase A knock out mice with human-like spontaneous mutation. *Neuroreport. 19*, 739–743.

Shih, J. C., Ridd, M. J., Chen, K., Meehan, W. P., Kung, M. P., Seif, I., & De Maeyer, E. (1999). Ketanserin and tetrabenazine abolish aggression in mice lacking monoamine oxidase A. *Brain Res, 835*, 104–112.

Sjöberg, R. L., Nilsson, K. W., Wargelius, H.-L., Leppert, J., Lindström, L., & Oreland, L. (2007). Adolescent girls and criminal activity: role of MAOA-LPR genotype and psychosocial factors. *Am J Med Genet B Neuropsychiatr Genet, 144B*, 159–164.

Skeem, J. L., & Monahan, J. (2011). Current directions in violence risk assessment. *Current Directions in Psychological Science, 20*, 38–42.

Sotres-Bayon, F., Cain, C. K., & LeDoux, J. E. (2006). Brain mechanisms of fear extinction: historical perspectives on the contribution of prefrontal cortex. *Biol Psychiatry, 60*, 329–336.

Sun, Y., Zhang, J., Yuan, Y., Yu, X., Shen, Y., & Xu, Q. (2012). Study of a possible role of the monoamine oxidase A (MAOA) gene in paranoid schizophrenia among a Chinese population. *Am J Med Genet B Neuropsychiatr Genet, 159B*, 104–111.

Syagailo, Y. V., Stöber, G., Grässle, M., Reimer, E., Knapp, M., Jungkunz, G., Okladnova, O., Meyer, J., & Lesch, K. P. (2001). Association analysis of the functional monoamine oxidase A gene promoter polymorphism in psychiatric disorders. *Am J Med Genet, 105*, 168–171.

Tochigi, M., Otowa, T., Hibino, H., Kato, C., Otani, T., Umekage, T., Utsumi, T., Kato, N., & Sasaki, T. (2006). Combined analysis of association between personality traits and three functional polymorphisms in the tyrosine hydroxylase, monoamine oxidase A, and catechol-O-methyltransferase genes. *Neurosci Res, 54*, 180–185.

Tuvblad, C., & Baker, L. A. (2011). Human aggression across the lifespan: genetic propensities and environmental moderators. *Adv Genet, 75*, 171–214.

Treadway, M. T., & Buckholtz, J. W. (2011). On the use and misuse of genomic and neuroimaging science in forensic psychiatry: current roles and future directions. *Child and Adolescent Psychiatry Clinics of North America, 20*, 533–546.

UK Home Office. (2007). *Understanding the prolific and other priority offender programme.* London: Home Office.

Vanyukov, M. M., Maher, B. S., Devlin, B., Kirillova, G.P., Kirisci, L., Yu, L.-M., & Ferrell, R. E. (2007). The MAOA promoter polymorphism, disruptive behavior disorders, and early onset substance use disorder: gene-environment interaction. *Psychiatr Genet, 17*, 323–332.

Varnäs, K., Halldin, C., & Hall, H. (2004). Autoradiographic distribution of serotonin transporters and receptor subtypes in human brain. *Hum Brain Mapp, 22*, 246–260.

Wargelius, H.-L., Malmberg, K., Larsson, J.-O., & Oreland, L. (2012). Associations of MAOA-VNTR or 5HTT-LPR alleles with attention-deficit hyperactivity disorder symptoms are moderated by platelet monoamine oxidase B activity. *Psychiatr Genet, 22*, 42–45.

Waters, H., Hyder, A., Rajkotia, Y., Basu, S., Rehwinkel, J. A., & Butchart, A. (2004). *The economic dimensions of interpersonal violence.* Geneva: Department of Injuries and Violence Prevention, World Health Organization.

Widom, C. S., & Brzustowicz, L. M. (2006). MAOA and the "cycle of violence:" childhood abuse and neglect, MAOA genotype, and risk for violent and antisocial behavior. *Bps, 60*, 684–689.

Williams, L. M., Gatt, J. M., Kuan, S. A., Dobson-Stone, C., Palmer, D. M., Paul, R. H., Song, L., Costa, P. T., Schofield, P. R., & Gordon, E. (2009). A polymorphism of the MAOA gene is associated with emotional brain markers and personality traits on an antisocial index. *Neuropsychopharmacology, 34*, 1797–1809.

Yu, Y. W.-Y., Yang, C.-W., Wu, H.-C., Tsai, S.-J., Hong, C.-J., Chen, M.-C., & Chen, T.-J. (2005). Association study of a functional MAOA-uVNTR gene polymorphism and personality traits in Chinese young females. *Neuropsychobiology, 52*, 118–121.

Zalsman, G., Huang, Y.-Y., Harkavy-Friedman, J. M., Oquendo, M. A., Ellis, S. P., & Mann, J. J. (2005). Relationship of MAO-A promoter (u-VNTR) and COMT (V158M) gene polymorphisms to CSF monoamine metabolites levels in a psychiatric sample of Caucasians: A preliminary report. *Am J Med Genet B Neuropsychiatr Genet, 132B*, 100–103.

Zhang, J., Chen, Y., Zhang, K., Yang, H., Sun, Y., Fang, Y., Shen, Y., & Xu, Q. (2010). A cis-phase interaction study of genetic variants within the MAOA gene in major depressive disorder. *Biol Psychiatry, 68*, 795–800.

9

Genetic Biomarker Research of Callous-Unemotional Traits in Children: Implications for the Law and Policymaking

ESSI VIDING AND EAMON McCRORY

CALLOUS-UNEMOTIONAL TRAITS AS A SUBGROUPING CRITERIA FOR CHILDREN WITH ANTISOCIAL BEHAVIOR

Antisocial behavior is one of the most common reasons for a childhood referral to mental health and educational services and represents a substantial public health cost (e.g., Romeo, Knapp, & Scott, 2006; Scott, Knapp, Henderson, & Maughan, 2001). We know that children with early-onset antisocial behavior are at risk of developing chronic life-course persistent antisocial problems, as well as several other psychiatric and physical health problems (Kim-Cohen et al., 2003; Odgers et al., 2007). It is also clear from decades of developmental psychopathology research that antisocial behavior symptoms that appear similar on the surface can be driven by different underlying vulnerabilities (Frick & Viding, 2009).

One subgrouping criterion that has received considerable attention is the presence of callous-unemotional (CU) traits. CU traits include lack of guilt and empathy, as well as shallow affect. Adults with a combination of CU traits and antisocial behavior are labelled psychopaths within the criminal justice system (Hare & Neumann, 2006). While no one would suggest that children are psychopaths, CU traits can be used to distinguish a subgroup of children who are capable of premeditated antisocial behavior and violence (AB/CU+) and who are at an elevated risk for developing psychopathy when they reach adulthood (Frick & Viding, 2009; Lynam et al., 2007). Longitudinal data show that children with AB/CU+ present with a more severe behavioral profile and more long-term problems than children who have AB but lower levels of CU (AB/CU−) (Fontaine, McCrory, Boivin, Moffitt, & Viding, 2011; Frick & Viding, 2009). Even in the absence of AB, CU traits can predict poorer long-term outcomes, including risk for developing delinquent behaviors (Frick, Cornell, Barry, Bodin, & Dane, 2003). Longitudinal data also show that CU traits add to the prediction of serious and persistent criminal behavior in boys (Pardini & Fite, 2010). Children with AB/CU+ are resistant to some forms of traditional interventions prescribed for childhood AB, such as time-out disciplinary strategies (Hawes & Dadds, 2005). Recent edition of the *Diagnostic and Statistical Manual of Mental Disorders* (American Psychiatry Association) has introduced a 'Limited Prosocial Emotions' specifier to the Conduct Disorder diagnoses that enables subtyping of children with Conduct Disorder based on their CU traits.

Cognitive experimental data suggest that children with AB/CU+ are poor at modulating their behavior in response to punishment in conditioning paradigms (Frick & Viding, 2009). In addition, they have difficulties in processing others' fearful and sad facial expressions, vocal tones, and body postures (see Blair & Viding, 2008; also Muñoz, 2009). Children with AB/CU+ may also have an impoverished personal experience of fear and guilt, which could in part explain why they have such difficulty processing others' distress (Jones, Happé, Gilbert, Burnett, & Viding, 2010; Marsh et al., 2011). Theoretical accounts of AB/CU+ propose that normal socialization is disrupted in these children because they do not form adequate associations between their transgressions and punishment outcome and because they do not find other people's distress aversive and consequently have difficulties in developing empathy (Blair & Viding, 2008). This affective profile is very different from that found for children with AB/CU-, who are often hypervigilant to threat emotions and do not show the pattern of difficulties seen in AB/CU+ (Frick & Viding, 2009). Figure 9.1 illustrates schematically how these subgroups of children with AB may be characterized by specific sets of neurocognitive, genetic, and environmental features that generate different developmental patterns of risk. Two trajectories, I and II, are shown. These trajectories present with similar behavioral characteristics but have only partly shared risk factors. For example, pathway I (comparable to AB/CU−) is potentiated by a greater number of specific environmental risk factors, whereas for pathway II (comparable to AB/CU+) increased risk emerges from the interaction between greater genetic vulnerability and a more limited exposure to environmental risk. Different factors (illustrated by the shaded circles) are likely to play different roles for each trajectory. Underlying differences for each trajectory may have implications for intervention as different genetic, neurocognitive, and environmental factors are likely to interact with therapeutic mechanisms that drive change.

Although there is now a substantial body of behavioral and cognitive experimental studies attesting to the distinct nature of AB/CU+, the biomarker research in this group is still in its infancy. The purpose of this chapter is to

CHILD

PATHWAY A   PATHWAY B

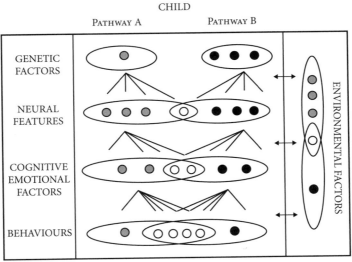

Figure 9.1 This schematic describes shows two hypothetical pathways (Pathway A: gray ellipses; Pathway B: black ellipses) that illustrate how different subgroups of children with antisocial behavior may present with different risk factors at different levels of explanation. Thus, while the example pathways shown may have a high level of similarity in terms of shared features at the behavioral level, this in fact conceals underlying differences at the genetic, neurocognitive, and environmental levels. (Colored circles: pathway-specific risk factors; open circles: shared risk factors.)

review genetic findings relevant for CU and AB/CU+. We begin by providing a short overview of the twin method and then consider four important points regarding the existing quantitative genetic data:

1. CU traits show heritable and mainly nonshared environmental influences in childhood/adolescence.
2. The same genetic and environmental influences are important in accounting for individual differences in CU traits for both males and females (although the magnitude of their influence may vary between sexes).
3. At least for males, genetic factors account for stability of CU traits across development.
4. Antisocial behavior in the presence of CU traits is strongly heritable.

The quantitative genetic work also provides an informative background to molecular genetic studies that may eventually provide us with concrete genetic "biomarkers." We then provide a brief overview of the few recent molecular genetic studies that have attempted to pinpoint specific genes involved in the etiology of CU traits and AB/CU+ in children (e.g., Fowler et al., 2009; Sadeh et al., 2010; Viding et al., 2010). These preliminary data suggest that neuro-developmental genes, as well as genes affecting emotional reactivity, may be involved in AB/CU+. Finally, we will consider potential implications of genetic biomarkers of AB/CU+ for law and policy. We think it is critical to establish a conceptual framework to facilitate responsible interpretation and application of biomarker research while the field is still emerging.

TWIN METHOD

The twin method is a natural experiment that relies on the different levels of genetic relatedness between identical and fraternal twin pairs to estimate the contribution of genetic and environmental factors to individual differences, or extreme scores in a phenotype of interest. Phenotypes include any behavior or characteristic that is measured separately for each twin, such as score on an antisocial behavior checklist. Statistical model-fitting techniques and regression analysis methods incorporating genetic relatedness parameters are used to investigate the etiology of the phenotype of choice. These techniques will not be covered in detail in this article, but there are textbooks on the topic available for the interested reader (Plomin, DeFries, McClearn, & McGuffin, 2008). The basic premise of the twin method is this: If identical twins, who share 100 percent of their genetic material, appear more similar on a trait than fraternal twins, who share on average 50 percent of their genetic material (like any siblings), then we infer that there are genetic influences on a trait. Identical twins' genetic similarity is twice that of fraternal twins'. If nothing apart from genes influences behavior, then we would expect the identical twins to be twice as similar with respect to the phenotypic measure as fraternal twins. Shared environmental influences—environmental influences that make twins similar to each other—are inferred if fraternal twin similarity is more than half of the identical twin similarity (as expected from sharing 50 percent, as opposed to 100 percent, of their genes). Finally, if identical twins are not 100 percent similar on a trait (as would be expected if only genes influenced a trait), nonshared environmental influences are inferred—in other words environmental influences that make twins different from each other. The nonshared environmental estimate also includes measurement error.

QUANTITATIVE GENETIC FINDINGS

CU traits show heritable and nonshared environmental influences in childhood/adolescence

A number of twin studies have examined the etiology of CU traits (or equivalent constructs) in children/youth.[1] These studies come from the United States,

Sweden, and the United Kingdom. The samples used in these studies vary in size from moderate (398 twin pairs) to large (3,687 twin pairs), represent different age ranges (7 to 24 years old), and have used a range of instruments that have relied on ratings by both self and others (parent or teacher). All studies, except one (Taylor, Loney, Bobadilla, Iacono, & McGue, 2003), include information from both sexes with a similar male/female composition (46 to 49 percent males). In this section we concentrate on giving an overview of univariate data documenting the relative importance of heritable and environmental influences on CU traits in children and youth. These data also give the first indication of the "modus operandi" of environmental influences—that is, whether environmental influences act to increase (shared) or decrease (nonshared) twin similarity.

Taylor et al. (2003) used items from a self-report questionnaire, the Minnesota Temperament Inventory (Loney, Taylor, Butler, & Iacono, 2002), to assess the CU (e.g., "I don't experience very deep emotions"). This self-report questionnaire was distributed to a sample of 398 adolescent male twin pairs (16 to 18 years old) from the Minnesota Twin Family Study (MTFS sample). In this study, genetic effects accounted for around 40 percent of the variation in CU traits. Nonshared environmental effects explained all of the remaining variance, whereas the influences of shared environment seemed to be of no importance (Taylor el al., 2003).

Blonigen, Hicks, Krueger, Patrick, and Iacono (2005, 2006) used factor scores on the primary scales of the self-report Multidimensional Personality Questionnaire (MPQ) to index fearless-dominance (a construct with considerable overlap with CU traits; from here onwards CU traits for consistency). In their first report on this sample of adolescents Blonigen et al. examined data from 626 17-year-old male and female twin pairs from the MTFS sample. Genetic influences accounted for 45 percent of the variance in the CU traits. The remainder of the variance in CU traits was accounted for by nonshared environmental influences. Very similar findings were reported for the same sample at age 24. Genetic influences accounted for 42 percent of the variance in the CU traits, and the remainder of the variance was accounted for by nonshared environmental influences.

Viding et al. studied the heritability of teacher-rated CU in the Twins Early Development Study (TEDS) sample of over 3,500 7-year-old twin pairs (both boys and girls) (Viding, Blair, Moffitt, & Plomin, 2005; Viding, Frick, & Plomin, 2007). The CU scale used in the TEDS analyses consisted of seven items: three Antisocial Process Screening Device items (Frick & Hare, 2001) and four items from the Strengths and Difficulties Questionnaire (SDQ; Goodman, 1997). Individual differences in CU were moderately heritable (48 (girls) to 67 (boys) percent of the variability in CU scores was due to genetic influences) (Viding et al., 2007). The group difference in CU between those scoring at the top 10 percent of the TEDS sample and the rest of the TEDS children was also strongly heritable ($h_g^2 = 0.67$). The group heritability estimates were very similar regardless of whether the CU occurred with ($h_g^2 = 0.80$) or without ($h_g^2 = 0.68$) elevated levels of conduct problems (Larsson, Viding, & Plomin, 2008). Fontaine, Rijsdijk, McCrory, and Viding (2010) conducted longitudinal trajectory analyses on the TEDS twins and demonstrated four trajectories related to development of CU between ages 7 and 12: low, decreasing, increasing, and high. There were no sex differences in the heritability estimates for those on the low trajectory ($h^2 = 0.68$). However, while CU trajectory membership was heritable for boys for high, increasing, and decreasing trajectories ($h^2 = 0.78$, 0.58, and 0.61 respectively), the heritability estimates for girls were significant only for the decreasing trajectory ($h^2 = 0.54$). Nonshared environmental influences made a significant contribution to CU at age 7 both across the continuum as well as at the extremes and were also a significant influence on longitudinal trajectory membership from ages 7 to 12 (Fontaine et al., 2010; Larsson et al., 2008; Viding et al., 2007). Shared environmental influences were detected in only few cases (Fontaine et al., 2010; Viding et al., 2007), but our longitudinal data indicate that such influences may be particularly important for a handful of girls who are on the high or increasing CU trajectory. In other words, elevated levels of CU traits may have a different origin for girls than boys. There may be factors such as sexual abuse that could affect development of CU in girls (Odgers et al., 2007), but specific investigations with measured environmental factors within twin designs are required to explore this further. Minimal contribution of shared environmental influences does not mean that family or neighborhood environments are not relevant for development of CU or AB/CU+ for boys. Rather, for boys the environmental risk factors are likely to promote differences between members of the same family (nonshared environment in the twin models).

Larsson, Andershed, and Lichtenstein (2006) used a sample of 1,090 male and female twin pairs, aged 16, from the Twin Study of Child and Adolescent Development (TCHAD; Lichtenstein, Tuvblad, Larsson, & Carlstrom, 2007) to examine the heritability of CU, as measured by the Youth Psychopathic Traits Inventory (YPI; Andershed, Kerr, Stattin, & Levander, 2002). They found that genetic effects accounted for 43 percent of the variation in the CU, with the remainder accounted for by nonshared environment.

Bezdjian, Raine, Baker, and Lynam (2011) examined a sample of 1,219 twins and triplets aged 9 and 10 years and found that heritability for CU, as measured by the Child Psychopathy Scale (Lynam, 1997, 2002) was moderate (0.49 for girls and 0.64 for boys). Nonshared environmental influences were also detected, but shared environmental influences were not.

CU traits in children/adolescents show moderate to strong genetic influence and moderate nonshared environmental influence. Shared environmental influences are not systematically found for CU traits but may be important for some girls exhibiting these traits. Generally this suggests that the environmental factors that make members of the twin pair similar to each other do not, as a rule, account for individual differences in CU traits in children/adolescents. These results are in line with previous adult data on psychopathic personality traits (Blonigen, Carlson, Krueger, & Patrick, 2003) as well as data on other personality dimensions (Bouchard & Loehlin, 2001). Importantly, these results do not preclude that risk factors, such as parental characteristics, exert an influence on CU traits. Such risk factors may act in a child-specific manner (nonshared environmental risk factors)—for example, an aspect of parenting experienced by one twin but not the other that serves to promote the development of CU.

In addition to reporting univariate heritablities for CU traits, some of the studies reviewed above have also addressed questions about etiology of sex differences in CU traits, etiology of stability of CU traits, as well as heritability of antisocial behavior with/without CU traits. The subsequent sections will review findings that have shed light on these questions.

Same genetic and environmental influences are important in accounting for individual differences in CU traits for both males and females

Four studies (Bezdjian et al., 2011; Fontaine et al., 2010; Larsson et al 2006; Viding et al., 2007) have incorporated dizygotic opposite-sex twin pairs in their analyses and formally explored the potential role of qualitative sex differences (i.e., different genes and environments influencing phenotypic variation for males and females) in the etiology of psychopathy. None of these studies reported qualitative sex differences in the genetic and environmental influences on psychopathic traits. Few studies have also assessed the impact of quantitative sex differences (i.e., the same genetic and environmental influences affecting males and females to a different degree). Two studies found little evidence of quantitative sex differences (Blonigen et al., 2006; Larsson et al., 2006), but there is also some support for a higher heritability of CU for males (Bezdjian et al., 2011; Fontaine et al., 2010; Viding et al., 2007). For instance, using data from 9,462 youths from TEDS, Fontaine et al. (2010) found that high heritability (nearly 80 percent) was observed for boys on a stable high CU trajectory (between 7 and 12 years old). Stable and high levels of CU in girls, however, appeared to be almost entirely driven by environmental influences that make twins similar to each other in their levels of CU. As we have already highlighted, replication of this finding is needed given the small number of children

(3.4 percent of the sample) who followed the stable and high CU trajectory, and the even smaller proportion of this already small group who were females (19.2 percent).

The findings so far indicate that although boys and girls show mean differences in CU trait scores at the phenotypic level, the same genetic and environmental influences are important for individual differences in CU traits for both sexes. Our data and that of others suggest that although the same genetic influences are important for both sexes, these may be more prominent for accounting for individual differences in CU traits in boys than in girls. Once we know more about the specific genetic and environmental influences and how they operate for boys and girls, there may be policy implications with regard to more targeted prevention and treatment provision for at-risk boys and girls.

Genetic factors account for stability of CU traits across development

A few twin studies to date have explored the genetic and environmental contributions to the stability of CU traits in childhood and adolescence. Blonigen et al. (2006) used their scale derived from the MPQ to examine the genetic and environmental contribution to stability of CU traits from adolescence to early adulthood. The authors applied model-fitting analyses on MPQ information from two timepoints 7 years apart, when the twins were 17 and 24 years old. Their results indicate that the heritability of CU traits remained consistent across time. Further, the decomposition of the covariance across time revealed that 58 percent of the stability of CU traits was due to genetic influences. This result indicates that the relatively high stability in CU traits is substantially influenced by genetic factors.

Using the TEDS sample, Fontaine et al. (2010) found that stable high trajectory of CU in childhood (between 7 and 12 years) was highly heritable in boys ($h^2 = 0.78$) but not in girls, where high and stable levels of CU were explained by shared environmental influences ($c^2 = 0.75$). This finding suggests that at least in childhood/early adolescence, genetic influences may drive the stability of CU traits for boys in particular.

Forsman, Lichtenstein, Andershed, and Larsson (2008) measured CU traits (as well as impulsivity and grandiosity) with the YPI and examined genetic and environmental contribution to the stability of these traits between ages 16 and 19 in the TCHAD sample. They found that CU traits were stable between middle and late adolescence. Most of the stability of CU traits was explained by genetic factors that were shared with the broader psychopathy construct. There was also some evidence of genetic effects that were unique to the CU dimension of psychopathic personality, and these unique genetic effects were also stable between middle and late adolescence.

In sum, longitudinal twin studies have found that the stability in CU traits in childhood (in males in particular) and from adolescence to early adulthood is substantially influenced by genetic factors. Nothing is known about how genetic and environmental factors contribute to psychopathic traits during the transition from childhood to adolescence. It would therefore be interesting to explore how genetic and environmental factors influence different developmental trajectories for antisocial children with and without CU. Another important research goal for future longitudinal twin studies of psychopathic personality traits is to test developmental hypothesis about different patterns of gene–environment correlations and gene–environment interaction.

Heritability of antisocial behavior with and without CU traits

Our group has used twin data to inform the utility of CU traits in subtyping individuals with antisocial behavior. Viding et al. (2005) used information from the TEDS sample to investigate whether the etiology of teacher-rated antisocial behavior differs as a function of teacher-rated CU at age 7. Antisocial behavior was assessed using the Strengths and Difficulties Questionnaire 5-item conduct problem scale. The authors separated children with elevated levels of antisocial behavior (in the top 10 percent for the TEDS sample) into two groups based on their CU score (in the top 10 percent or not). Antisocial behavior in children with CU was under strong genetic influence ($h_g^2 = 0.81$) and no influence of shared environment. In contrast, antisocial behavior in children without elevated levels of CU showed moderate genetic influence ($h_g^2 = 0.30$) and substantial environmental influence ($c_g^2 = 0.34$, $e_g^2 = 0.26$). Viding, Jones, Frick, Moffitt, and Plomin (2008) replicated the finding of different heritability estimates for the CU and non-CU groups using the 9-year teacher data from the TEDS study. Their results indicate that the heritability differences hold even after hyperactivity scores of the children are controlled for, suggesting that the result is not driven by any differences in hyperactivity between the two groups. Taken together, these findings clearly suggest that while the CU subtype is genetically vulnerable to antisocial behavior, children with the non-CU subtype manifest a more strongly environmental etiology to their antisocial behavior.

In sum, children with the combination of antisocial behavior and CU traits appear more genetically vulnerable to antisocial behavior than their non-CU counterparts. This finding does not mean that these children are genetically destined to become antisocial, but just as some of us are more genetically vulnerable to hypertension or heart disease (given the appropriate environmental risk factors), it may be that there is a group of children who has an inborn vulnerability to antisocial outcomes, given sufficiently unfortunate environmental circumstances. These findings need to be replicated by other groups.

MOLECULAR GENETIC STUDIES

Despite the substantial literature demonstrating heritable components of CU traits, we know of only three published molecular genetic studies of child/adolescent CU traits. The first of these was carried out on a relatively small sample of adolescents with attention-deficit/hyperactivity disorder and reported associations between the val allele of the cathecol-o-methyl-transferase (COMT) gene, the low-activity allele of the monoamine oxidase A gene (MAOA-L), the short allele of the serotonin transporter gene (5HTTLPRs), and "emotional dysfunction" scores of psychopathy (Fowler et al., 2009). The latter two of these associations were unexpected based on imaging genetic data suggesting that MAOA-L and 5HTTLPRs confer opposite patterns of amygdala reactivity (heightened; e.g., Meyer-Lindenberg et al., 2006; Munafò, Brown, & Hariri, 2008) to that typically seen in adults with psychopathy and children with AB/CU+ (dampened; e.g., Birbaumer et al., 2005; Jones, Laurens, Herba, Barker, & Viding, 2009; Kiehl et al., 2001; Marsh et al., 2008). A more recent study reported that the long allele of the 5HTTLPR (i.e., the allele conferring low amygdala reactivity) was associated with CU traits in those adolescents from lower socioeconomic backgrounds (Sadeh et al., 2010). Finally, new technologies, such as DNA pooling,[2] are enabling genome-wide association studies that search for novel single nucleotide polymorphisms (SNPs) that may be associated with the combination of antisocial behavior and CU traits. We recently conducted such a study and our preliminary data are suggestive of several SNPs, some of them near neurodevelopmental genes, associated with AB/CU+ (Viding et al., 2010). If these findings are replicated, such SNPs could be assessed in relation to psychopathy/antisocial behavior in several existing studies that span beyond our own collaborations. They could also be incorporated into imaging genetic investigations of psychopathy. The latter avenue is particularly interesting, as we have recently used twin design and structural brain scans to document that aberrant structural brain development in AB/CU+ reflects genetic rather than environmental vulnerability to this behavioral outcome (Rijsdijk, Viding, et al., 2010).

Research on molecular genetics of CU traits is thus still very much in its infancy. Potentially useful research directions can, however, be gleaned from molecular genetic research on antisocial behavior. Genes regulating serotonergic neurotransmission, in particular MAOA, have been highlighted in the search for a genetic predisposition to antisocial behavior (Lesch, 2003). The MAOA gene contains a well-characterized functional polymorphism consisting of a variable number of tandem repeats in the promoter region, with high-activity (MAOA-H) and low-activity (MAOA-L) allelic variants. The MAOA-H variant is associated with a lower concentration of intracellular serotonin, whereas the MAOA-L variant is associated with a higher concentration of intracellular serotonin. Recent research suggests that genetic vulnerability to antisocial behavior conferred by the MAOA-L may only become evident in the presence of an environmental trigger, such as maltreatment (e.g., Caspi et al., 2002; Kim-Cohen et al., 2006). Despite the demonstration of genetic influences on individual differences in antisocial behavior, it is important to note that no genes *for* antisocial behavior exist. Instead, genes code for proteins that influence characteristics such as neurocognitive vulnerabilities that may in turn increase risk for antisocial behavior. Thus, although genetic risk alone may be of little consequence for behavior in favorable conditions, the genetic vulnerability may still manifest at the level of brain/cognition.

Imaging genetics studies that we have already alluded to above attest to genotype differences being associated with variation in brain structure and function in nonclinical samples (Meyer-Lindenberg & Weinberger, 2006). We can think of this as the neural fingerprint that has the potential to translate into disordered behavior in the presence of unfortunate environmental triggers. Meyer-Lindenberg et al. (2006) provided the first demonstration of the MAOA-L genotype being associated with a pattern of neural hypersensitivity to emotional stimuli. Specifically, they reported increased amygdala activity coupled with lesser activity in the frontal regulatory regions in MAOA-L than in MAOA-H carriers. Similar findings have been reported in subsequent studies (reviewed in Buckholtz & Meyer-Lindenberg, 2008). Buckholtz and Meyer-Lindenberg speculated that the brain imaging findings of poor emotion regulation in MAOA-L carriers relate to threat-reactive and impulsive rather than psychopathic antisocial behavior. They based this speculation on the findings of individuals with psychopathy displaying underreactivity of the brain's emotional circuit, particularly the amygdala (Birbaumer et al., 2005; Kiehl et al., 2001).

It is interesting to note that some studies have reported increased vulnerability to antisocial behavior in the presence of the MAOA-H allele (e.g., Manuck et al., 1999). These may reflect false-positive findings, but it is also possible that the amygdala's hyporeactivity as opposed to hyperreactivity in individuals with psychopathy is influenced by the MAOA-H, rather than the MAOA-L genotype. This suggestion remains highly speculative, and as for any behavior, the genetic influences will not be limited to a single candidate gene. However, it is entirely possible that different alleles of the same gene may predispose to different types of antisocial behavior, with one type related to emotional overreactivity to perceived threat and the other to emotional underreactivity to someone's distress (see Glenn, 2010, for a review of this in relation to 5-HTTLPR and Viding & Jones, 2008, for a more general proposal of differential genetic vulnerability). Sadeh et al.'s (2010) study is in line with this possibility, as it demonstrated not only that the long allele of the 5-HTTLPR predisposed individuals to CU traits in low socioeconomic environments, but also that the short allele of the same gene predisposed individuals to impulsive antisocial behavior. Preliminary genome-wide association and twin neuroimaging data from Viding and colleagues (Rijsdijk et al., 2010; Viding et al., 2010) suggest that neurodevelopmental genes may be important in the pathophysiology of AB/CU+ and that we should expect to find genes with small effect size that incrementally increase risk for CU and/or AB/CU+. We also cannot rule out that a subset of individuals with CU and/or AB/CU+ may have rare copy number variants that have a large risk effect. No studies have been conducted examining this possibility.

There are no immediate policy implications that can be drawn from the current data. We are not able to reliably infer from genes (or genetic effects on brain structure/function) to individual behavior. However, as we come to know more about the exact genes that are involved in increasing risk for CU and or AB/CU+ and the mechanisms by which they operate at the neural level, it may be possible to better infer the probability of future behavior and more importantly the type of individualized provision that could help reduce risk traits and behaviors. Such inference is likely to be stronger once we know about more than one genetic risk marker and once we also have information about likely levels of environmental risk.

OVERVIEW

Research suggests that CU traits are moderately to strongly heritable (Viding, Fontaine, & Larsson, in press). This applies particularly for boys with elevated and persistent levels of CU traits (Fontaine et al., 2010). Antisocial behavior is strongly heritable in children with AB/CU+, while antisocial behavior in AB/CU− children shows stronger environmental influence (Viding et al., 2005, 2008). Our and others' recent data suggest that the genetic vulnerability to CU and AB/CU+ is conferred by multiple genes of small effect size probabilistically increasing the risk for poor behavioral outcome (e.g., Sadeh et al., 2010; Viding et al., 2010). Based on data from candidate gene and imaging genetic studies, it is possible to speculate that the risk genes for AB/CU+ may confer low reactivity to emotional stimuli (Glenn, 2010; Sadeh et al., 2010; Viding & Jones, 2008). Neurodevelopmental genes may also be important (Viding et al., 2010) and may partly explain the differences in brain structure seen between typically developing and AB/CU+ adolescents (Rijsdijk et al., 2010). The molecular genetic research into CU traits, as well as AB/CU+ and AB/CU- subgroups, is in its infancy and will doubtless advance greatly in the coming decade, including novel epigenetic approaches that may help us uncover mechanisms of gene–environment interaction. It is important to note that the genetic variants implicated in CU and AB/CU+ are likely to include several common polymorphisms that confer advantages, as well as disadvantages, depending on the environmental context.

Because it is such early days for genetic research on CU traits and AB/CU+, several questions remain outstanding. What genes are involved in vulnerability to AB/CU+? In the coming years we are likely discover that some of the polymorphisms we thought were important may represent a false-positive finding and others that may at first sight appear less intuitive could represent true genetic risk. It is also of interest to study genetic risk longitudinally. Are genetic biomarkers predictive of long-term outcome and treatment response? These are continuing challenges to biomarker research. Because our diagnostics systems are based on behavioral criteria, we can comfortably predict that there will not be a single basis to any given disorder (genetic or otherwise). We currently have a fairly rudimentary understanding of genes–brain and brain–mind relationships, as well as environmental and developmental contingencies. All of these considerations represent a challenge to basic science research and give a glimpse of the even greater challenges for law and policymaking that considers biomarker information.

GENETIC RESEARCH TO CU TRAITS: IMPLICATIONS FOR THE LAW AND POLICYMAKING

All legal and policymaking changes must proceed with extensive ethical consultation and should consider several issues, including discrimination, stigma, and labeling (see Singh & Rose, 2009). The research base into genetic influences on child/adolescent CU traits is still sparse and requires considerable replication and extension before any legal or policy recommendations can be reliably based on these findings.

The current studies do suggest a degree of genetic vulnerability to CU traits, as well as etiological differences between children with/without CU-type antisocial behavior. These findings tie in with much of the neurocognitive, behavioral, and treatment research on CU traits. The existing, nongenetic research base strongly suggests that children/adolescents with CU traits form a specific, particularly high-risk group of youngsters (Frick & Viding, 2009). Prevention, therefore, remains an important policymaking goal. In this context it is important to note three things. First, *genetic vulnerability does not denote immutability.* Levels of CU traits are malleable throughout childhood (Fontaine et al., 2011), and we know from recent studies that CU traits can change in response to interventions that focus on rewarding good behavior (e.g., Hawes & Dadds, 2007). The current findings do suggest, however, that understanding the nature of genetic vulnerability and how it may differ between individuals may provide important understanding for tailoring interventions to individual needs. Second, *behavioral genetic designs suggest that environment drives change.* Genetic risk for developing CU traits or AB/CU+ could be buffered by prevention and treatment, which could be considered as positive gene–environment interaction. For example, recent research has suggested that warm parenting reduces the risk of conduct problems in children with high levels of CU traits (Pasalich, Dadds, Hawes, & Brennan, 2011), and treatments promoting positive child–parent interactions might be helpful. Future research is needed to better inform what environmental factors may exert maximal influence on the change of CU traits in children. In most cases these are likely to be behavioral and systemic interventions that are specifically tailored to these children's profile of neurocognitive strengths (e.g., spared or increased neural reactivity to rewards) and weaknesses (e.g., deficits in empathic arousal). These may also, in the future, include pharmacological interventions that could be tailored to fit particular genotype risks. We consider the latter type of intervention to be less promising in the immediate term. Third, *gene therapy is not an appropriate form of intervention.* From time to time, we hear people express concerns with regard to gene therapy. Gene therapy refers to the insertion, alteration, or removal of genes within an individual's cells to treat disease. We do not consider such an approach to be a viable option for the treatment of complex, polygenic traits. This is particularly obvious given that "risk" genes are usually common polymorphisms implicated in a range of normative developmental processes. In addition, these genes typically only confer a small increase in the probability of problem behavior.

The law and policymaking communities have expressed worries about scientific findings on "risk genes" in two ways. Some are concerned that such findings can be used to argue for more lenient sentences for the carriers of "risk genes. Others worry that they may result in prosecutors demanding harsher and longer ("preventive") sentences for the carriers of "risk genes." Although the current data suggest that there is genetic vulnerability for CU traits, we need to remember that there are no *genes* for CU traits. Instead we know that genes act in a probabilistic manner and in concert with environmental factors to make some individuals more vulnerable for developing CU traits (see, e.g., Moffitt, 2005; Viding, Larsson, & Jones, 2008). Policymakers may be interested in probabilities, but the court of law, which also uses probabilities, is not probabilistic in the same way that science is; more generally, it is recognized that science and law have different goals (Eastman & Campbell, 2006; Mobbs, Lau, Jones, & Frith, 2007). The legal system considers the probability of a given individual being guilty as well as likelihood that he or she might reoffend. While they may use population or group data to inform this judgment, this is very different from behavioral genetic research. Such research focuses on the causes of individual differences and is not concerned with determining the risk for a single individual. We may find genes that show reliable and consistent association with individual differences in CU traits and identify the specific environmental risk factors that serve to increase the likelihood that genetic risk is expressed. However, whether such information should play a role in sentencing decisions would depend on carefully conducted research that demonstrates that such information can inform prediction over and above that gained by relying on other well-established risk factors, such as prior history.

SUMMARY

Genetic research into CU traits is off to a very promising start, with several research groups in different countries publishing in the area. Overall, CU traits appear to be moderately to strongly heritable and show little shared environmental influence. The same genetic and environmental influences appear important in accounting for individual differences in CU traits for both males and females, with the possible exception of girls with high levels of CU traits, who appear to show a different etiology to CU (predominantly influenced by shared environmental factors). Genetic factors are important in explaining the stability of CU traits across development, perhaps particularly for boys. Much more work using genetically informative study designs is required. First of all, the quantitative genetic research findings need more replications. Secondly, the molecular genetic research base on CU and AB/CU+ is currently very small, and we predict this will be an area of substantial future research activity. New avenues, such as imaging genetic studies, should also be engaged in. The current behavioral genetic findings are not "ready for the courtroom" or for policy initiatives, but neither are similar findings on most other phenotypes. Given the probabilistic nature by which most genetic risk on behavior operates, it is questionable whether genotype information can be reasonably considered as a mitigating or extenuating factor on sentencing decisions. However, knowing more about specific mechanistic pathways from genetic vulnerability to behavioral outcome (both maladaptive and resilient) has scope to inform interventions and as such may come to inform policy in the future.

ACKNOWLEDGMENTS

During the writing of this chapter E.V. was supported by a research grant from the ESRC (RES-062-23-2202) and E.McC. was supported by a research grant from the ESRC (RES-061-25-0189). We thank Patricia Lockwood for her help in preparing this chapter.

NOTES

1. We include in this section studies that have used measures comparable to CU and report straightforward univariate heritability estimate for CU somewhere in the paper. We exclude studies that have assessed heritability of "composite" psychopathic traits that include items of impulsivity and narcissism in addition to CU. If multiple papers from the same dataset have reported the same univariate heritability estimate in different contexts, we refer to the paper where the estimate first appeared.
2. DNA pooling refers to a genetic screening method that combines DNA from many individuals in a single molecular genetic analysis to generate a representation of allele frequencies. A DNA pool can thus be generated for all cases and all controls and allele frequencies can be compared between these pools.

REFERENCES

Andershed, H., Kerr, M., Stattin, H., & Levander, S. (2002). Psychopathic traits in non-referred youths: Initial test of a new assessment tool. In E. Blaauw & L. Sheridan (Eds.), *Psychopaths: Current international perspectives* (pp. 131–158). The Hague: Elsevier.

Bezdjian, S., Raine, A., Baker, L., & Lynam, D. (2011). Psychopathic personality in children: genetic and environmental contributions. *Psychological Medicine, 1*(3), 1–12.

Birbaumer, N., Veit, R., Lotze, M., Erb, M., Hermann, C., Grodd, W., et al. (2005). Deficient fear conditioning in psychopathy: a functional magnetic resonance imaging study. *Archives of General Psychiatry, 62*(7), 799–805.

Blair, R. J. R., & Viding, E. (2008). Psychopathy. In Rutter, M., Bishop, D., Pine, D., Scott, S., Stevenson, J., Taylor, E., & Thapar, A. (Eds.), *Rutter's child and adolescent psychiatry* (5th ed., pp. 852–863). John Wiley and Son.

Blonigen, D. M., Carlson, S. R., Krueger, R. F., & Patrick, C. J. (2003). A twin study of self-reported psychopathic personality traits. *Personality and Individual Differences, 35*(1), 179–197.

Blonigen, D. M., Hicks, B. M., Krueger, R. F., Patrick, C. J., & Iacono, W. G. (2005). Psychopathic personality traits: heritability and genetic overlap with internalizing and externalizing psychopathology. *Psychological Medicine, 35*(5), 637–648.

Blonigen, D. M., Hicks, B. M., Krueger, R. F., Patrick, C. J., & Iacono, W. G. (2006). Continuity and change in psychopathic traits as measured via normal-range personality: a longitudinal-biometric study. *Journal of Abnormal Psychology, 115*(1), 85–95.

Bouchard, T. J., & Loehlin, J. C. (2001). Genes, evolution, and personality. *Behavior Genetics, 31*(3), 243–273.

Buckholtz, J. W., & Meyer-Lindenberg, A. (2008). MAOA and the neurogenetic architecture of human aggression. *Trends in Neurosciences, 31*(3), 120–129.

Caspi, A., McClay, J., Moffitt, T., Mill, J., Martin, J., Craig, I. W., et al. (2002). Role of genotype in the cycle of violence in maltreated children. *Science, 297*(5582), 851–854.

Eastman, N., & Campbell, C. (2006). Neuroscience and legal determination of criminal responsibility. *Nature Reviews Neuroscience, 7*(4), 311–318.

Fontaine, N. M. G., Rijsdijk, F. V., McCrory, E. J. P., & Viding, E. (2010). Etiology of different developmental trajectories of callous-unemotional traits. *Journal of the*

American Academy of Child and Adolescent Psychiatry, 49(7), 656–664.

Fontaine, N. M. G., McCrory, E. J. P., Boivin, M., Moffitt, T. E., & Viding, E. (2011). Predictors and outcomes of joint trajectories of callous-unemotional traits and conduct problems in childhood. *Journal of Abnormal Psychology, 120*(3), 730–742.

Forsman, M., Lichtenstein P., Andershed H., & Larsson H. (2008). Genetic effects explain the stability of psychopathic personality from mid-to late adolescence. *Journal of Abnormal Psychology, 117*(3), 606–617.

Fowler, T., Langley, K., Rice, F., van den Bree, M., Ross, K., Wilkinson, L. S., Owen, M. J., O'Donovan, M. C., & Thapar, A. (2009). Psychopathy trait scores in adolescents with childhood ADHD: The contribution of genotypes affecting MAOA, 5HTT and COMT activity. *Psychiatric Genetics, 19*(6), 312–319.

Frick, P. J., & Hare, R. D. (2001). *Antisocial Process Screening Device.* Toronto: Multi Health Systems.

Frick P. J., Cornell, A. H., Barry, C. T., Bodin, S. D., & Dane, H. E. (2003). Callous-unemotional traits and conduct problems in the prediction of conduct problem severity, aggression, and self-report of delinquency. *Journal of Abnormal Child Psychology, 31*(4), 457–470.

Frick, P. J., & Viding, E. (2009). Antisocial behavior from a developmental psychopathology perspective. *Development and Psychopathology, 21*(4), 1111–1131.

Glenn, A. L. (2010). The other allele: Exploring the long allele of the serotonin transporter gene as a potential risk factor for psychopathy: A review of the parallels in findings. *Neuroscience and Biobehavioral Reviews, 35*(3), 612–620.

Goodman, R. (1997). The Strengths and Difficulties Questionnaire: A research note. *Journal of Child Psychology & Psychiatry, 38*(5), 581–586.

Hare, R. D., & Neumann, C. N. (2006). The PCL-R Assessment of Psychopathy: development, structural properties, and new directions. In C. Patrick (Ed.), *Handbook of Psychopathy* (pp. 58–88). New York: Guilford.

Hawes, D. J., & Dadds, M. R. (2005). The treatment of conduct problems in children with callous-unemotional traits. *Journal of Consulting & Clinical Psychology, 73*(4), 737–741.

Hawes, D. J., & Dadds, M. R. (2007). Stability and malleability of callous-unemotional traits during treatment for childhood conduct problems. *Journal of Clinical Child and Adolescent Psychology, 36*, 347–355.

Jones, A. P., Laurens, K. R., Herba, C. M., Barker, G. J., & Viding, E. (2009). Amygdala hypoactivity to fearful faces in boys with conduct problems and callous-unemotional traits. *American Journal of Psychiatry, 166*(1), 95–102.

Jones, A. P., Happé, F. G. E., Gilbert, F., Burnett, S., & Viding, E. (2010). Feeling, caring, knowing: different types of empathy deficit in boys with psychopathic tendencies and autism spectrum disorder. *Journal of Child Psychology and Psychiatry, 51*(11), 1188–1197.

Kiehl, K. A., Smith, A. M., Hare, R. D., Mendrek, A., Forster, B. B., Brink, J., et al. (2001). Limbic abnormalities in affective processing by criminal psychopaths as revealed by functional magnetic resonance imaging. *Biological Psychiatry, 50*(9), 677–684.

Kim-Cohen, J., Caspi, A., Moffitt, T. E., Harrington, H., Milne, B. J., & Poulton, R. (2003). Prior juvenile diagnoses in adults with mental disorder: developmental follow-back of a prospective-longitudinal cohort. *Archives of General Psychiatry, 60*(7), 709–717.

Kim-Cohen, J., Caspi, A., Taylor, A., Williams, B., Newcombe R, Craig, I. W., et al. (2006). MAOA, maltreatment, and gene-environment interaction predicting children's mental health: new evidence and a meta-analysis. *Molecular Psychiatry, 11*(10), 903–913.

Larsson, H., Andershed, H., & Lichtenstein, P. (2006). A genetic factor explains most of the variation in the psychopathic personality. *Journal of Abnormal Psychology, 115*(2), 221–230.

Larsson, H., Viding, E., & Plomin, R. (2008). Callous unemotional traits and antisocial behavior: Genetic, environmental, and early parenting characteristics. *Criminal Justice and Behavior, 35*(2), 197–211.

Lesch, K. P. (2003). The serotonergic dimension of aggression and violence. In *Neurobiology of aggression: understanding and preventing violence.* Totawa, NJ: Humana Press..

Lichtenstein, P., Tuvblad, C., Larsson, H., & Carlstrom, E. (2007). The Swedish Twin study of CHild and Adolescent Development: the TCHAD-study. *Twin Research and Human Genetics, 10*(1), 67–73.

Loney, B. R., Taylor, J., Butler, M., & Iacono, W. G. (2002). *The Minnesota Temperament Inventory: A psychometric study of adolescent self-reported psychopathy.* Unpublished manuscript.

Lynam, D. R. (1997). Pursuing the psychopath: capturing the fledgling psychopath in a nomological net. *Journal of Abnormal Psychology, 106*(3), 425–438.

Lynam, D. R. (2002). Fledgling psychopathy: A view from personality theory. *Law and Human Behavior, 26*(2), 255–259.

Lynam, D. R., Caspi, A., Moffitt, T. E., Loeber, R., & Stouthamer-Loeber, M. (2007). Longitudinal evidence that psychopathy scores in early adolescence predict adult psychopathy. *Journal of Abnormal Psychology, 116*(1), 155–165.

Manuck, S. B., Flory, J. D., Ferrell, R. E., Dent, K. M., Mann, J. J., & Muldoon, M. F. (1999). Aggression and anger-related traits associated with a polymorphism of the tryptophan hydroxylase gene. *Biological Psychiatry, 45*(5), 603–614.

Marsh, A. A., Finger, E. C., Mitchell, D. G. V., Reid, M. E., Sims, C., Kosson, D. S., et al. (2008). Reduced amygdala response to fearful expressions in children and adolescents with callous-unemotional traits and disruptive behavior disorders. *American Journal of Psychiatry, 165*(6), 712–720.

Marsh, A. A, Finger, E. E., Schechter, J. C., Jurkowitz, I. T. N., Reid, M. E., & Blair, R. J. R. (2011). Adolescents with psychopathic traits report reductions in physiological responses to fear. *Journal of Child Psychology & Psychiatry, 52*(8), 834–841.

Meyer-Lindenberg, A., Buckholtz, J. W., Kolachana, B., Hariri, A. R., Pezawas, L., Blasi, G., et al. (2006). Neural mechanisms of genetic risk for impulsivity and violence in humans. *Proceedings of the National Academy of Sciences USA, 103*(16), 6269–6274.

Meyer-Lindenberg, A., & Weinberger, D. (2006). Intermediate phenotypes and genetic mechanisms of psychiatric disorders. *Nature Review Neuroscience, 7*(10), 818–827.

Mobbs, D., Lau, H. C., Jones, O. D., & Frith, C. D. (2007). Law, responsibility, and the brain. *PLOS Biology, 5*(4), 693–700.

Moffitt, T. E. (2005). The new look of behavioral genetics in developmental psychopathology: gene–environment interplay in antisocial behaviors. *Psychological Bulletin, 131*(4), 533–554.

Moffitt, T. E., Arseneault, L., Jaffee, S. R., Kim-Cohen, J., Koenen, K. C., Odgers, C. L., et al. (2008). Research review: DSM-V conduct disorder: research needs for an evidence base. *Journal of Child Psychology and Psychiatry, 49*(1), 3–33.

Munafò, M. R., Brown, S. M., & Hariri, A. R. (2008). Serotonin transporter (5-HTTLPR) genotype and amygdala activation: A meta-analysis. *Biological Psychiatry, 63*(3), 852–857.

Muñoz, L. C. (2009). Callous-unemotional traits are related to combined deficits in recognizing afraid faces and body poses. *Journal of the American Academy of Child and Adolescent Psychiatry, 48*(5), 554–562.

Odgers, C. L., Caspi, A., Broadbent, J. M., Dickson, N., Hancox, R. J., Harrington, H., et al. (2007). Prediction of differential adult health burden by conduct problem subtypes in males. *Archives of General Psychiatry, 64*(4), 476–484.

Pardini, D. A., & Fite, P. J. (2010). Symptoms of conduct disorder, oppositional defiant disorder, attention-deficit/hyperactivity disorder, and callous-unemotional traits as unique predictors of psychosocial maladjustment in boys: advancing an evidence base for DSM-V. *Journal of the American Academy of Child and Adolescent Psychiatry, 49*(11), 1134–1144.

Pasalich, D. S., Dadds, M. R., Hawes, D. I., & Brennan, J. (2011). Do callous-unemotional traits moderate the relative importance of parental coercion versus warmth in child conduct problems? An observational study. *Journal of Child Psychology and Psychiatry, 52,* 1308–1315.

Plomin, R., DeFries, J., McClearn, G., & McGuffin, P. (2008). *Behavioral Genetics* (5th ed.). New York: Worth Publishers.

Rijsdijk, F. V., Viding, E., et al. (2010). Heritable variations in gray matter concentration as a potential endophenotype for psychopathic traits. *Archives of General Psychiatry, 67*(4), 406–413.

Romeo, R., Knapp, M., & Scott, S. (2006). Economic cost of severe antisocial behaviour in children—and who pays it. *British Journal of Psychiatry, 188,* 547–53.

Sadeh, N., Javdani, S., Jackson, J. J., Reynolds, E. K., Potenza, M. N., Gelernter, J., et al. (2010). Serotonin transporter gene associations with psychopathic traits in youth vary as a function of socioeconomic resources. *Journal of Abnormal Psychology, 119*(3), 604–609.

Scott, S., Knapp, M., Henderson, J., & Maughan, B. (2001). Financial cost of social exclusion: follow up study of antisocial children into adulthood. *British Medical Journal, 323*(7306), 191.

Singh, I., & Rose, N., (2009). Biomarkers in psychiatry. *Nature, 460*(7252), 202–207.

Taylor, J., Loney, B. R., Bobadilla, L., Iacono, W. G., & McGue, M. (2003). Genetic and environmental influences on psychopathy trait dimensions in a community sample of male twins. *Journal of Abnormal Child Psychology, 31*(6), 633–645.

Viding, E., Blair, R. J. R., Moffitt, T. E., & Plomin, R. (2005). Evidence for substantial genetic risk for psychopathy in 7-year-olds. *Journal of Child Psychology & Psychiatry, 46*(6), 592–597.

Viding, E., Frick, P. J., & Plomin, R. (2007). Aetiology of the relationship between callous-unemotional traits and conduct problems in childhood. *British Journal of Psychiatry, 190*(49), 33–38.

Viding, E., Jones, A., Frick, P. J., Moffitt, T. E., & Plomin, R. (2008). Heritability of antisocial behaviour at nine-years: Do callous-unemotional traits matter? *Developmental*

Science, 11(1), 17–22.Viding, E., Larsson, H., & Jones, A. P. (2008). Quantitative genetic studies of antisocial behaviour. *Philosophical Transactions of the Royal Society: B, 363*(1503), 2519–2527.

Viding, E., Hanscombe, K., Curtis, C. J. C., Davis, O. S. P., Meaburn, E. L., & Plomin, R. (2010). In search of genes associated with risk for psychopathic tendencies in children: A two-stage genome-wide association study of pooled DNA. *Journal of Child Psychology and Psychiatry, 51*(7), 780–788.

10

The Neural Code for Intentions in the Human Brain

JOHN-DYLAN HAYNES

To understand how intentions are encoded in the human brain, one should first consider the general principles for identifying neural representations of any kind of mental state. One of the key assumptions of modern neuroscience is that every mental state is realized by brain activity. Instead of a dualistic model that would allow an independence of mental from neural, neuroscience postulates that for each mental state it is possible to identify a specific neural state that "encodes," "represents," or "correlates with" it. One can think of the brain as the "neural carrier" in which the mental states occur, and the different states of the carrier (i.e., brain) encode different mental states (Haynes, 2009).

Several theoretical approaches have been proposed for identifying the neural correlates of specific mental states. These typically distinguish between "enabling" or background conditions and "content-specific" conditions.[1] An enabling condition would be a necessary condition for a mental state, but it would also be necessary for a number of other mental states. For example wakefulness (along with its neural correlates in the brain stem) is necessary for sensory percepts, memories, and intentions alike. Similarly, activity in the inferior frontal junction might be necessary for intentions (Brass et al., 2005), but it is active in task switching across various different intentions and thus does not distinguish between the specific intentions that are being implemented (Haynes et al., 2007). Then there are specific conditions that are necessary only for a subset of mental states or even one individual mental state to occur.

In the visual system, specific patterns of neural activity are necessary for the conscious percept of a very specific image. Similarly, it is reasonable to assume that also intentions are coded by specific patterns of activity. Such specific conditions have been termed the "core neural correlates of conscious-ness" (NCC). This means a minimal set of neurons with a "direct correlation" or "tight mapping"[2] with a specific class of experiences (Block, 2007; Chalmers, 2000; Haynes, 2009; Koch, 2004). Importantly, every class of mental states (sensory percepts, memories, intentions, etc.) can have a different core NCC. The big question is: What is the core NCC for conscious intentions? What is needed is a way to translate the general formula mentioned above into a scien-tific research program. How would one be able to identify the core NCC of a specific intention?[3] How would one know which of the approximately 85 billion neurons in the human brain (Azevedo et al., 2009; Williams & Herrup, 1988) is relevant? And what is the coding format? This chapter will focus on *coding principles* for intentions, rather than providing an overview of the entire cogni-tive neuroscience of intentions, for which several excellent reviews are avail-able (e.g. Andersen, Hwang, & Mulliken, 2010; Blankertz et al., 2006; Brass & Haggard, 2008; Burgess, Gilbert, & Dumontheil, 2007; Haggard, 2008; Miller & Coher, 2001; Passingham, Bentsson, & Lau, 2010; Ramnani & Owen, 2004; Sakai, 2008).

As with any mental representation, various neural coding formats could be possible for intentions (Fig. 10.1). First of all, the neural code for lossless encod-ing of six intentions in a neural carrier could in principle either be univariate or multivariate. Univariate means that it is would be based upon a *single* aspect of neural processing, say the mean activity level of a single neuron or small group of neurons. Multivariate means that it would be based on multiple parameters of neural processing, such as the activity of a set of individual neurons. In Figure 10.1 (left) the grayscale indicates a hypothetical univariate code where each intention is represented by a specific level of firing of cells. In another domain, perception, a univariate code is used to code the perceived intensity of a sensory stimulus (Haynes, 2009). For intentions one might envisage specific *graded* dimensions to be encoded in this way (say, for example, the degree of *commitment* to an inten-tion or the *time delay* after which an intention will be implemented).

An alternative is to use a *multivariate* code where a pattern of activity in a *group* of neurons encodes the different intentions. Multivariate codes come in different flavors. The most important distinction is between sparse codes and distributed codes. Sparse codes use one (and only one) neuron for each inten-tion, like a labeled line (or "cardinal cell") that is active only when this intention occurs. Examples of labeled line codes from other fields are the somatosen-sory homunculus (where one location in the brain encodes one region of the body; Penfield & Rasmussen, 1950) and retinotopic coding (where one loca-tion in the brain encodes one region of the visual field; Wandell, 1999). For intention representation, the advantage of this code would be that one could directly monitor the presence of an intention by only measuring the activity in

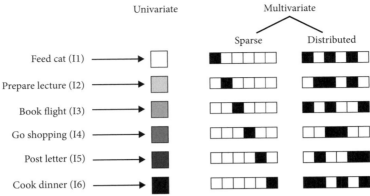

Figure 10.1 Possible coding formats for six intentions (I1 through I6). "Univariate" refers to a single graded parameter of neural activity, such as the average firing rate of a group of cells; "multivariate" refers to the multiple parameters of a neural population; "sparse" refers to a multivariate labeled line code (also known as cardinal cell or grandmother cell code); "distributed" refers to a multivariate code that uses arbitrary combinations of activity levels of individual units.

its corresponding labeled line. A further advantage is that it provides a natural way to solve the problem of *superposition*: Say a person is holding two intentions in mind at the same time, "prepare lecture" and "go shopping." With a sparse code the representation of this conjoint set of intentions could be to simply activate *both* of the labeled lines (i.e., 2 and 4 in Fig. 10.1). However, there is also a severe disadvantage of this code: N neurons can only encode N different intentions, so one needs one neuron for each intention that is to be encoded. Thus, the disadvantage of a sparse neural code for intentions is that one might find oneself running out of neurons for coding all the different intentions one might have throughout the lifespan. In contrast, a *distributed* multivariate code can be advantageous, because any state (or state vector) of an ensemble of neurons can be used to code the content of a given intention. This makes it possible to code for a very high number of intentions with just a few neurons.

MULTIVARIATE DECODING

Recently, with the advent of multivariate decoding a powerful approach has emerged that allows us to identify how mental states are encoded in brain activity (see Haynes & Rees, 2006, for an overview). This can just as well be applied to intentions as to any other mental state (such as sensory percepts or memories). The idea is to invert the problem of identifying the code by assessing from which neural signals it is possible to *decode* the intention a person is currently holding in mind (Fig. 10.2A,B). Specifically, the method is to first

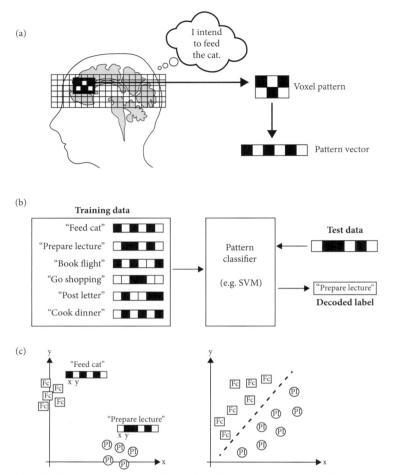

Figure 10.2 Multivariate decoding of intentions from neural signals. (**A**) The prefrontal activation pattern in a region of prefrontal cortex while a person is holding an intention (say, "I am going to feed the cat"). This voxel pattern is then translated into a pattern vector and entered into a decoding analysis. (**B**) Pattern vectors for a set of six intentions are entered as training data into a pattern classifier. The classifier uses a classification algorithm (e.g., a support vector machine) to optimally distinguish between the different training patterns. Then, pattern vectors from an independent test dataset are fed into the classifier to assess whether it can correctly assign the label. Please note that the data shown here are noise-free and would thus be very easy to classify. In typical neural data there are many irrelevant background signals and technical artifacts that make the patterns less distinguishable. (**C**) The classification problem shown in a two-dimensional coordinate system where measurements points are defined by x (activity in first voxel) and y values (activity in second voxel). Left shows an easy case where classification would be possible based either on the first voxel (x) or second voxel (y) alone. The right shows a more complicated case where classification can be performed only if the values in both voxels are taken into account simultaneously.

measure the brain response of a person while he or she is holding various intentions and then train a computer to recognize the intentions from these brain signals. It is very useful to *simultaneously* measure as many parameters (such as fMRI voxels, EEG channels, multielectrode units, etc.) of brain activity as possible, for several reasons: (1) It is not always clear *a priori* which neurons will be most informative about a particular mental state. Measuring many locations at once (as with fMRI) has the advantage that one does not have to preselect *a priori* where the information will be. This approach thus removes spatial biases. (2) If information is distributed across multiple units (see Fig. 10.1), then it is essential to obtain as much information as possible about this ensemble. The reason is that information can be encoded in the *conjoint* activity of multiple units that cannot be extracted by measuring the individual units on their own (Fig. 10.2C).

The first step in multivariate decoding is to repeatedly measure the multivariate brain responses for each intention one wants to be able to decode. Part of this data is then fed as *training data* labeled with the corresponding intentions into a multivariate pattern classifier that learns to optimally classify the activity patterns for different intentions, which means it has to assign the correct labels. The evidence that a multivariate neural signal (say from a region of prefrontal cortex) contains information about an intention is given if the classifier can correctly assign the labels for an independent dataset, such as the remaining rest of the data (typically referred to as *test data*). The accuracy of this classifier is a measure of information a particular region of the brain has about a person's current intention. Please note that this approach is very different from more conventional analyses of neuroimaging signals, because it allows us to pinpoint exactly where a specific representation is encoded in the brain. In contrast, the more routine analyses of neuroimaging data (based, e.g., on general linear models) focus on the overall activation of a brain region and do not distinguish between different representational contents (see Sakai, 2008, and Haggard, 2008, for reviews).[4]

In a first experiment on this topic (Haynes et al., 2007) we attempted to decode conscious intentions from fMRI signals. Our subjects performed a number of trials in an MR scanner. At the beginning of each trial the instruction "select" appeared on a screen that told subjects to "freely choose" whether they wanted to add or subtract numbers that would appear a few seconds later. Afterwards, subjects were instructed to focus on the selected intention and to wait until two numbers appeared, then perform the chosen calculation as fast as possible and report the result. We chose adding and subtracting since they are sufficiently similar and we were interested in a maximally pure representation of intention that is not contaminated by a differential preparation for different types of tasks (see, e.g., Sakai & Passingham, 2003). If we had allowed them to select between "adding numbers" and "identifying faces," this would have likely caused large-scale differences in activity patterns in the brain due to the differential preparation of the different processing modules involved in mental calculation and face recognition. With adding and subtracting we hoped to have two intentions that would be processed by a maximally similar set of networks and that would thus only differ in the representation of the intention itself, at least during the preparation phase.[5]

We then split our data into training and test data and trained a computer algorithm (a linear support vector machine, see Müller et al., 2001) to optimally classify the intention subjects were holding in mind based only on the brain signals. We found that the classifier could predict the intention with around 70 percent accuracy based on patterns of brain signals from medial prefrontal cortex (MPFC), specifically a region known as Brodmann area (BA) 10 (Fig. 10.3A). This finding is compatible with neuropsychology, where it is known that BA 10 is involved in so-called prospective memory (i.e., our ability to memorize action plans for later execution; see, e.g., Burgess, Gilbert, & Dumontheil 2007). Furthermore, the anatomical connections of medial prefrontal cortex make it suitable for initiating self-generated behavior (Passingham, Bengtsson, & Lau, 2010), and in particular BA 10 has been argued to have a connectivity profile that makes it suitable for high-level control (Ramnani & Owen, 2004). Although we were able to decode the self-chosen prospective intention also from lateral prefrontal cortex, decoding accuracy in this region was considerably lower (maximally around 65 percent). From a different, more posterior subregion of medial prefrontal cortex we were also able to decode the intention at a later stage while it was being executed ("intention in action"). This study has several implications for the neural coding of intentions. First, it is possible to read out freely chosen intentions after a person has decided what he or she wants to do but in absence of any reports and before he or she puts this into action. One might call this decoding of "hidden" or "concealed" intentions. Furthermore, different regions seem to be responsible for encoding of prospective plans versus plans that are determining our current behavior. This reveals something important about intention coding: The representation of an intention seems to shift across medial prefrontal cortex, depending on the stage it is currently in (prospective intention versus intention in action). One speculation is that BA 10 might contain a neural buffer that stores or "cues" intentions waiting to be executed in the near future.

In another experiment (Bode & Haynes, 2009) we investigated the storage of intentions that had come about in a different way: Instead of being "freely" self-chosen we instructed subjects on each trial which task to perform. We used two simple tasks that consisted of two different ways of mapping two colorful pattern images to two responses (movement of joystick to left versus right).

Before each trial subjects received a cue telling them whether to (A) respond to image 1 with moving the joystick left and image 2 with joystick right, or (B) respond to image 1 with joystick right and image 2 with joystick left. Again, we trained a pattern classifier to decode from brain activity which intention subjects were holding in mind. This time we found that the task was encoded in lateral (rather than medial) prefrontal cortex. This difference from the adding and subtracting task could potentially reflect either the switch from a mental calculation task to a simpler response-mapping task, or it could reflect the switch from freely chosen to instructed tasks. To date it is unknown whether cued and self-chosen intentions share a similar neural code.

INTENTIONS ACROSS TIME

If medial prefrontal cortex were to contain a buffer for future intentions, one important question would be what happens to an intention stored in the buffer when competing intentions are present. Say you have planned to go give a lecture in the late afternoon, but first you have to do some shopping. While you are busy working on one intention (shopping) you still have to keep the prospective intention (lecture) in memory. We investigated the encoding of such prospective intentions using a task that involved storing an intention across a delay period while working on other intentions during the delay. In this experiment (Momennejad & Haynes, 2012) participants formed an instructed intention and maintained it over a self-organized time delay during which they were busy with another task. Our aim was to decode the future intention in spite of the distracting intermediate task that filled the delay. More specifically, at the beginning of each trial subjects were told to memorize and later perform either a parity or magnitude judgment task. Both tasks could be performed on the same upcoming single-digit numbers. Parity judgment involved assessing whether the number is odd or even; magnitude involved judging whether the number is smaller or larger than 5. Throughout the experiment, a continuous stream of colored single-digit numbers appeared on the screen. At instruction, subjects were also given a time period (15, 20, or 25 seconds) after which they were to start performing the parity or magnitude task. This required them to monitor when the delay was elapsed and to then spontaneously start doing the memorized task without any additional external cue. During this time delay subjects had to perform a color judgment on the digits, which allowed us to assess whether it is possible to decode the memorized intention even when another intention was currently being acted upon. We found that it is possible to decode which prospective intention the subjects were holding in mind even across the "occupied" delay period during which they were busy performing another task (Fig. 10.3C). Again, the region encoding this delayed intention was medial prefrontal cortex. Importantly, during the recall period of the intention we found that the information switched to a more lateral region. Thus, the lateral–medial distinction might also be related to storage versus retrieval processes from prospective memory.

Interestingly, this study allowed us to also look for the encoding not only of the content of the intention ("what" is going to be done), but also for the encoding of the time information ("when" it is going to be done). For this we trained the classifier to distinguish from brain activity *after which delay* a subject would start performing the prospective task. We found time information in several regions of prefrontal and parietal cortex, some of which have previously been indicated in timekeeping functions (see Momennejad & Haynes, 2012). Importantly, the regions encoding task (magnitude/parity) and time (15/20/25 seconds) did not overlap. Furthermore, the regions encoding the task were the same for different delays, and the regions encoding the delay were the same across different tasks. Thus, there appears to be considerable independence between these two aspects of intentions. It is only when the delay reaches zero and the intention has to be acted upon immediately that the intention representation shifts to a different location.

Whereas the previous set of experiments addressed the question where intentions are encoded *after* they have been consciously decided upon or memorized, a different set of experiments (Haggard & Eimer, 1999; Lau et al., 2004; Libet et al., 1983) addressed whether it would be possible to predict intentions even before a person has decided what he or she wants to do. Most of these Libet experiments typically use one variant of a free-choice paradigm in combination with EEG or fMRI. In most cases subjects can choose freely, either between moving a finger or not, or between moving one or the other finger. The time of conscious decision is behaviorally measured using a reference stimulus, typically a rotating clock dial. Although there has been some debate (see Haynes, 2011, for an overview), these studies have typically found that signals in movement-related brain regions (readiness potentials, lateralized readiness potentials) begin to deviate from baseline a few hundred milliseconds before a person consciously makes his or her choice. Unfortunately (with the exception of the lateralized readiness potential) the EEG signal is not specific enough to distinguish between the encoding of different intentions. Moreover, the EEG only provides information about a relatively late stage of decision preparation. We thus performed a variant of the original Libet experiment (Bode et al., 2011; Soon et al., 2008) using fMRI in combination with a classifier to obtain a more detailed resolution of brain signals preparing free decisions between different intentions. Again, we trained a pattern classifier to distinguish between brain signals that were indicative of one of two possible intentions: either left-hand or right-hand button presses. We found that it was possible to partially predict the upcoming decision up to 7 seconds before subjects believed they were making up their mind (Fig. 10.3B). Maximally choice-predictive brain activity patterns could be found in medial parietal cortex and also in medial prefrontal cortex, that is in similar regions that encode free chosen intentions *after* subjects had made up their mind (see above). Predictive accuracy was low (around 60 percent) but still significantly above chance. This begs the question whether the limited predictability is due to the lack of resolution of fMRI signals, or due to an in-principle lack of predictability at such an early stage. However, taken together, the Libet-type experiments demonstrate that the brain starts preparing the outcome of free decisions long before we believe we are making up our mind (for a discussion of the implications of this experiment, see Haynes, 2011).

Importantly, as in the study discussed above (Momennejad & Haynes, 2012), we also looked for information that would allow us to predict when (as opposed to how) the subject would decide (Soon et al., 2008). We were able to predict the timepoint of the subjective decision up to 6 seconds before the decision from medial brain regions (SMA/pre-SMA). Thus, presumably the timing and the outcome of the decision are determined by two independent networks, as suggested also by our work on prospective intentions above (Momennejad & Haynes, 2012).

CHALLENGES IN INTENTION DECODING

Based on the above-mentioned examples, one might get the impression that it is just a matter of time until a technical device will be available that can read our intentions for everyday applications. Imagine a machine that would allow us to control our computer (car, TV, or similar) using a brain–computer interface. Simple versions of such techniques are in development today (Blankertz et al., 2006), but they require cooperation on the side of the user. Such a technology could be highly useful in crime prevention, by allowing us to prevent a crime even before it has happened by detecting the unlawful intention in a person's brain. The consequences of a similar technology have been portrayed in movies, most spectacularly in *Minority Report*. I would like to spend the remainder of this section discussing what makes it so difficult to build such a generic real-world intention-detection device, and why it is likely to remain science fiction for quite some time.

Imagine the extreme case: You are responsible for airline safety and want to install a machine that can detect if a person is planning to detonate an explosive on your plane. You might envisage a brain scanner that can detect a "terrorist intention" by measuring and analyzing a person's brain activity at the gate. We have already shown (Momennejad & Haynes, 2012) that it is possible to decode prospective intentions and that it is even possible to do so while someone is thinking about something else (e.g., another intention). But, for several

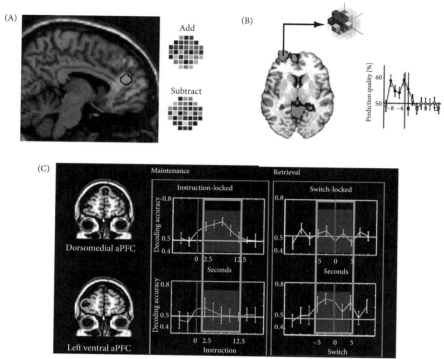

Figure 10.3 Multivariate decoding of intentions from fMRI signals in prefrontal cortex.
(**A**) This medial view of the brain shows in green the region around Brodmann area
10, where the fine-scaled activity patterns (right) could be used to decode whether a
subject had the intention to add or subtract two numbers (Haynes et al., 2007). (**B**) fRMI
signal patterns in frontopolar Brodmann area 10 could be used to predict a subject's
decision to press one of two buttons several seconds before the subject believed to have
decided which button to take (Soon, Brass, Heinze, & Haynes, 2008). (**C**) Intention
representations in anterior medial prefrontal cortex encode a prospective intention
across a delay ("maintenance") while the subject is busy working on another task
(top). Thus, prospective intention representations are stable across time even in the
presence of other competing goals. Signals in anterior lateral prefrontal cortex encode
the intention at a later stage when it is retrieved from memory in order to be executed
(Momennejad & Haynes, 2012).

reasons, building an intention detector is not as easy as it seems. Besides the
technical limitations of current neuroimaging, there are also several theoretical
points that still need to be solved.

Commitment

You would need to be able to distinguish between people with a full-blown
intention to blow up a plane and normal people who are just imagining their

plane blowing up, say because they are scared to go on board. Even worse: When confronted with such an intention-detection device before boarding, persons with obsessive-compulsive disorder (OCD) might find themselves compulsively having to think about blowing up the plane, even if they have no intention of doing so. It is a well-known fact in psychology that suppressing thoughts can make them even stronger (Wegner et al., 1987), and it is also well known that attention can modulate processing of intentions (Lau et al., 2004). Thus, one needs to be able to distinguish between *thinking about* an intention and *having* an intention. In other words: One would have to assess the degree of *commitment* to an action plan.

Multitude of intentions

To build a "terrorist intention detector" one would need to know the *entire set* of possible terrorist intentions because one would need to train a computer to recognize their corresponding brain patterns. Imagine you have a detector for the intention "blowing up a plane with TNT," and someone boards the plane with a plan to blow up the plane with a to-date-unknown type of improvised explosive device. So another major open question is: How can we know the brain patterns for so many different intentions we might not even be able to envisage ourselves?

Architecture of intentions

The intentions used in the studies above are all very simple: they involve simple tasks such as adding, subtracting, or pressing buttons in response to particular pictures. The real-world intention, however, is a more complex data structure. It involves multiple components (see Brass & Haggard, 2008, for a related distinction): (a) **What** a person is going to do; (b) **Triggering conditions** that determine **when** or under which conditions to start implementing the intention; for example, the implementation of an intention can occur either in response to an external event (cue-based prospective memory) or after a certain time has elapsed (time-based prospective memory); detailed lesion analyses suggest that these two triggering conditions might rely on dissociable regions of prefrontal cortex (Volle et al., 2011); successful triggering of intentions improves their cortical representation (Gilbert et al., 2012); and once triggered, an intention can also be suppressed (or "vetoed," see Brass & Haggard, 2008); (c) **Hierarchies** between intentions and a goal–subgoal structure, such as when one intention is part of another intention (e.g., the subgoal of opening the can of cat food as part of the goal of feeding the cat); (d) **Prioritization** of specific goals over others; say, while driving a car staying on the road is more

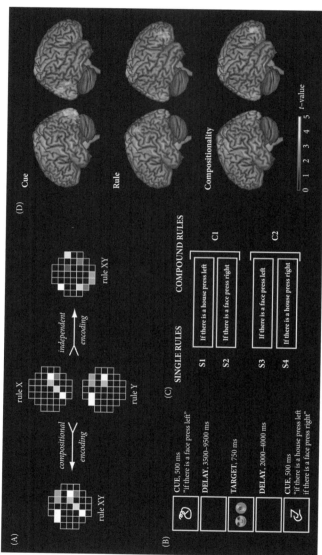

Figure 10.4 Compositionality of rule representations in human prefrontal cortex (Reverberi, Görgen, & Haynes, 2011). (**A**) Two possible neural coding schemes could be used to encode a complex intention XY that consists of two simple intentions: If the code is compositional it means that the neural representation XY can be predicted from the neural codes for the ingredient rules X and Y. If the coding is independent it can't. (**B**) We performed an experiment where subjects were cued to either form simple or complex intentions that involved pressing buttons in response to various pictures. (**C**) We had two levels of rules: single rules that associated one picture with one response, and compound rules that associated two pictures with a response each and that were composed of two single rules. (**D**) The rules upon which compound intentions were based could be decoded from parietal and lateral prefrontal cortex. However, only the prefrontal code was compositional and could be predicted from a pattern classifier trained only on the single rules from which the compound rules were composed.

important than operating the music system. This will require establishing the link between intentions and reward expectations, values, and reasons.

The neural code for many of these above-mentioned components of intentions is to date unknown. At least there might be a solution to the problem of training a computer on a multitude of different intentions. It appears as if the brain might use a systematic way to store intentions, such that complex intentions are built out of the neural building blocks of simple intentions (Reverberi, Görgen, & Haynes 2011). We directly addressed this question in a study that investigated a simple form of neural compositionality of intentions (Fig. 10.4). Specifically, we used complex rule-based intentions, each of which consisted of two simpler intentions. The simple rule might be: "If you see a face picture then press the left button," or "If you see a house picture then press the right button." A complex rule would be "If you see a face picture then press the left button OR if you see a house picture then press the right button." We then trained a pattern classifier on the simple intentions and tried to use this classifier on the complex rules. Indeed, in lateral prefrontal cortex we were able to predict which complex intention a person was holding in mind, based on the classifier trained on the simple rules it was composed of. This speaks for a compositional code for encoding of intentions in lateral prefrontal cortex. Extending this finding to the set of all possible intentions, however, would require knowing the space in which these intentions are coded. If the similarity space between intentions were understood better, this would allow us to interpolate the neural patterns encoding intentions that have not to date been measured.

NOTES

1. Please note that in studies on NCCs, "conditions" and "correlates" are often not sufficiently differentiated. This reflects the fact that only a few causal studies are performed in cognitive neuroscience.
2. In the sense of a high mutual information.
3. This chapter addresses intention representation in the human brain. There is a considerable work reviewed elsewhere on coding of *motor* intentions in nonhuman primates (see, e.g., Miller & Cohen, 2001, or Andersen, Hwang, & Mulliken, 2011, for reviews) and on noninvasive brain–computer interfaces in humans (see, e.g., Müller et al., 2008).
4. The lateralized readiness potential (LRP) used by Haggard & Eimer (1999) can be used to differentially index two different motor intentions. However, the LRP is restricted to late stages of movement preparation in motor-related brain regions and cannot be used to reveal intention coding in other cortical regions.
5. Please note that even adding and subtracting are known to partially involve different networks (Fehr, Code, & Herrmann 2007), but this choice allowed us to minimize such effects.

REFERENCES

Andersen, R. A., Hwang, E. J., & Mulliken, G. H. (2010). Cognitive neural prosthetics. *Annual Review of Psychology, 61*, 169–190.

Azevedo, F. A., Carvalho, L. R., Grinberg, L. T., Farfel, J. M., Ferretti, R. E., Leite, R. E., Jacob Filho, W., Lent, R., & Herculano-Houzel, S. (2009). Equal numbers of neuronal and nonneuronal cells make the human brain an isometrically scaled-up primate brain. *Journal of Comparative Neurology, 513*(5), 532–541.

Blankertz, B., Müller, K. R., Krusienski, D. J., Schalk, G., Wolpaw, J. R., Schlögl, A., Pfurtscheller, G., Millán, J. del R, Schröder, M., & Birbaumer, N. (2006). The BCI competition. III: Validating alternative approaches to actual BCI problems. *IEEE Transactions on Neural Systems and Rehabilitation Engineering 14*(2). 153–159.

Block, N. (2007) Consciousness, accessibility and the mesh between psychology and neuroscience. *Behavioral and Brain Sciences, 30*, 481–548.

Bode, S., & Haynes, J. D. (2009). Decoding sequential stages of task preparation in the human brain. *Neuroimage, 45*(2), 606–613.

Bode, S., He, A. H., Soon, C. S., Trampel, R., Turner, R., & Haynes, J. D. (2011). Tracking the unconscious generation of free decisions using ultra-high field fMRI. *PLoS One, 6*(6), e21612.

Brass, M., Derrfuss, J., Forstmann, B., & von Cramon, D. Y. (2005). The role of the inferior frontal junction area in cognitive control. *Trends in Cognitive Sciences,, 9*(7), 314–316.

Brass, M., & Haggard, P. (2008). The what, when, whether model of intentional action. *Neuroscientist, 14*(4), 319–325.

Burgess, P. W., Gilbert, S. J., & Dumontheil, I. (2007). Function and localization within rostral prefrontal cortex (area 10). *Philosophical Transactions of the Royal Society of London B Biological Sciences, 362*(1481), 887–899.

Chalmers, D. (2000). What is a neural correlate of consciousness? In T. Metzinger (Ed.), *Neural correlates of consciousness: conceptual and empirical questions* (pp. 17–40). Cambridge, MA: MIT.

Fehr, T., Code, C., & Herrmann, M. (2007). Common brain regions underlying different arithmetic operations as revealed by conjunct fMRI-BOLD activation. *Brain Research, 1172*, 93–102.

Gilbert, S. J., Armbruster, D. J., & Panagiotidi, M. (2012). Similarity between brain activity at encoding and retrieval predicts successful realization of delayed intentions. *Journal of Cognitive Neuroscience, 24*(1), 93–105.

Haggard, P. (2008). Human volition: towards a neuroscience of will. *Nature Reviews Neuroscience, 9*(12), 934–946.

Haggard, P., & Eimer, M. (1999). On the relation between brain potentials and the awareness of voluntary movements. *Experimental Brain Research,, 126*(1), 128–133.

Haynes, J. D. (2009). Decoding visual consciousness from human brain signals. *trends in Cognitive Sciences, 13*(5), 194–202.

Haynes, J. D. (2011). Decoding and predicting intentions. *Annals of the New York Academy of Sciences, 1224*, 9–21.

Haynes, J. D., & Rees, G. (2006). Decoding mental states from brain activity in humans. *Nature Reviews Neuroscience, 7*(7), 523–534.

Haynes, J. D., Sakai, K., Rees, G., Gilbert, S., Frith, C., & Passingham, R. E. (2007). Reading hidden intentions in the human brain. *Current Biology, 17*(4), 323–328.

Koch, C. (2004). *The quest for consciousness: a neurobiological approach.*Englewood: Roberts.

Roberts Lau, H. C., Rogers, R. D., Haggard, P., & Passingham, R. E. (2004). Attention to intention. *Science, 303*(5661), 1208–1210.

Libet, B., Gleason, C. A., Wright, E. W., & Pearl, D. K. (1983). Time of conscious intention to act in relation to onset of cerebral activity (readiness-potential). The unconscious initiation of a freely voluntary act. *Brain, 106*(Pt 3), 623–642.

Miller, E. K., & Cohen, J. D. (2001). An integrative theory of prefrontal cortex function. *Annual Review of Neuroscience, 24,* 167–202.

Momennejad, I., & Haynes, J.D. (2012). Human anterior prefrontal cortex encodes the "what" and "when" of future intentions. *Neuroimage 61,* 139–148.

Müller, K. R., Mika, S., Rätsch, G., Tsuda, K., & Schölkopf, B. (2001). An introduction to kernel-based learning algorithms. *IEEE Transactions on Neural Networks, 12,* 181–202.

Müller, K. R., Tangermann, M., Dornhege, G., Krauledat, M., Curio, G., & Blankertz, B. (2008). Machine learning for real-time single-trial EEG-analysis: from brain-computer interfacing to mental state monitoring. *Journal of Neuroscience Methods, 167*(1), 82–90.

Passingham, R. E, Bengtsson, S. L., & Lau, H. C. (2010). Medial frontal cortex: from self-generated action to reflection on one's own performance. *Trends in Cognitive Sciences, 14*(1), 16–21.

Penfield, W., & Rasmussen, T. (1950). *The cerebral cortex of man: a clinical study of localization of function.* New York: Macmillan.

Ramnani, N., & Owen, A. M. (2004). Anterior prefrontal cortex: insights into function from anatomy and neuroimaging. *Nature Reviews Neuroscience, 5*(3), 184–194.

Reverberi, C., Görgen, K., & Haynes, J. D. (2011). Compositionality of rule representations in human prefrontal cortex. *Cereb Cortex,* Aug 4. [Epub ahead of print].

Sakai, K. (2008). Task set and prefrontal cortex. *Annual Review of Neuroscience, 31,* 219–245.

Sakai, K., & Passingham, R. E. (2003). Prefrontal interactions reflect future task operations. *Nature Neuroscience 6*(1), 75–81.

Soon, C. S., Brass, M., Heinze, H. J., & Haynes, J. D. (2008). Unconscious determinants of free decisions in the human brain. *Nature Neuroscience, 11*(5), 543–545.

Volle, E., Gonen-Yaacovi, G., Costello Ade, L., Gilbert, S. J., & Burgess, P. W. (2011). The role of rostral prefrontal cortex in prospective memory: a voxel-based lesion study. *Neuropsychologia, 49*(8), 2185–2198.

Wandell, B. A. (1999). Computational neuroimaging of human visual cortex. *Annual Review of Neuroscience, 22,* 145–173.

Wegner, D. M., Schneider, D. J., Carter, S., & White, T. (1987). Paradoxical effects of thought suppression. *Journal of Personality and Social Psychology, 53,* 5–13.

Williams, R. W., & Herrup, K. (1988). The control of neuron number. *Annual Review of Neuroscience, 11,* 423–453.

11

Biomarkers: Potential and Challenges

MICHAEL RUTTER

INTRODUCTION

A biomarker is generally defined as a biological feature that can be objectively measured and that serves as an indicator of normal or pathogenic biological processes, or a pharmacological response to a therapeutic intervention (Biomarkers Definition Working Group, 2001). The interest in development of good biomarkers arose because both clinical diagnoses and risk characteristics for mental disorders, as well as mental states, rely on behavioral judgments that are open to biases and uncertainties over reliability, but especially and more importantly validity, at an individual level. In internal medicine, the pathophysiology of many conditions is known, but this is not the case in the field of mental disorders (with just a few exceptions such as Alzheimer's disease [AD]). Biomarkers cannot, in themselves, define the pathophysiology of the conditions for which they are a marker, but, if successful, they could enable a conceptualization that is much closer to the biological basis of whatever condition is being considered.

The first major goal of biomarkers has been to enable diagnoses to be made on the basis of biological features rather than on descriptive symptom patterns. The second goal has been to provide early presymptomatic diagnoses. This chapter will be focused entirely on these two goals—giving examples from diverse forms of psychopathology. In most cases, the main interest lies in the implications for behavior, but the rationale is that these have to be reflected in the biology.

However, it needs to be noted that a third goal has been to validate mental phenomena such as telling lies (see Buchman & Iles, 2010; Greely & Wagner, 2011). This is of particular importance in the forensic field. The polygraph (measuring autonomic processes) constitutes one of the earliest approaches of this kind. Although research has shown that it performs well above a chance level, it has also indicated that it involves errors leading to both false positives and false negatives (see National Research Council, 2002). More recently, it has been hoped that brain imaging may be able to improve on polygraph performance. Although that is possible, there is too little evidence for any firm conclusions to be drawn. It needs to be added that it is likely that people can be trained how to fake responses. In a somewhat related fashion, it has been suggested that brain imaging may be used to validate or invalidate forensic claims of mental capacity/incapacity. The rationale is that mental capacity must be based on brain functioning and that if imaging can reflect the latter it can be employed to assess the former. At the present, it seems very dubious whether imaging can provide an individual measure of level of mental capacity that is both quantified and valid at an individual level. This chapter will not discuss the various examples of this third goal in the forensic field. Nevertheless, the principles discussed in relation to diagnosis apply equally to these broader uses.

Forms of challenge or stimulus have also been used as a way of studying neural functioning. For example, these have included fear-eliciting stimuli (Meyer-Lindenberg & Weinberger, 2006) and exposure to high levels of carbon dioxide (Battaglia et al., 2008; Spatola et al., 2011). Both of these were used as an intermediate phenotype to study the biological pathways involved in psychopathology. Neither was designed to be used as a diagnostic test as such, but the challenges have been found to induce neural effects and, therefore, eventually might be used as a biomarker.

CLINICAL EXAMPLES

In this section, attempts to develop biomarkers for the diagnosis of various forms of psychopathology will be discussed. The examples have been deliberately chosen to represent disorders with both a high likelihood (because of knowledge on the pathophysiology) that a biomarker might be possible (e.g., AD) and those where the possibility seems much more distant because of both heterogeneity and ignorance on the pathophysiology (e.g., antisocial behavior). They also illustrate the range of rather different types of biomarker.

Alzheimer's disease

Many of the issues are well illustrated by the findings on AD. As noted above, AD is unusual in the field of medical disorders in that a lot is known about the basic pathophysiology. It appears that the disease begins with abnormal processing of amyloid precursor protein, which then leads to excessive β amyloid

(A β42). This is followed by neurofibrillary tangles formed by hyperphosphory-lated tau together with synaptic dysfunction, cell death, and brain shrinkage (Jack et al., 2010). However, the neuropathological changes associated with AD are not infrequently found in asymptomatic individuals without either cognitive decline or functional deterioration (Mitsis et al., 2009).

It has often been assumed that minor cognitive impairment (MCI) neces-sarily precedes dementia, but meta-analyses have shown that typically only about half the individuals with MCI progress to dementia over the next decade, with the annual conversion rate being about 5 to 15 percent (Kelley & Petersen, 2009; Mitchell & Shivi-Felski, 2009); a significant proportion even improve. It appears that MCI is a rather heterogeneous category. Accordingly, there has been much interest in using biomarkers to identify those likely to proceed to dementia (Trojanowski et al., 2010) because of the possible value in prevention (see Ritchie et al., 2010).

In that connection, it is relevant that different biomarkers are most effective at different phases of the disease (see Aisen et al., 2010; Jack et al., 2010). Of course, there is also interest in differentiating AD from other types of dementia (see Kapaki, 2003). Hort et al. (2010) have usefully summarized the various different measures that may be employed. The longest established comprise assessment of memory and other neuropsychological functions—with both the pattern and degree of impairment being of diagnostic significance. Structural and functional brain imaging findings may also be useful—perhaps particu-larly in identifying vascular changes associated with dementia other than AD. Genetic testing is useful for identifying presenilin mutations, which account for about half of the familial form of early-onset AD. Although the ApoE ε 4 allele has consistently been implicated in the much commoner non-Mendelian late-onset form of AD, it is far from diagnostic and cannot be recommended for detecting vulnerability for AD. Potentially, cerebrospinal fluid (CSF) analy-ses to detect decreased levels of A β 42 and increased tau (especially in com-bination) may have the greatest potential for detecting AD because they tap into the neuropathology (Blennow and Hampel, 2003); Kapaki et al., 2003). Unfortunately, it seems that there is considerable inter-laboratory variation in measurement (Hort et al., 2010). Most crucially, with all these possible bio-markers, a key question is the extent to which the specific biomarkers (such as the CSF measures) can improve on clinical prediction that includes the use of cognitive measures.

Autism spectrum disorder

Although numerous brain imaging disorders have produced findings point-ing to abnormal neural connectivity in autism, the details have been strikingly inconsistent across studies (Amaral et al., 2008; Frith & Frith, 2008; Toal et al., 2005). Ecker et al. (2010) argued that a multidimensional approach to morphology (including volumetric and geometric factors) might provide a more useful method. Twenty volunteer adult controls were compared with 20 adults with autism spectrum disorder (ASD) and 19 adults with attention-deficit/hyperactivity disorder (ADHD), using magnetic resonance imaging (MRI). A support vector machine analytic approach followed, with findings showing good separation between the groups. As a "proof of concept" demonstration, the paper was valuable, but numerous questions remain. To begin with, discriminative function analyses (of which this is a more sophisticated modern example), are notorious for capitalizing on chance differences, and independent cross-validation using an entirely different sample is essential. Secondly, the findings showed substantial spread—indicating that although *group* differentiation was excellent, the application to individual diagnosis would be much less satisfactory. Third, for a biomarker to be useful, it must provide a better index than that available on clinical measures, and that has not been shown. That is a highly relevant issue in view of the evidence that neuropsychological measures do quite a good job (Losh et al., 2009). Fourth, it is crucial to determine whether the biomarker can differentiate ASD from a range of neurodevelopmental disorders.

The discovery of mirror neurons (meaning neurons that responded to a person or animal watching the actions of others) in the 1990s by Rizzolatti and his colleagues (see Rizzolatti & Craighero, 2004) led to the suggestion that autism might be due to "broken" mirror neurons because autism is associated with an impaired ability to understand the meaning of others' actions (Dapretto et al., 2006; Ramachandran & Oberman, 2006). The possibility arose that a biomarker indexing the neural dysfunction might be possible. Mu suppression as evident on the electroencephalograph (EEG) may do the job. The evidence so far suggests that the notion that "broken mirror neurons" account for autism is not supported (Fan et al., 2010). However, Rizzolatti and Fabbri-Destro (2010) have pointed out that the mirror neuron system is sufficiently multifaceted that a single role and a single index are unlikely to work. On the evidence to date, mirror neurons are unlikely to constitute the basis for an effective biomarker.

In recent years, the interest in identifying biomarkers that could pick out children who will later show ASD has been increased by a range of "baby sibling" studies of the younger siblings of a child known to have an ASD (Bryson et al., 2007; Landa et al., 2007; Zwaigenbaum et al. 2005). Clinical measures do a reasonable job at 2 years and older (Zwaigenbaum et al., 2009), but they are much less effective under the age of 18 months. Event-related potentials (ERP) in response to direct gaze, differences in visual attention, and eye-tracking have been reported as being able to provide an effective group differentiation by 12 to 18 months of age (Elsabbagh & Johnson, 2009; Elssabagh et al., 2009a and

2009b; Gliga et al., 2009; Holmboe et al., 2010), but, so far, it has not been shown that they provide an adequate differentiation at the individual level. Clearly, that is a requirement if the biomarkers are to be used to identify children to be treated with some form of preventive intervention.

Attention-Deficit/Hyperactivity Disorder

The situation with respect to ADHD is quite different in that although animal models have pointed to anatomical and functional disturbances in cortico-striato-thalamo-centered circuits (see Sagvolden et al., 2005; Sobel et al., 2010), the pathophysiology of the condition remains speculative and inferential, despite evidence implicating frontostriatal or mesocorticolimbic circuits (Plessen & Peterson, 2009). On the whole, brain imaging has pointed to reduced brain volume, but the details of findings have been highly variable. The evidence from meta-analyses suggests the existence of biases in both publication and data analysis (Ioannidis, 2011). Sobel et al. (2010) undertook a cross-sectional MRI study comparing children with ADHD and normal controls. The main finding was a decrease in the volume of the putamen in the ADHD group, deriving from marked inward deformations across multiple portions of the surface. It was speculated that the deformations may have arisen from dopamine dysfunction. Within the ADHD group, the use of stimulant medication attenuated the imaging differences associated with ADHD, suggesting that medication might have altered morphological features in a normalizing direction. The findings are provocative and interesting but, clearly, they fall well short of providing a biomarker for the condition.

Event-related potentials have also been used to provide a physiological marker for the feedback-related negativity that might index the abnormal responses to reinforcement thought to characterize ADHD (Luman et al., 2005). The finding of significant differences from the control group suggests that the approach has promise. However, the small sample size, the confounding effects of low IQ, and the high rate of comorbidity with disruptive behavior disorders make clear that ERPs require much further study before their utility as a biomarker can be accepted.

Schizophrenia

During the last several decades or so there has been a revolution in thinking about the nature of schizophrenia, moving from a concept that it was just an adult-onset psychosis to a recognition that it has its beginnings in neurodevelopmental impairments in early childhood (Keshavan et al., 2004). General-population longitudinal studies showed that this early pan-developmental impairment was specific to schizophreniform disorders (Cannon et al., 2002). At about the same time, the Dunedin longitudinal study showed the predictive value of psychotic-like symptoms at 11 to 12 years of age for the later development of schizophreniform disorders in adult life (Poulton et al., 2000). This finding was replicated in other samples, and it has been shown that this clinical syndrome shares many central risk factors with schizophrenia itself (see review by Kelleher & Cannon, 2011). Clearly this presents the possibility of early intervention in late childhood. However, only some individuals with psychotic-like experiences (PLE) go on to develop schizophrenia, and this highlighted the need to develop effective biomarkers to identify those individuals at risk who will actually show schizophrenia.

The Edinburgh High Risk Study (see Johnstone et al., 2005) focused on the 16-to-24-years age group in a sample at risk because they had at least two first- or second-degree relatives with schizophrenia. Again, there was a significantly raised rate of schizophrenia (relative to controls) 8 years later, but many did not develop any evidence of a psychosis. Moreover, of those who did develop schizophrenia, some had not shown PLE in adolescence at the time of entering the study. The strongest predictor of later schizophrenia was the presence of schizotypal features. The question that arose was whether brain imaging biomarkers could do a better job. The imaging findings so far (Borgwardt et al., 2007; Haller et al., 2009; Harris et al., 2007) have shown reasonable predictive value with respect to the degree of prefrontal cortical folding (A-GI) but they do not provide an individual diagnosis that can be relied on. It is relevant that individuals with an increased right prefrontal A-GI did not all develop schizophrenia and, conversely, some individuals without this imaging feature did develop schizophrenia (see also Borgwardt et al., 2007; Haller et al., 2009; Milev et al., 2003, and Pantelis et al., 2003, for similar imperfect predictions from different imaging indices).

Depression

About half of all patients with major depression have a raised cortisol output that returns to normal after recovery (Goodwin, 2009). Accordingly, it seemed promising as a possible basis for the development of a biomarker. The dexamethasone suppression test (DST) seemed to be an effective marker for the melancholic variety of depression (Carroll et al., 1981). Unfortunately, the high specificity and moderate sensitivity found in comparing melancholic patients and controls was not matched when comparing major depression with other groups. As a result, the DST was largely discarded as a marker of depression. Taylor and Fink (2006; Fink, 2005) have argued that the demise of the DST reflected the inadequacies of the prevailing classification of depression rather than the inadequacy of the test itself. Accordingly, it was suggested that the DST ought to be viewed as a reasonable biomarker for melancholia, and for predicting treatment response, but not for depressive disorders as a whole (see also Berman et al., 2009).

Antisocial behavior

Three main methods have been used to find possible biomarkers of antisocial behavior: (1) peripheral and electrocortical psychophysiology; (2) structured and functional neuroimaging; and (3) neurochemical assays to assess differences in brain neurotransmitter levels and activity (Patrick & Bernat, 2009). In children and adolescents, aggression is associated with lowered baseline levels of autonomic arousal but higher autonomic reactivity to stressful events. Much the same has been seen with adults except that those with psychopathy have shown a normal baseline and a *reduced* electrodermal response to stress. EEG studies have shown enhanced cortical slow-wave activity in violent criminal offenders and a reduced P300 response to intermittent target stimuli. However, these findings seem not to apply to those showing premeditated, rather than impulsive, explosive aggression. Neuroimaging studies point to deviations in the structure and functions of the frontal, temporal, and anterior cingulate brain regions in impulsive-aggressive individuals, but the nature of the processing abnormalities remains unclear.

Neuroendocrinological studies have produced mixed results but, as with findings on autonomic arousal, the implication is that the pattern probably varies according to the presence or absence of psychopathy (van Goozen & Fairchild, 2009). Antisocial behavior is often associated with parental neglect or abuse (see Wilson, Stover, & Berkowitz, 2009), and this association largely reflects a causal effect (Eaves et al., 2010; Jaffee et al., 2004). Because it is known that abuse and neglect have marked biological effects (Gunar & Vasquez, 2006; Twardosz & Lutzker, 2010), there is a need (usually unmet) to determine whether biomarker findings concern abuse/neglect or antisocial behavior.

With respect to brain neurotransmitters, the greatest attention has focused on serotonin metabolism (see Rutter et al., 1998, for a review). There is ample evidence from whole blood serotonin findings, monoamine oxidase activity in platelets, and CSF findings on 5-hydroxyindoleacetic acid (5H1AA) levels that there are differences in serotonin functioning associated with impulsive violence. However, there are inconsistencies between findings in children and adults, and between males and females. As with other biomarkers, the findings probably also reflect the heterogeneity of antisocial behavior. Thus, it is evident that the findings with respect to reactive and instrumental aggression differ, as do the findings on antisocial behavior that is versus that which is not associated with psychopathy (Blair, 2009; Patrick & Bernat, 2009). Moreover, findings may also differ according to whether antisocial behavior is associated with psychosis or substance abuse. In addition, there is the uncertainty over the extent to which the findings reflect adverse experiences or social context, and the difficulty in knowing whether the differences reflect cause or consequence. It is all too clear that there is a long way to go in the identification of biomarkers for antisocial behavior.

CONCLUSIONS

Inferences from findings

The uncertainties over inferences from biomarker findings are well brought out in relation to structural and functional brain imaging (see Frith & Frith, 2008; Lu & Yang, 2009). There have been important technical advances, particularly with respect to the study of connectivity within and across neural networks (see Ramnani et al., 2004), and the findings on possible false positives in imaging genetics are reassuring (see Meyer-Lindenberg et al., 2008). Nevertheless, Paus (2005) has pointed to the problem posed by interindividual variability in the exact location of any given cortical area and its connectivity. Even if these technical difficulties can be overcome, there is the major problem of determining which between-group differences are a function of cause, consequence, compensation, or correlation (see Frith & Frith, 2008). With respect to the last possibility, perhaps best illustrated by the neuroendocrine findings, the correlation possibility arises because of the uncertainty over whether the group differences reflect the results of experiences such as abuse or neglect (see McCrory et al., 2010) rather than the disorder to which they provided a predisposition. Moreover, even with imaging, it needs to be appreciated that they provide only a rather indirect index of neural functioning. Quantification of the measure of brain activity will be influenced by details of the measure being used, the details of the task challenges, and the details of sample comparisons. This problem applies similarly to cognitive patterns because of the major uncertainties in inferring the neural functioning that they are thought to index (Pennington, 2006).

Heterogeneity in the disorder being studied

Most studies of biomarkers are based on groups defined according to one of the major classification systems, but it is clear that these have many serious weaknesses (Rutter, 2011). Furthermore, the relevant biological pathway involved in pathogenesis may well not be diagnosis-specific and may, indeed, occur in the normal population (Meyer-Lindenberg & Weinberger, 2006). In addition, there is often heterogeneity within diagnostic categories—as exemplified by the biological differences within antisocial behavior according to the presence/ absence of psychopathy (see above). Similarly, Happé and Ronald (2008) have argued on the basis of persuasive but somewhat inconclusive evidence that the different domains of symptomatology in ASD reflect different causal pathways. Or, again, it has been found that the catechol-o-methyltransferase (COMT) findings apply strictly to antisocial behavior within individuals with ADHD and not to either antisocial behavior or ADHD as such (Caspi et al., 2008; see also Fowler et al., 2009). Such heterogeneity may, at least in part, account for the many inconsistencies in biomarker findings. The success or failure of biomarkers should not be judged solely in relation to existing diagnostic classifications. It is possible that replicated biomarker findings might lead to a better reconceptualization of diagnostic categories based on biological causal pathways.

Developmental changes

Karmiloff-Smith (2009) has argued convincingly that the development of the brain is characterized by plasticity, with dynamic restructuring of itself over the course of ontogeny. In putting this case, she pointed, for example, to the changes over the course of development in the cognitive patterns found in both Williams syndrome and autism. As a consequence, the similarities and differences between the two vary markedly according to the age of the children studied. Similarly, children with a severe developmental receptive language disorder but a normal IQ in middle childhood show a marked drop in nonverbal IQ when older (Clegg et al., 2005; Mawhood et al, 2000; Rutter, 2008). Other follow-up studies have shown much the same (Botting & Conti-Ramsden 2003; Conti-Ramsden, et al., 2001). Of course, the change in cognitive patterns does not necessarily mean a change in the biology, but quite likely it does. In addition, studies of children experiencing an early brain injury have shown neural adaptation by which noninjured brain regions take over functions that are ordinarily carried out elsewhere in the brain (see, e.g., Lidzba et al., 2006; Stiles et al., 2005). Brain functioning (both normal and abnormal) is far from fixed.

The discussion of this issue has mainly been in relation to developmental disorders, but the points apply more widely across the whole field of mental disorders. Thus, schizophrenic psychoses first overtly manifest in adult life have their origins in childhood, as discussed above. Will the biomarker findings be the same at all points in this progression? Quite possibly not. Similarly, a progressive disease in later life, such as AD, goes through several phases. Will the biomarker findings be the same throughout? The limited available evidence suggests not.

Cause or pathophysiology

Most biomarker studies have been concerned to measure some aspect of a postulated biological pathway, and it is necessary to question why, instead, there has not been more attention to causes and, hence, the use of DNA as a possible biomarker. Some geneticists have, indeed, argued for diagnosing diseases by their causes, but there are several reasons why this has not proved fruitful. First, most mental disorders involve multifactorial causation—meaning an individually varying mixture of multiple genes and multiple environmental influences. As a consequence, there can be no single basic cause. Some geneticists have argued for the value of composites involving multiple genes (De Quervain & Papassotiropoulos, 2006; Harlaar et al., 2005; McCrae et al., 2010). However, at least so far, this has not given rise to an effective biomarker. Second, the risk effect of individual genes in the field of psychopathology is very low (Kendler, 2005)—so low that there is now debate on what has been termed the "missing heritability" (Maher, 2008), meaning the apparent gap between the often high heritability and the tiny effect of individual genes (McClellan & King, 2010). Third, the risk effect of individual genes may be dependent on gene–environment interaction (Karg et al., 2011; Rutter et al., 2006, 2009). As Kendler (2006) has noted, there is a high potential for molecular genetic findings to be important in the discovery of pathophysiological mechanisms, but it is not likely that they will be diagnostically informative in their own right.

Biomarkers to predict treatment response

There have been high hopes that genetic findings may be used for this purpose (Collins, 2010; Mrazek, 2010). Uher (2011) has argued, too, that findings on gene–environment interaction may also be helpful in deciding, when treating someone with depression, *which* form of treatment (pharmacological or psychological) might be most effective in the individual case, or whether their combination might be more appropriate. There will be a place for biomarkers in predicting treatment response, but the payoff so far has been modest.

Nevertheless, individual differences in drug response are quite substantial, and it has come to be appreciated that these are not simply a function of the blood levels achieved. As a result, brain imaging has been used to examine the impact of particular drugs on the relevant receptors in the brain (see Kapur et al., 1999; Volkow et al., 2002). This approach has been well established in research as a most important means of studying drug action. It is not likely to be practical at a clinical level, but it is conceivable that it could constitute the basis of a clinical application.

Assumptions

Much of the research on biomarkers has used straightforward intergroup comparisons without paying much attention to the assumptions that need to underlie the study of biomarkers. To begin with, it is obvious that strong connections between the biomarker and the phenotype being studied are crucial. The intergroup comparisons will do that. But, in addition, there is a need for good data on the reliability and validity of the biomarker in relevant populations. The emphasis here has to be on "relevant." For example, if the focus is on differentiation between different forms of mental disorder, the comparisons must involve multiple disorders and not just comparison with a control group of some kind. Similarly, if the biomarker is to be used as a predictor in nonsymptomatic populations, it must be determined whether the biomarker is reliable and valid in such populations. Most crucially, the inferences based on the biomarker findings must be shown to be robust and valid at an individual level. That is more of a challenge than many people appreciate. It is a universal finding that the confidence interval around the mean score on any test or marker being investigated is very wide. That necessarily means that the generalization from mean levels in two populations may not work as well as an individual predictor within any population. Finally, the conclusions must not be affected by the complexities and individual variation in multifactorial interplay. The basic point here is that when any disorder is due to the interplay among multiple genetic and multiple environmental factors, the specifics of the mix are likely to vary, and may vary substantially, among individuals.

Group validity and individual diagnoses

Scientific validity is ordinarily assessed by showing effective group identification, and this has been done for many biomarkers. However, individual diagnostic validity requires much more than that. That is, it is crucial to determine whether or not the biomarker provides an effective diagnostic indicator with a low rate of false positives and false negatives. Although claims have been made that that has been done with some biomarkers, in most cases the differentiation applies to whether or not they are a case or control. There are far fewer examples where differentiation has been established with respect to the differentiation among various competing diagnoses, and even less has been tested with respect to the prediction, within a high-risk group of some kind, of whether a disorder actually develops. It is necessary to ask what the individual base rates are and how they are affected by sampling variations, as well as what features or contexts are likely to bias the individual application of biomarkers.

Overall conclusions

Technical and conceptual advances are likely to overcome some of the current problems, as outlined here. The use of biomarkers for diagnosis is likely to be dependent on their being a unifying pathophysiology, and it remains quite uncertain how far that will prove to be the case. To a substantial extent the development of sound biomarkers will be dependent on new research that can elucidate the pathophysiology of different disorders. Biomarkers need to be thought of as tools that should greatly aid objective quantification in relation to psychopathological issues, rather than as something that can replace clinical approaches. Nevertheless, given the many findings that cast doubt on the validity of diagnostic distinctions in the prevailing classifications today, we need to consider the possibility that there may be advantages of making diagnoses on the basis of biological findings, rather than of symptom patterns. While we do not know how biomarkers will develop in the years ahead, it is already clear that they constitute an area that is well worth substantial research investment.

REFERENCES

Amaral, D. G., Schumann, C. M., & Nordahl, C. W. (2008). Neuroanatomy of autism. *Trends in Neuroscience, 31*, 137–145.

Aisen, P. S., Petersen, R. C., Donohue, M. C., Gamst, A., Raman, R., Thomas, R. G., et al. (2010). Clinical core of the Alzheimer's disease neuroimaging initiative: Progress and plans. *Alzheimer's & Dementia, 6*, 239–246.

Battaglia, M., Pesenti-Gritti, P., Spatola, C.A., Ogliari, A., & Tambs, K. (2008). A twin study of the common vulnerability between heightened sensitivity to hypercapnia and panic disorder. *American Journal of Medicine B: Neuropsychiatric Genetics, 147B*, 586–593.

Berman, R. M., Sporn, J., Charney, D. S., & Matthew, S. J. (2009). Prinicples of the pharmacotherapy of depression. In D. S. Charney & E. J. Nestler (Eds.), *Neurobiology of mental illness* (3rd ed., pp. 491–514). New York: Oxford University Press.

Biomarkers Definition Working Group. (2001). *Clinical Pharmacoology & Therapeutics, 69*, 89–95.

Blair, R. J. R. (2009). Neurobiology of reactive and instrumental aggression. In D. S. Charney & E. J. Nestler (Eds.), *Neurobiology of mental illness* (3rd ed., pp. 1307–1320). New York: Oxford University Press.

Blennow, K., & Hampel, H. (2003). CSF markers for incipient Alzheimer's disease. *Lancet Neurology, 2*, 605–613.

Borgwardt, S. J., McGuire, P. K., Aston, J., et al. (2007). Structural brain abnormalities in individuals with an at-risk mental state who later develop psychosis. *British Journal of Psychiatry, 191*, 69–75.

Botting, N., & Conti-Ramsden, G. (2003). Autism, primary pragmatic difficulties, and specific language impairment: Can we distinguish them using psycholinguistic markers? *Developmental Medicine & Child Neurology, 45*, 515–524.

Bryson, S. E., Saigenbaum, L., Brian, J., et al. (2007). A prospective case series of high-risk infants who developed autism. *Journal of Autism & Developmental Disorders, 37,* 12–24.

Buchman, D. Z., & Iles, J. (2010). Imaging genetics for our neurogenetic future. *Minnesota Journal of Science. & Technology, 11*(1), 79–97.

Cannon, M., Caspi, A., Moffitt, T. E., Harrington, H. L., Taylor, A., Murray, R. M., & Poulton, R. (2002). Evidence for early-childhood, pan-developmental impairment specific to schizophreniform disorder: Results from a longitudinal birth cohort. *Archives of General Psychiatry, 59,* 449–456.

Carroll, B. J., Feinberg, M., Greden, J. F., et al. (1981). A specific laboratory test for the diagnosis of melancholia. Standardization, validation and clinical utility. *Archives of General Psychiatry, 38,* 15–22.

Caspi, A., Langley, K., Milne, B., Moffitt, T., O'Donovan, M., Owen, M., Polo-Tomas, M., Poulton, R., Rutter, M., Taylor, A., Williams, B., & Thapar, T. (2008). A replicated molecular genetic basis for subtyping antisocial behavior in children with attention-deficit/hyperactivity disorder. *Archives of General Psychiatry, 65,* 203–210.

Clegg, J., Hollis, C., Mawhood, L., & Rutter, M. (2005). Developmental language disorder—a follow-up in later adult life. Cognitive, language, and psychosocial outcomes. *Journal of Child Psychology & Psychiatry, 46,* 128–149.

Collins, F. S. (2010). *The language of life: DNA and the revolution in personalized medicine.* New York: Harper Collins.

Conti-Ramsden, G., Botting, N., Simkin, Z., & Knox, E. (2001). Follow-up of children attending infant language units: Outcomes at 11 years of age. *International Journal of Language & Communication Disorders, 36,* 207–219.

Dapretto, M., Davies, M. S., Pfeifer, J. H., Scott, A. A., Sigman, M., Bookheimer, S. Y., & Iacoboni, M. (2006). Understanding emotions in others:Mmirror neuron dysfunction in children with autism spectrum disorders. *Nature Neuroscience, 9,* 28–30.

De Quervain, D. J. F., & Papassotiropoulos, A. (2006). Identification of a genetic cluster influencing memory performance and hippocampal activity in humans. *Proceedings of the National Academy of Sciences, 103,* 4270–4274.

Eaves, L. J., Prom, E. C., & Silberg, J. L. (2010). The mediating effect of parental neglect on adolescent and young adult anti-sociality: A longitudinal study of twins and their parents. *Behavioral Genetics, 40,* 425–437.

Ecker, C., Marquand, A., Mourão-Miranda, Johnston, P., Daly, E. M., Brammer, M. J., et al. (2010). Describing the brain in autism in five dimensions—magnetic resonance imaging-assisted diagnosis of autism spectrum disorder using a multiparameter classification approach. *Journal of Neuroscience, 30,* 10612–10623.

Elsabbagh, M., & Johnson, M. H. (2010). Getting answers from babies about autism. *Trends in Cognitive Science, 4,* 81–87.

Elsabbagh, M., Volein, A., Csibra, G., Holmboe, K., Garwood, H., Tucker, L., et al. (2009a). Neural correlates of eye gaze processing in the infant broader autism phenotype. *Biological Psychiatry, 65,* 31–38.

Elsabbagh, M., Volein, A., Holmboe, K., Tucker, K., Csibra, G., Baron-Cohone, S., et al. (2009b). Visual orienting in the early broader autism phenotype: disengagement and facilitation. *Journal of Child Psychology & Psychiatry, 50,* 637–642.

Fan, Y-T., Decety, J., Yang, C-Y., Liu, J-L., & Cheng, Y. (2010). Unbroken mirror neurons in autism spectrum disorders. *Journal of Child Psychology & Psychiatry, 51,* 981–988.

Fink, M. (2005). Should the dexamethasone suppression test be resurrected? *Acta Psychiatrica Scandanavia, 112,* 245–249.

Fowler, T., Langley, K., Rice, F., van den Bree, M. B., Ross, K., Wilkinson, L. S., Owen, M. J., O'Donovan, M. C., & Thapar, A. (2009). Psychopathy trait scores in adolescents with childhood ADHD: the contribution of genotypes affecting MAOA, 5HTT and COMT activity. *Psychiatric Genetics, 19,* 312–319.

Frith, C., & Frith, U. (2008). What can we learn from structural and functional brain imaging? In M. Rutter, D. Bishop, D. Pine, S. Scott, J. Stevenson, E. Taylor, & A. Thapar (Eds.), *Rutter's child and adolescent psychiatry* (5th ed., pp. 134–144). Oxford: Blackwell.

Greely, H. T., & Wagner, A. D. (2011). Reference guide on neuroscience. In: *Reference manual on scientific evidence* (3rd ed., pp. 747–812). U.S. National Academy of Sciences.

Gliga, T., Esabbagh, M., Andravizou, A., & Johnson, M. (2009). Faces attract infants' attention in complex displays. *Infancy, 14,* 550–562.

Goodwin, G. (2009). Neurobiological aetiology of mood disorders. In M. G. Gelder, N. C. Andreasen, J. J. Lopez-Ibor, & J. R. Geddes (Eds.), *New Oxford textbook of psychiatry* (2nd ed., pp. 658–665). New York: Oxford University Press.

Haller, S., Borgwardt, S. J., Schindler, C., Aston, J., Radue, E. W., & Riecher-Rössler, A. (2009). Can cortical thickness asymmetry analysis contribute to detection of at-risk mental state and first-episode psychosis? A pilot study. *Radiology, 250,* 212–221.

Happé, F., & Ronald, A. (2008). The 'fractionable autism triad': A review of evidence from behavioral, genetic, cognitive and neural research. *Neuropsychological Review, 18,* 287–304.

Harlaar, N., Butcher, L. M., Meaburn, E., Sham, P., Craig, I.W., Plomin, R. (2005). A behavioural genomic analysis of DNA markers associated with general cognitive ability in 7-year-olds. *Journal of Child Psychology & Psychiatry, 46,* 1097–1107.

Harris, J. M., Moorhead, T. W. J., Miller, P., McIntosh, A. M., Bonnici, H. M., Owens, D. G. C., Johnstone, E. C., & Lawrie, S. M. (2007). Increased prefrontal gyrification in a large high-risk cohort characterizes those who develop schizophrenia and reflects abnormal prefrontal development. *Biological Psychiatry, 62,* 722–729.

Holmboe, K., Elsabbagh, M., Volein, A., Tucker, L. A. A., Baron-Cohen, S., Bolton, P., et al. (2010). Frontal cortex functioning in the infant broader autism phenotype. *Infant Behavior & Development, 33,* 482–491.

Hort, J., O'Brien, J. T., Gainotti, G., Pirttila, T., Popescu, B. O., Rektorova, I., et al. (2010). EFNS guidelines for the diagnosis and management of Alzheimer's disease. *European Journal of Neurology, 17,* 1236–1248.

Ioannidis, J. P. A. (2011). Excess significance bias in the literature on brain volume abnormalities. *Archives of General Psychiatry, 68,* 773–780.

Jack, C. R., Knopman, D. S., Jagust, W. J., Shaw, L. M., Aisen, P. S., Weiner, M. W., Petersen, R. C., & Trojanowski, J. Q. (2010). Hypothetical model of dynamic biomarkers of the Alzheimer's pathological cascade. *Lancet, 9,* 119–128.

Jaffee, S. R., Caspi, A., Moffitt, T. E., & Taylor, A. (2004). Physical maltreatment victim to antisocial child: Evidence of an environmentally mediated process. *Journal of Abnormal Psychology, 113*, 44–55.

Johnstone, E. C., Ebmeier, K. P., Miller, P., Owens, D. G. C., & Lawrie, S. M. (2005). Predicting schizophrenia: findings from the Edinburgh High-Risk study. *British Journal of Psychiatry, 186*, 18–25.

Kapaki, E., Paraskevas, G. P., Salonis, I., & Zournas, C. (2003). CSF tau protein and β-amyloid (1-42) in Alzheimer's disease diagnosis: discrimination from normal ageing and other dementias in the Greek population. *European Journal of Neurology, 10*, 119–128.

Kapur, S., Zipursky, R. B., & Remmington, G. (1999). Clinical and theoretical implications of 5-HT2 and D2 receptor occupancy of clozapine, risperidone, and olanzapine in schizophrenia. *American Journal of Psychiatry, 156*, 286–293.

Karg, K., Burmeister, M., Shedden, K., & Sen, S. (2011). The serotonin transporter promoter variant (5-HTTLPR), stress and depression meta-analysis revisisted: evidence of genetic moderation. *Archives of General Psychiatry, 68*, 444–454.

Karmiloff-Smith, A. (2009). Nativism versus neuroconstructivism: rethinking the study of developmental disorders. *Developmental Psychology, 45*, 56–63.

Kelleher, I., & Cannon, M. (2011). Psychotic-like experiences in the general population: charaterizing a high-risk group for psychosis. *Psychological Medicine, 41*, 1–6.

Kelley, B. J., & Petersen, R. C. (2009). Mild cognitive impairment. In D. S. Charney & E. J. Nestler (Eds.), *Neurobiology of mental illness* (3rd ed., pp. 1066–1081). Oxford University Press.

Kendler, K. S. (2005). 'A gene for...' The nature of gene action in psychiatric disorders. *American Journal of Psychiatry, 162*, 1243–1252.

Kendler, K. S. (2006). Reflections on the relationship between psychiatric genetics and psychiatric nosology. *American Journal of Psychiatry, 163*, 1138–1146.

Keshavan, M., Kennedy, J., & Murray, R. (2004). *Neurodevelopment and schizophrenia.* Cambridge: Cambridge University Press.

Landa, R. J., Holman, K. C., & Garrett-Mayer, E. (2007). Social and communication development in toddlers with early and later diagnosis of autism spectrum disorders. *Archives of General Psychiatry, 64*, 853–864.

Lidzba, K., Staudt, M., Wilke, M., & Krageloh-Mann, I. (2006). Visuospatial deficits in patients with early left-hemispheric lesions and functional reorganization of language: consequence of lesion or reorganizing? *Neuropsychologi, 44*, 1088–1094.

Losh, M., Adolphs, R., Poe, M. D., Couture, S., Penn, D., Baranek, G. T., & Piven, J. (2009). The neuropsychological profile of autism and the broad autism phenotype. *Archives of General Psychiatry, 66*, 518–526.

Lu, H., & Yang, Y. (2009). Neuroimaging methods using nuclear magnetic resonance. In D. S. Charney & E. J. Nestler (Eds.), *Neurobiology of mental illness* (3rd ed., pp. 179–191). Oxford University Press.

Luman, M., Oosterlaan, J., & Sergeant, J. A. (2005). The impact of reinforcement contingencies on AD/HD: A review and theoretical appraisal. *Clinical Psychology Review, 25*, 183–213.

Maher, B. (2008). Personal genomes: The case of the missing heritability. *Nature, 456*, 18–21.

Mawhood, L., Howlin, P., & Rutter, M. (2000). Autism and developmental receptive language disorder—a comparative follow-up in early adult life. I: Cognitive and Language outcomes. *Journal of Child Psychology & Psychiatry, 41*, 547–559.

McCrae, R. R., Scally, M., Abecasis, G. R., & Terracciano, A. (2010). An alternative to the search for single polymorphisms: toward molecular personality scales for the five-factor model.*Journal of Personality & Social Psychology,9*, 1014–1024

McCrory, E, De Brito, S. A., & Viding, E. (2010). Research review: The neurobiology and genetics of maltreatment and adversity. *Journal of Child Psychology & Psychiatry, 51*, 1079–1095.

McClellan J., & King, M-C. (2010). Genetic heterogeneity in human disease. *Cell, 141*, 210–217.

Meyer-Lindenberg, A., Mervis, C. B., & Berman, K. F. (2006). Neural mechanisms in Williams syndrome: a unique window to genetic influences on cognition and behaviour. *Nature Reviews Neuroscience, 7*, 380–393.

Meyer-Lindenberg, A., Nicodemus, K. K., Egan, M. F., Callicott, J. H., Mattay, V., & Weinberger, D. R. (2008). False positives in imaging genetics. *NeuroImage, 40*, 655–661.

Milev, P., Beng-Choon, H., Arndt, S., Nopoulos, P., & Andreasen, N. C. (2003). Initial magnetic resonance imaging volumetric brain measurements and outcome in schizophrenia: A prospective longitudinal study with 5-year follow-up. *Biological Psychiatry, 54*, 608–615.

Mitchell, A. J., & Shiri-Feshki, M. (2009). Rate of progression of mild cognitive impairment to dementia—meta-analysis of 41 robust inception cohort studies. *Acta Psychiatrica Scandanvia, 119*, 252–265.

Mitsis, E. M., Bobinski, M., Brys, M., Glodzik-Sobanska, L., DeSanti, S., Li, Y., et al. (2009). Neuropathological and neuroimaging studies of the hippocampus in normal aging and in Alzheimer's disease. In D. S. Charney & E. J. Nestler (Eds.), *Neurobiology of mental illness* (3rd ed., pp. 936–957). Oxford University Press.

Mrazek, D. A. (2010). *Psychiatric pharmacogenomics.* New York: Oxford University Press.

National Research Council. (2002). *Scientific research in education.* Washington DC: National Academy Press.

Pantelis, C., Velakoulis, D., McGorry, P. D., Wood, S. J., Suckling, J., Phillips, L. J., et al. (2003). Neuroanatomical abnormalities before and after onset of psychosis: a cross-sectional and longitudinal MRI comparison. *Lancet, 361*, 281–288.

Patrick, C. J., & Bernat, E. M. (2009). From markers to mechanisms: Using psychophysiological measures to elucidate basic processes underlying aggressive externalizing behavior. In S. Hodgins, E. Viding, & A. Plodowski (Eds.), *The neurobiological basis of violence: Science and rehabilitation* (pp. 223–250). Oxford University Press.

Paus, T. (2005). Inferring causality in brain images: a perturbation approach. *Philosophical Transactions of Royal Society B, 360*, 1109–1114.

Pennington, B. (2006). From single to multiple deficit models of developmental disorders. *Cognition, 101*, 385–413.

Plessen, K. J., & Peterson, B. S. (2009). The neurobiology of impulsivity and self-regulatory control in children with attention-deficit/hyperactivity disorder. In D. S. Charney & E. J. Nestler (Eds.), *Neurobiology of mental illness* (3rd ed., pp.1129–1152). Oxford University Press.

Poulton, R. P., Caspi, A., Moffitt, T. E., Cannon, M., Murray, R. & Harrington, H. L. (2000). Children's self-reported psychotic symptoms predict adult schizophreniform disorders: A 15-year longitudinal study. *Archives of General Psychiatry, 57*, 1053–1058.

Ramachandran, V. S., & Oberman, L. M. (2006). Broken mirrors: a theory of autism. *Scientific American, 295*, 62–69.

Ramnani, N., Behrens, T. E. J., Penny W., & Matthews, P. M. (2004). New approaches for exploring anatomical and functional connectivity in the human brain. *Biological Psychiatry, 56*, 613–619.

Ritchie, K. (2010). Designing prevention programmes to reduce incidence of dementia: prospective cohort study of modifiable risk factors. *British Medical Journal, 341*, C3885.

Rizzolatti, G., & Craighero, L. (2004). The mirror-neuron system. *Annual Review of Neuroscience, 27*, 169–192.

Rizzolatti, G., & Fabbri-Destro, M. (2010). Mirror neurons: from discovery to autism. *Experimental Brain Research, 200*, 223–237.

Rutter, M. (2008). Autism and specific language impairments: A tantalising dance. In V. Joffe, M. Cruice, & S. Chiate (Eds.), *Language disorders in children and adults* (pp. 122–137). London: Wiley.

Rutter, M. (2011). Child psychiatric diagnosis and classification: Concepts, findings, challenges and potential. *Journal of Child Psychology & Psychiatry, 52*(6), 647–660.

Rutter, M., Giller, H., & Hagell, A. (1998). *Antisocial behavior by young people.* New York: Cambridge University Press.

Rutter, M., Moffitt, T. E., & Caspi, A. (2006). Gene-environment interplay and psychopathology: Multiple varieties but real effects. *Journal of Child Psychology & Psychiatry, 47*, 226–261.

Rutter, M., Thapar, A., & Pickles, A. (2009). Gene-environment interactions: biologically valid pathway or artifact? *Archives of General Psychiatry, 66*, 1287–1289.

Sagvolden, T., Russell, V. A., Aase H., Johansen, E. B., & Farshbaf, M. (2005). Rodent models of attention-deficit/hyperactivity disorder. *Biological Psychiatry, 57*, 1239–1247.

Sobel, J. L., Bansal, R., Maia, T. V., Sanchez, J., Mazzone, L., Durkin, K., et al. (2010). Basal ganglia surface morphology and the effects of stimulant medications in youth with attention deficit hyperactivity disorder. *American Journal of Psychiatry, 167*, 977–986.

Spatola, C. A. M., Scaini, S., Presenti-Gritti, P., Medland, S. E., Moruzzi, S., Ogliari, A., Tambs, K., & Battaglia, M. (2011). Gene-environment interactions in panic disorder and CO_2 sensitivity: Effects of events occurring early in life. *American Journal of Medical Genetics, 156*, 79–88.

Stiles, J., Reilly, J., Paul, B., & Moses, P. (2005). Cognitive development following early brain injury: Evidence for neural adaptation. *Trends in Cognitive Science, 9*, 136–143.

Toal, F., Murphy D. G., & Murphy, K. C. (2005). Autistic-spectrum disorders: lessons from neuroimaging. *British Journal of Psychiatry, 187*, 395–397.

Taylor, M. A., & Fink, M. (2006). *Melancholia: the diagnosis, pathophysiology, and treatment of depressive illness.* Cambridge, New York: Cambridge University Press.

Trojanowski, J. Q., Vandeerstichele, H., Korecka, M., Clark, C. M., Aisen, P. S., Petersen, R. C., Blennow, K., et al. (2010). Update on the biomarker core of the Alzheimer's disease neuroimaging initiative subjects. *Alzheimer's & Dementia, 6,* 230–238.

Twardosz, S., & Lutzker, J. R. (2010). Child maltreatment and the developing brain: A review of neuroscience perspectives. *Aggression & Violent Behavior, 15,* 59–68.

Uher, R. (2011). Genes, environment & personalized treatment for depression. In K. Dodge & M. Rutter (Eds.), *Genes, environment and policies in mental health* (pp. 140–158). New York: Guilford Press.

van Goozen, S. H. M., & Fairchild, G. (2009). The neuroendocrinology of antisocial behavior. In S. Hodgins, E. Viding, & A. Plodowski (Eds.), *The neurobiological basis of violence: Science and rehabilitation* (pp. 201–221). Oxford University Press.

Volkow, N. D., Wang, G. J., Fowler, J. S., Logan, J., Franceschi, D., Maynard, L., et al. (2002). Relationship between blockage of dopamine transporters by oral methylphenidate and the increases in extracellular dopamine: therapeutic implications. *Synapse, 43,* 181–187.

Wilson, H. W., Stover, C. S., & Berkowitz, S. J. (2009). Research review: The relationship between childhood violence exposure and juvenile antisocial behavior: A meta-analytic review. *Journal of Child Psychology & Psychiatry, 50,* 769–779.

Zwaigenbaum, L., Bryson, S., Lord, C., Rogers, S., Carter, A., Carver, L., et al. (2009). Clinical assessment and management of toddlers with suspected autism spectrum disorder: Insights from studies of high-risk infants. *Pediatrics, 5,* 1383–1391.

Zwaigenbaum, L., Bryson, S., Rogers, T., Roberts, W., Brian, J., & Szatmari, P. (2005). Behavioral manifestations of autism in the first year of life. *International Journal of Developmental Neuroscience, 23,* 143–152.

12

Neuroimaging-Based Automatic Classification of Schizophrenia

VINCE D. CALHOUN AND MOHAMMAD R. ARBABSHIRANI

INTRODUCTION

Population studies show that the lifetime prevalence of all psychotic disorders is as high as 4 percent (http://www.nimh.nih.gov/statistics/SMI_AASR.shtml). These disorders be significantly impairing and impose huge societal cost (Rice, 1999). Clinically, the patient's self-reported experiences and observed behavior over the longitudinal course of the illness constitute the basis for diagnosis. The overlapping symptoms of mental disorders and the absence of standard biologically based clinical tests make differential diagnosis a challenging task. Early diagnosis of these diseases can significantly improve treatment response and reduce associated costs. In addition, biomarker discovery can help us better understand the effects of the disease in the brain, which can result in more effective drugs.

Human brain has a well-identified structural anatomy as well as a functional anatomy. Advances in neuroimaging technologies in the past two decades have opened a new window into the structure and function of the healthy human brain as well as many brain disorders such as schizophrenia. Modalities such as magnetic resonance imaging (MRI) and magnetoencephalography (MEG), along with more traditional methods such as electroencephalography (EEG), have made it possible to noninvasively study various aspects of the human brain.

MRI-related techniques such as structural MRI (SMRI), functional MRI (fMRI), and diffusion tensor imaging (DTI), have the benefit of providing localized spatial information. These MRI-related techniques have provided new insight into the human brain and have brought hope to researchers trying to unravel the secrets of one of the most complex systems in the universe, the human brain.

SMRI has made it possible to visualize the brain at high spatial resolution (1 mm^3 or less). SMRI high-resolution images of the brain are ideal for studying various brain structures as well as detecting physical abnormalities, lesions, and damages. DTI allows mapping the diffusion process of water in biological tissues. In brain imaging, DTI at each voxel is represented by a symmetrical 3×3 matrix, called diffusion tensor. In the white matter regions of the brain, there is a higher rate of diffusion along the direction of the fibers. This property enables this imaging technique to visualize anatomical connections between different brain regions. fMRI, in contrast to the mentioned MRI-based techniques, measures brain activity by detecting changes in the blood flow. fMRI makes it possible to study functional regions and networks of the brain as well as temporal association among them.

There are several biological markers (so-called biomarkers) that can be extracted from each of these complementary imaging techniques. These biomarkers have the potential to explain effects of psychiatric disorders on the brain. Recently, there has been a growing interest in designing objective prognostic/diagnostic tools based on neuroimaging and other data that display high accuracy and robustness. Promising results of these studies in detecting and predicting mental disorders such as schizophrenia suggest potential clinical utility of neuroimaging data. In this chapter, we focus on automatic diagnosis of schizophrenia as a good example of heterogeneous mental disorders based on different MRI-based techniques. However, most of the methods are applicable to other disorders, such as Alzheimer's disease, mild cognitive impairment, bipolar disorder, and even disorders such as psychopathy.

WHAT IS SCHIZOPHRENIA?

Schizophrenia is among the most prevalent mental disorders, affecting about 1 percent of the population worldwide (Bhugra, 2005; Wyatt et al., 1995). This chronic heterogeneous disease is usually characterized by disintegration in perception of reality, cognitive problems, and a chronic course with lasting impairment (Heinrichs & Zakzanis, 1998). Social isolation, paranoia, and difficulties in memory (both working and long-term) are other common symptoms of schizophrenia. The average age of onset of schizophrenia is 18 and 25 for men and women respectively. Schizophrenia is thought to be related to a combination of genetic and environmental factors, although the exact cause is still unknown. Several psychological and neurological mechanisms have been associated with schizophrenia. Unfortunately, there is no clinical test for schizophrenia, and the diagnosis is based on either the American Psychiatric Association's *Diagnostic and Statistical Manual of Mental Disorders* (DSM-IV) or the World Health Organization's *International Statistical Classification of Diseases and Related Health Problems.* The criteria for diagnosis are usually based on self-reported symptoms and abnormalities in behavior.

AUTOMATIC DIAGNOSIS BASED ON STRUCTURAL BIOMARKERS

Volumetric structural abnormalities measured by MRI are the main category of structural studies (Caan et al., 2006; Csernansky et al., 2004; Fan et al., 2005; Kawasaki et al., 2007; Nakamura et al., 2004; Sun et al., 2009; Takayanagi et al., 2011). Neuroimaging studies using MRI have documented reductions in gray matter (GM) volume accompanied by proportionate increases in ventricular cerebrospinal fluid (CSF) volume. Also, some studies showed volumetric abnormalities in subcortical structures such as thalamus and hippocampus (Csernansky et al., 2004; Honea et al., 2005). Various methods such as voxel-based morphometry (VBM) (Davatzikos et al., 2005; Fan et al., 2007), cortical pattern matching (Sun et al., 2009), cortical thickness surface based approach (Yoon et al., 2007), and manually selected regions of interest (ROIs) (Nakamura et al., 2004; Takayanagi et al., 2010) have been used to differentiate schizophrenia patients from healthy controls.

Davatzikos et al. (2005) extracted GM, white matter, and CSF volumes in number of brain regions as features and trained and tested a classifier on a cohort of 69 patients and 79 healthy controls. They reported 81.1 percent mean classification accuracy. Fan et al. (2007) used a combination of deformation-based morphometry and machine learning methods to distinguish schizophrenia patients from healthy controls. First they computed local tissue volumes based on extracted tissue density maps. By using support vector machine (SVM), they selected the most important features, and then they trained and tested the SVM classifier using the leave-one-out strategy. Figure 12.1 illustrates the brain regions with most group difference between patients and controls. Their method demonstrated high classification accuracy (91.8 percent for female and 90.8 percent for male subjects), which is very promising.

Yoon et al. (2007) proposed pattern classification based on cortical thickness. They computed the cortical thickness based on Euclidean distance between linked vertices on inner and outer cortical surfaces. They demonstrated that the thickness of several brain regions, such as precentral, postcentral, superior frontal and temporal, cingulate and parahippocampal gyri, have high discriminative power between the patient and control groups. They reported 88 to 94 percent accuracy for the automatic classification based on these cortical thicknesses.

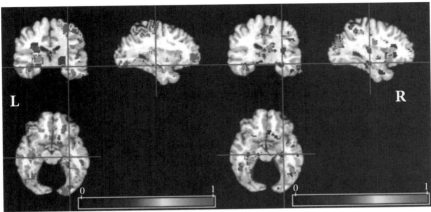

Figure 12.1 Brain regions with most group differences for male (right) and female subjects (left). (Courtesy of Fan et al., 2007)

Sun et al. (2009) used cortical pattern matching method to differentiate patients from controls. This method is able to capture correspondence between brain surfaces. Figure 12.2 shows the maps of average GM density of patients with recent onset of psychosis and controls. It is evident from Figure 12.2 that patients show lower GM density, especially in the lateral surface of the prefrontal and temporal lobes, limbic regions, cingulate sulci, and parieto-occipital fissures.

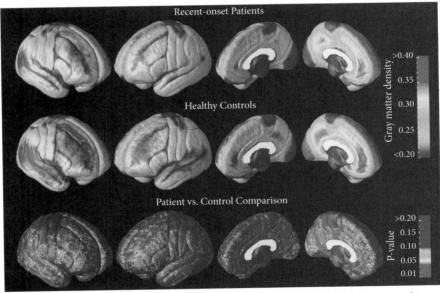

Figure 12.2 GM density and P-maps of patients and healthy controls. (Courtesy of Sun et al., 2009)

By using multinomial logistic regression classifier, they reported 86.1 percent accuracy for automatic classification of patients from controls using GM densities as features.

Takayanagi et al. (2010) used volumes of 19 ROIs for differentiating first-episode schizophrenia patients from healthy controls. They reported 75.6 and 82.9 percent accuracy for male and female subjects respectively. They combined regional brain volumes with cortical thickness features and achieved above 80 percent accuracy in automatic classification of first-episode schizophrenia patients. Figure 12.3 illustrates the selected regions for their model based on volume or cortical thickness. Cortical thinning and volume reductions are evident in prefrontal and temporal cortices of the patients.

Another major category of structural studies is based on DTI technique. There are a number of parameters that can be computed based on tensor matrices of each brain voxel in DTI imaging. One of these measures, fractional anisotropy (FA), shows the anisotropy of the self-diffusion of water molecules (Kingsley, 2006). Since in the white matter of the brain, water tends have a higher rate of diffusion along the direction of fibers, it is anisotropic. Therefore, FA can reflect white matter fiber integrity, which has been shown to be associated with a number of brain disorders, such as schizophrenia (Kubicki et al., 2007; Szeszko et al., 2008). Another measure calculated from tensor matrices is mean diffusivity (MD), which shows the magnitude of self-diffusion of water molecules. MD abnormality has been reported in schizophrenia patients in a number of studies (Ardekani et al., 2005; Lee et al., 2009; Narr et al., 2009). FA and MD features have been used in automatic classification of schizophrenia patients in several studies (Ardekani et al., 2011; Caan et al., 2006; Caprihan et al., 2008).

Caprihan et al. (2008) proposed applying discriminant principal component analysis (DPCA) to FA images of DTI of healthy controls and schizophrenia patients. They reported 80 percent accuracy using FA features for automated classification of patients. Ardekani et al. (2011) used both FA and MD maps to discriminate patients from controls. Using linear discriminant analysis they achieved a very promising classification accuracy of 94 percent. Figure 12.4 illustrates most discriminative white matter regions of classification in their study.

AUTOMATIC DIAGNOSIS BASED ON FUNCTIONAL BIOMARKERS

The other main category of automatic diagnosis of schizophrenia is based on functional biomarkers. fMRI is a powerful tool used to noninvasively investigate the working brain. This neuroimaging modality has opened a new window into the complexity of brain function based on blood oxygen-level dependent

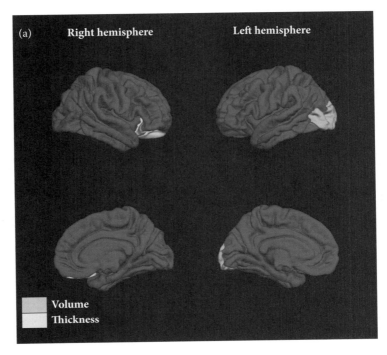

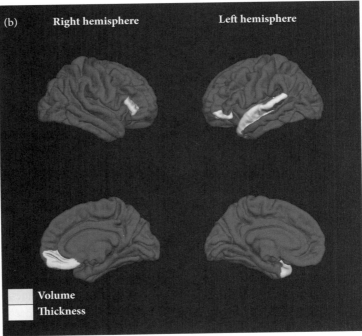

Figure 12.3 Discriminative brain regions based on volume or cortical thickness for male (left) and female (right) subjects.

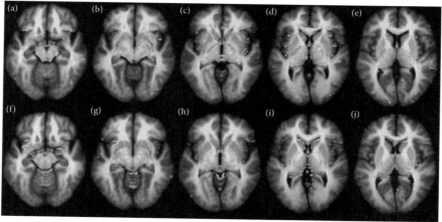

Figure 12.4 Slices from FA (a–e) and MD (f–j) images. Subjects with higher values in yellow regions tend to be classified as healthy controls, while those with higher blue values tend to be classified as patients. (Figure courtesy of Ardekani, et al., 2011)

(BOLD) signal changes. This modality also has been used to measure the functional connectivity in the brain.

Functional connectivity (FC) is defined as correlation (or other kinds of statistical dependency) among spatially remote brain regions (Friston, 2002). FC analysis documents interactions among brain regions during a task as well as during resting state scans. Two widely used FC approaches are (a) seed-based analysis (Biswal, Van Kylen, & Hyde, 1997; Biswal, Yetkin, Haughton, & Hyde, 1995; Cordes, Haughton, Carew, Arfanakis, & Maravilla, 2002; Cordes et al., 2000; Fox et al., 2005; Lowe, Mock, & Sorenson, 1998; Stein et al., 2000) and (b) spatial independent component analysis (ICA) (Calhoun, Adali, Pearlson, & Pekar, 2001; Esposito et al., 2005; Garrity et al., 2007; McKeown et al., 1998; van de Ven, Formisano, Prvulovic, Roeder, & Linden, 2004). In the seed-based approach, individual seed voxels from predefined brain ROIs are chosen and the cross-correlation of other voxels' time courses with the selected seeds are then computed to derive a correlation map. This map can then be thresholded to identify voxels showing significant FC with the seed voxels.

An alternative approach is based on ICA, a multivariate data-driven method that, as a blind source separation method, can recover a set of signals from their linear mixtures and has yielded fruitful results with fMRI data (Calhoun, Liu, & Adali, 2009). ICA estimates maximally independent components using independence measures based on higher-order statistics. ICA requires no specific temporal model (task-based design matrix), making it ideal for analyzing resting state data. Spatial ICA (sICA) is the predominant ICA approach used for fMRI data (Calhoun et al., 2001a; McKeown et al., 1998). sICA decomposes fMRI data into a set of maximally spatially independent maps and their corresponding time courses. Each thresholded sICA map may consist of several remote brain regions forming a brain functional network. sICA generates consistent spatial maps while modeling complex fMRI data collected during a task or in the resting state (Turner & Twieg, 2005) although the task can result in a subtle modulation of the spatial patterns (Calhoun et al., 2008). The dynamics of the BOLD signal within a single component is described by that component's time course. Regions contributing significantly within a given component are strongly functionally connected to each other.

There is growing interest in studying FC among brain functional networks. This type of connectivity, which can be considered as a higher level of FC, is termed functional network connectivity (FNC) (Jafri et al., 2008) and measures the statistical dependencies among brain functional networks. Each functional network may consist of multiple remote brain regions. Spatial components resulting from sICA are maximally spatially independent but their corresponding time courses can show a considerable amount of temporal dependency. This property of sICA makes it an excellent choice for studying FNC, which can be studied by analyzing these weaker dependencies among sICA time courses. These dependencies can be analyzed by correlation methods (Jafri et al., 2008) or algorithms such as dynamic causal modeling (Stevens et al., 2007) or Granger causality (Havlicek et al., 2010; Stevens et al., 2009).

Using FC methods, researchers have shown disrupted functional integration in schizophrenia patients (Bokde et al., 2006; Jafri, Pearlson, Stevens, & Calhoun, 2008; Liang et al., 2006; Mikula & Niebur, 2006; Salvador et al., 2010). Liang et al. (2006) reported decreased FC among insula, prefrontal lobe, and temporal lobe and increased connectivity between cerebellum and several other brain regions. (Meyer-Lindenberg et al., 2005) reported abnormal FC in frontotemporal interactions in schizophrenia in selected ROIs using positron emission tomography (PET) brain scans on a working memory task. Salvador et al. (2010) reported hyperconnectivity within medial and orbital structures of the frontal lobe and hyperconnectivity between these regions and several cortical and subcortical structures in schizophrenia patients.

Automatic diagnosis of schizophrenia based on functional biomarkers is relatively new. These studies fall into two main groups based on the functional biomarker features used: activation pattern of functional regions and networks of the brain and functional connectivity among brain regions and networks. (Arribas et al., 2010; Calhoun et al., 2008; Castro et al., 2011; Demirci et al., 2008a; Du et al., 2012; Georgopoulos et al., 2007; Michael et al., 2008; Shen et al., 2010; Yang et al., 2010).

Calhoun, Maciejewski, Pearlson, & Kiehl (2008) extracted temporal and default mode networks from fMRI data during the performance of an auditory oddball task using the ICA method. These networks were selected based on previous studies suggesting alteration of activation pattern of these networks in schizophrenia patients (Bluhm et al., 2007; Calhoun et al., 2004; Garrity et al., 2007). They used the combined maps of these two networks as the feature set to differentiate schizophrenia patients, bipolar disorder patients, and healthy controls from each other. Figure 12.5 illustrates the temporal and the default mode networks for the three groups.

Pairwise comparison of these three groups is illustrated in Figure 12.6. They reported an average sensitivity and specificity of 90 and 95 percent, which is very significant given the highly overlapping symptoms of bipolar and schizophrenia patients.

Demirci et al. (2008) proposed applying projection pursuit algorithm on several ICA components of fMRI data obtained during an auditory oddball task. The reported accuracy of their automatic classification method for differentiating schizophrenia patients from healthy controls was 80 to 90 percent.

Castro et al. (2011) proposed a framework based on composite kernels and recursive feature elimination for distinguishing patients with schizophrenia from healthy controls. Their proposed framework evaluates nonlinear

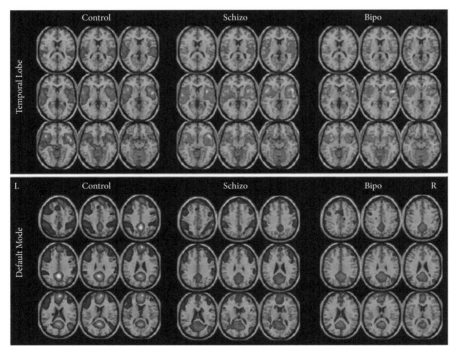

Figure 12.5 Temporal and default mode networks for schizophrenia, bipolar disorder, and healthy controls. (Figure Courtesy of Calhoun et al., 2008)

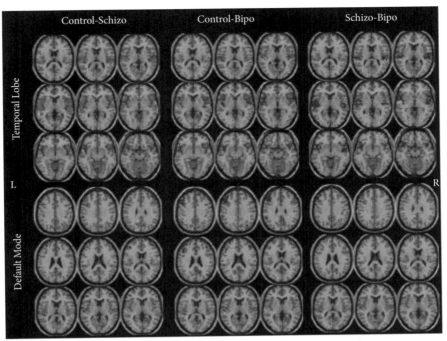

Figure 12.6 Pairwise comparison of temporal and default mode networks for schizophrenia, bipolar disorder, and healthy controls. (Figure courtesy of Calhoun et al., 2008)

relationships between voxels and analyzes whole-brain fMRI data from an auditory task experiment. They analyze the data with both ICA and general linear model (GLM) methods and feed the classifier with GLM spatial maps and temporal lobe and default mode network ICA components. Using leave-two-out cross-validation, they reported 95 percent mean classification accuracy. Discriminative brain regions and their associated weights used for the classification in their study are shown in Figure 12.7.

Du et al. (2012) reported a very high accuracy (98 percent) for classification of schizophrenia using rest and task fMRI data. In their proposed method, 14 ICA components were selected and then a two-level feature selection consisting of kernel principal component analysis (KPCA) and Fisher's linear discriminant (FLD) analysis was applied to select the best feature set. Their proposed method for feature selection is shown in Figure 12.8. Their results show that features extracted from default mode network and motor-temporal components lead to a very successful classification accuracy.

The other category of diagnosis based on functional biomarkers is mainly based on temporal interaction between the brain regions and networks. In recent years, spontaneous modulations of BOLD during the resting condition

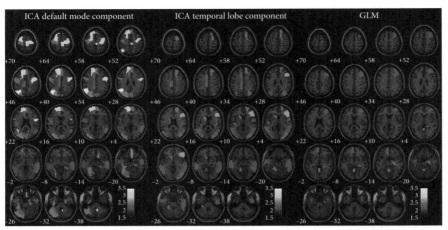

Figure 12.7 Discriminative brain regions color-coded for their associated discriminative power. (Figure courtesy of Castro et al., 2011)

have found fruitful clinical applications (Fox & Greicius, 2010). Resting-state fMRI experiments are less prone to multisite variability, allow a wider range of patients to be scanned, and make it possible to study multiple cortical systems from one dataset (Fox & Greicius, 2010). Moreover, more accurate connectivity maps can be detected using resting-state fMRI data compared to task-based fMRI data (Xiong et al., 1999). With considerable literature on resting-state fMRI group comparisons, researchers have started tackling the more challenging task of using the found abnormalities or so-called biomarkers to discriminate patients from healthy controls. The main target of these studies has been Alzheimer's disease (Greicius et al., 2004; Li et al., 2002; Supekar et al., 2008; Wang et al., 2006). However, resting-state fMRI data have been rarely used to discriminate schizophrenia patients (Shen et al., 2010).

Shen et al. (2010) used an atlas-based method to extract mean time courses of 116 brain regions in the resting state for both healthy controls and schizophrenia subjects. The correlation between these features made the feature vector for each subject. By using feature selection and dimensionality reduction techniques, they reduced the dimensionality down to three, where they classified

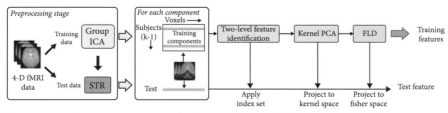

Figure 12.8 Feature extraction and selection framework. (Figure courtesy of Du et al., 2012)

patients from controls with a high accuracy rate (93 percent for patients and 75 percent for healthy controls). Figure 12.9 illustrates brain regions with a high discriminative power in their study.

It has been shown that there are significant FNC differences between schizophrenic patients and the control group in the resting state, possibly showing deficiencies in the brain functional processing in the patients (Jafri et al., 2008). Jafri et al. (2008) reported increased FNC among frontal, temporal, visual and default-mode networks and decreased FNC between temporal and parietal networks. We hypothesized that disrupted functional integration in schizophrenia patients as captured by FNC analysis entails valuable information that can be used to discriminate patients automatically. In our recent study we used functional network connectivity features to classify schizophrenia patients from healthy controls. The block diagram of our proposed method is depicted in Figure 12.10.

One session of resting-state fMRI data was collected from 28 healthy and 28 schizophrenic patients. We divided the data into training (16 healthy subjects + 16 patients) and testing (12 healthy subjects + 12 patients) randomly. The raw fMRI data were first preprocessed. Then the training data were analyzed with group ICA. Subject specific spatial maps and time courses were computed using back reconstruction. Next, FNC analysis was performed on the subject-specific ICA time courses. Since we selected nine IC components, we ended up with 36 FNC features for each subject (FNC was computed for each pair of networks).

Then, several classifiers were trained using the training data and were evaluated using the testing data. For classifiers that required setting parameters,

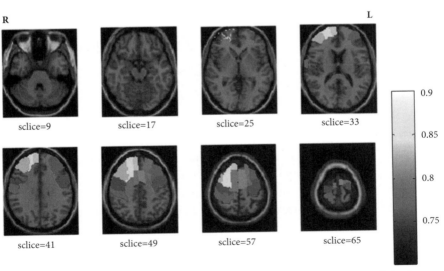

Figure 12.9 Statistically significant regions with high discriminative power. Color bar indicates mean correlation between the functional connectivity pairs and class labels. (Figure courtesy of Shen et al., 2010)

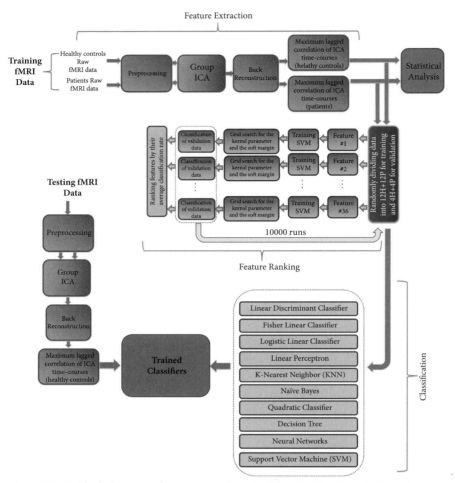

Figure 12.10 Block diagram of our proposed method for classification of schizophrenia patients based on FNC features.

cross-validation was used. The training data were divided into training (14 healthy subjects + 14 patients) and validation (2 healthy subjects + 2 patients) randomly (leave-four-out validation). To show that our method can provide significant results regardless of the type of machine learning algorithm, we report the results for several linear and nonlinear classification methods such as minimum least square linear classifier, Fisher's linear discriminant classifier, quadratic classifier, binary decision tree, SVM, k-nearest neighbor, artificial neural networks, naïve Bayes, logistic linear classifier, and dissimilarity-based classifier. Caution was used to avoid common pitfalls in automatic classification studies such as using a very small cohort, using testing dataset information in the training phase, and incomplete report of the results (Demirci et al., 2008b).

The functional networks (ICA spatial maps) in our study are illustrated in Figure 12.11. The classification accuracy of different classifiers in our experiment ranged from 67 to 100 percent.

The high accuracy of different classifiers in this study consolidates the disconnection hypothesis in schizophrenia patients (Bokde et al., 2006; Friston & Frith 1995; Frith et al., 1995; Josin & Liddle 2001; Mikula & Niebur 2006; Salvador et al., 2010). Some recent DTI studies have shown anatomical disconnection in several brain regions in temporal and frontal lobe in schizophrenia patients (Buchsbaum et al., 2006). Moreover. some studies have associated anatomical damage and FC disconnection in patients by analyzing DTI and functional data together (Zhou et al., 2008). This anatomical–functional association may be the reason for successful automatic diagnosis studies using DTI (Ardekani et al., 2011; Caprihan et al., 2008) and fMRI studies (Arribas et al., 2010; Calhoun et al., 2008; Demirci et al., 2008a; Georgopoulos et al., 2007; Michael et al., 2008; Shen et al., 2010).

There are few studies on the classification of schizophrenia patients based on the combination of genetics and functional neuroimaging data (Yang et al., 2010). These studies are motivated by the fact that researchers have shown that schizophrenia stems from both genetic and environmental factors. Yang et al. (2010) proposed classification of schizophrenia patients based on both fMRI data and single nucleotide polymorphism (SNP) data. They used an ensemble of three classifiers based on SNP features, fMRI map, and components of fMRI activation obtained by ICA. A majority voting among the three classifiers was used to classify patients. They reported 87 percent accuracy for their proposed combined SNP–fMRI method. Figure 12.12 illustrates selected fMRI voxels and the top 15 SNPs in their study.

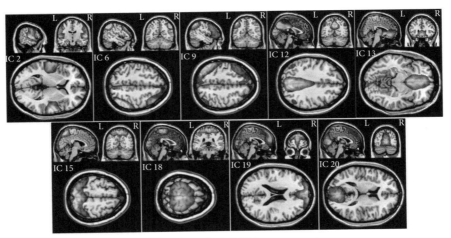

Figure 12.11 Spatial maps of the nine selected ICA components.

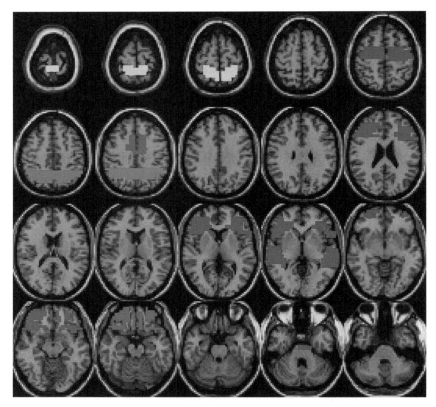

Area	Broadmann area	L/R volume (cc)	L/R importance: value (x,y,z)
Postcentral gyrus	: 3: 5: 2: 7	0.7/0.6	1 (–24,–29,71)/1 (18,–34,71)
Precentral gyrus	: 4: 6: 44: 9	0.9/1.0	1 (–12,–29,71)/1 (18,–29,71)
Paracentral lobule	: 6: 4: 5: 31	0.2/0.2	1 (0,–34,71)/1 (6,–29,71)
Cingulate gyrus	: 31: 32: 24	1.8/1.6	0.341 (–6,–42,44)/0.341 (12,–42,44)
Superior parietal lobule	: 7	0.3/0.2	0.341 (–30,–47,44)/0.341 (30,–53,44)
Inferior parietal lobule	: 40	0.6/0.4	0.341 (–30,–42,44)/0.341 (48,–42,44)
Precuneus	: 7: 31	1.0/0.9	0.341 (0,–42,44)/0.341 (30,–42,44)
Medial frontal gyrus	: 11: 32: 10: 6: 9	1.1/1.1	0.268 (–6,49,–15)/0.268 (6,49,–15)
Superior temporal gyrus	: 38: 22:*: 41: 42	1.0/1.0	0.268 (–48,20,–14)/0.268 (48,20,–14)
Middle frontal gyrus	: 11: 10: 47: 6: 46: 9	3.9/2.3	0.268 (–42,49,–15)/0.268 (24,37,–14)
Inferior frontal gyrus	: 47: 11:*: 46: 45: 9: 13	3.2/1.9	0.268 (–36,14,–8)/0.268 (42,20,–14)
Superior frontal gyrus	: 11: 10: 9	1.0/0.6	0.268 (–18,60,–16)/0.268 (18,60,–16)
Anterior cingulate	: 32: 24	0.2/0.3	0.036 (–6,39,23)/0.121 (12,43,–10)
Middle temporal gyrus	: 22: 19: 21: 20	0.8/0.6	0.024 (–53,–32,4)/0.024 (65,–32,4)
Caudate	:	0.1/0.2	0.024 (–36,–32,4)/0.024 (36,–32,4)
Transverse temporal gyrus	: 42: 41	0.2/0.3	0.012 (–59,–14,9)/0.012 (59,–14,9)
Posterior cingulate	: 31:*: 30	0.2/0.1	0.012 (–30,–60,17)/0.012 (30,–66,17)
Insula	: 13	0.1/0.2	0.012 (–30,27,18)/0.073 (30,26,1)
Cuneus	: 19: 18: 30: 17: 23	0.8/0.7	0.012 (–18,–89,24)/0.012 (12,–95,24)

Figure 12.12 Selected fMRI voxels (left) and top 15 SNPs (right) for classification of schizophrenia patients. (Figure courtesy of Yang et al., 2010)

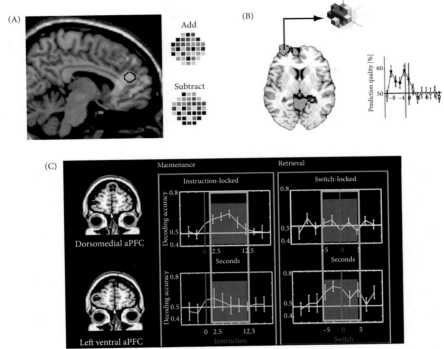

Figure 10.3 Multivariate decoding of intentions from fMRI signals in prefrontal cortex. (**A**) This medial view of the brain shows in green the region around Brodmann area 10, where the fine-scaled activity patterns (right) could be used to decode whether a subject had the intention to add or subtract two numbers (Haynes et al., 2007). (**B**) fRMI signal patterns in frontopolar Brodmann area 10 could be used to predict a subject's decision to press one of two buttons several seconds before the subject believed to have decided which button to take (Soon, Brass, Heinze, & Haynes, 2008). (**C**) Intention representations in anterior medial prefrontal cortex encode a prospective intention across a delay ("maintenance") while the subject is busy working on another task (top). Thus, prospective intention representations are stable across time even in the presence of other competing goals. Signals in anterior lateral prefrontal cortex encode the intention at a later stage when it is retrieved from memory in order to be executed (Momennejad & Haynes, 2012).

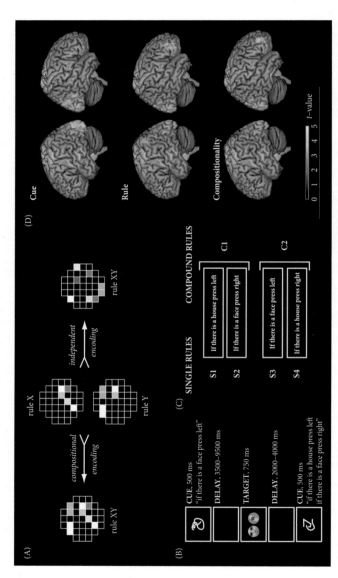

Figure 10.4 Compositionality of rule representations in human prefrontal cortex (Reverberi, Görgen, & Haynes, 2011). (**A**) Two possible neural coding schemes could be used to encode a complex intention XY that consists of two simple intentions: If the code is compositional it means that the neural representation XY can be predicted from the neural codes for the ingredient rules X and Y. If the coding is independent it can't. (**B**) We performed an experiment where subjects were cued to either form simple or complex intentions that involved pressing buttons in response to various pictures. (**C**) We had two levels of rules: single rules that associated one picture with one response, and compound rules that associated two pictures with a response each and that were composed of two single rules. (**D**) The rules upon which compound intentions were based could be decoded from parietal and lateral prefrontal cortex. However, only the prefrontal code was compositional and could be predicted from a pattern classifier trained only on the single rules from which the compound rules were composed.

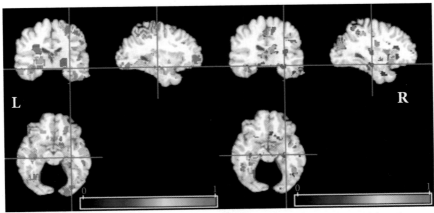

Figure 12.1 Brain regions with most group differences for male (right) and female subjects (left). (Courtesy of Fan et al., 2007)

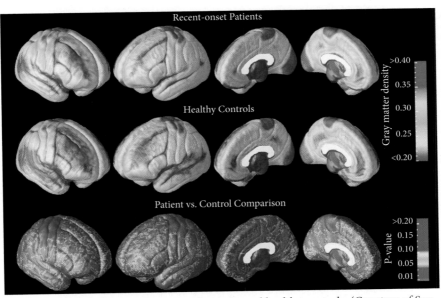

Figure 12.2 GM density and P-maps of patients and healthy controls. (Courtesy of Sun et al., 2009)

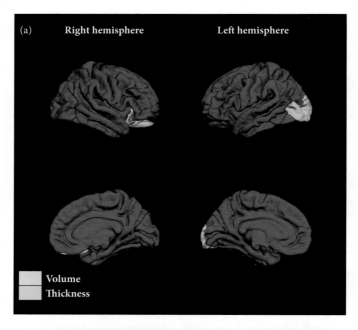

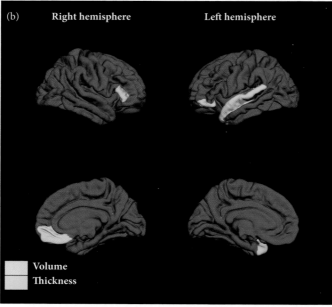

Figure 12.3 Discriminative brain regions based on volume or cortical thickness for male (left) and female (right) subjects.

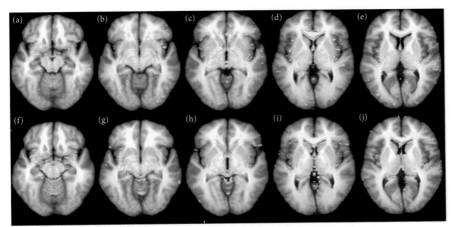

Figure 12.4 Slices from FA (a–e) and MD (f–j) images. Subjects with higher values in yellow regions tend to be classified as healthy controls, while those with higher blue values tend to be classified as patients. (Figure courtesy of Ardekani, et al., 2011)

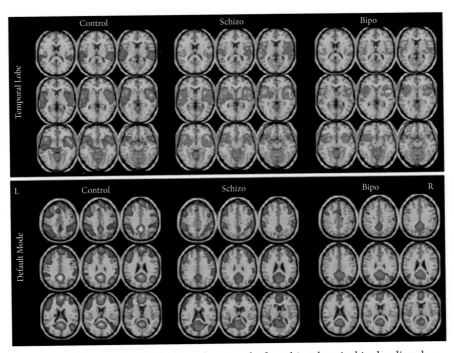

Figure 12.5 Temporal and default mode networks for schizophrenia, bipolar disorder, and healthy controls. (Figure Courtesy of Calhoun et al., 2008)

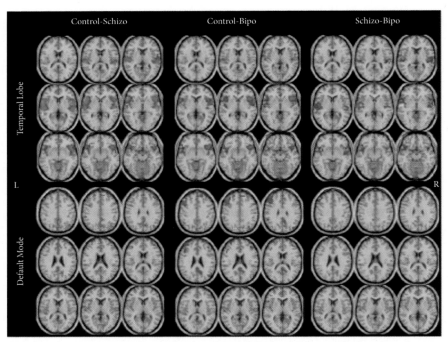

Figure 12.6 Pairwise comparison of temporal and default mode networks for schizophrenia, bipolar disorder, and healthy controls. (Figure courtesy of Calhoun et al., 2008)

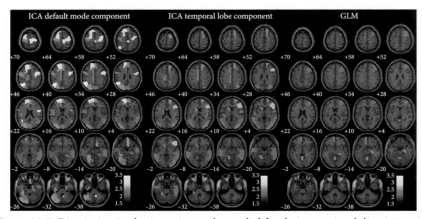

Figure 12.7 Discriminative brain regions color-coded for their associated discriminative power. (Figure courtesy of Castro et al., 2011)

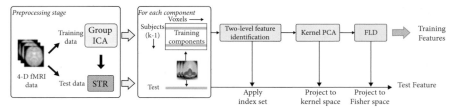

Figure 12.8 Feature extraction and selection framework. (Figure courtesy of Du et al., 2012)

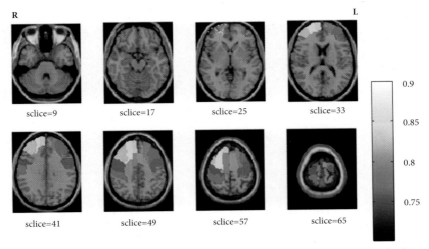

Figure 12.9 Statistically significant regions with high discriminative power. Color bar indicates mean correlation between the functional connectivity pairs and class labels. (Figure courtesy of Shen et al., 2010)

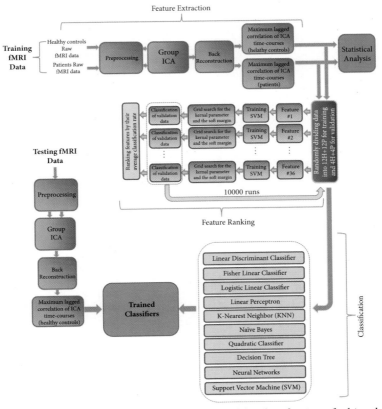

Figure 12.10 Block diagram of our proposed method for classification of schizophrenia patients based on FNC features.

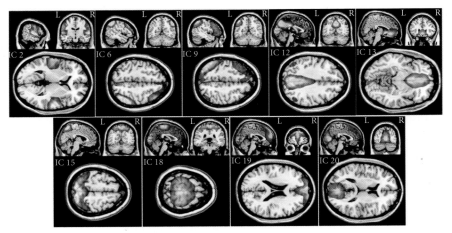

Figure 12.11 Spatial maps of the nine selected ICA components.

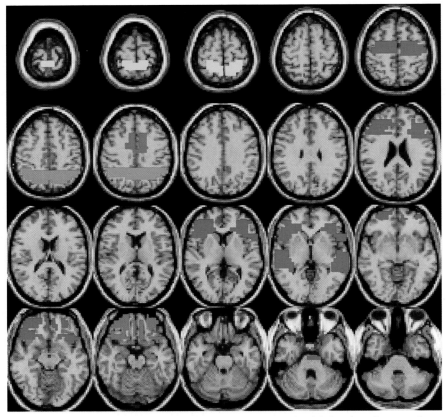

Figure 12.12 Selected fMRI voxels (left) and top 15 SNPs (right) for classification of schizophrenia patients. (Figure courtesy of Yang et al., 2010)

DISCUSSION

In this chapter we reviewed some of the main studies in automatic diagnosis of schizophrenia using neuroimaging data. Studies were categorized based on the biomarker nature into structural (sMRI and DTI) and functional (fMRI). A summary of the studies is provided in Table 12.1.

Several limitations and considerations make it very hard to compare different approaches of automatic classification of mental disorders. For example, study size, MRI scanner parameters, nature of extracted features, type of classifier, medication use, and disease severity in the patient group varied among the different studies. In the absence of standard training and testing datasets, comparison of different approaches based only on the classification rate is ambiguous.

Even though the accuracies of the studies do not necessarily reflect the performance of the method in general, consistently high automatic reported accuracies of these studies suggest that a reliable, biologically based diagnostic indicator of these diseases (a biomarker) could provide a helpful tool for the diagnosis of mental disorders.

As numerous studies have shown, we think that neuroimaging-based automatic diagnostic methods have proven to be useful, but there are some remaining issues preventing these methods from entering the clinical environment. First of all, most of these studies have a limited dataset (smaller than 100 patients). To be able to generalize these results, larger datasets should be collected. The other problem is the lack of standard procedures. This is more serious in fMRI, since there are variables such as imaging parameters, scanner parameters, type of task, length of task, patient behavior inside the scanner, and medication use. It is highly desirable to evaluate the strength of automatic diagnosis methods on diagnosed but not yet medicated patients, but most of the studies are performed using medicated patients. Although the effect of antipsychotic medication on the brain has not been fully understood, it has been shown that antipsychotic medications have a normalizing effect on the functionality of the schizophrenia patient's brain (Davis et al., 2005). Moreover, prior fMRI and EEG studies on nonmedicated schizophrenia patients have reported altered FC (Meyer-Lindenberg et al., 2005; Omori et al., 1995). In general, lack of standard procedure has proven challenging and has delayed the adoption of these methods in the clinic.

Establishing brain disorder prediction methods is much harder compared to diagnostic ones since prediction requires longitudinal studies. These studies are observational and hard to conduct since many variables change over time. However, some of the results from diagnostic studies are applicable to prediction studies. fMRI has been used successfully in predictive/information retrieval studies in other fields, such as extracting text from fMRI data (Pereira et al., 2011) and

Table 12.1 SUMMARY OF NEUROIMAGING-BASED AUTOMATIC DIAGNOSIS OF SCHIZOPHRENIA STUDIES

	Modality	Features	Disorder	Results	References
1	DTI	FA, MD	Schizophrenia	98% overall accuracy	Ardekani et al., 2011
2	DTI	FA	Schizophrenia	75% overall accuracy	Caan et al., 2006
3	DTI	FA	Schizophrenia	80% overall accuracy	Caprihan et al., 2008
4	sMRI	Thalamic and hippocampal shape and volume	Schizophrenia	78% overall error	Csernansky et al., 2004
5	sMRI	GM, white matter, and ventricular CSF volumes	Schizophrenia	81% overall accuracy	Davatzikos et al., 2005
6	sMRI	GM, white matter, and CSF	Schizophrenia	92% overall accuracy	Fan et al., 2005
7	sMRI	Distribution of GM	Schizophrenia	80–90% overall accuracy	Kawasaki et al., 2007
8	sMRI	22 neuropsychological test scores and 23 structural brain measurements	Schizophrenia & Bipolar	100% overall accuracy	Pardo et al., 2006
9	sMRI	Principal components of cortical thickness	Schizophrenia	88–93% overall accuracy	Yoon et al., 2007
10	sMRI	Regional brain volume and cortical thickness	First-episode schizophrenia	80% overall accuracy	Takayanagi et al., 2011
11	sMRI	Structural brain measurements	Schizophrenia	~80% overall accuracy	Nakamura et al., 2004
12	sMRI	Volume of 29 ROIs	First-episode schizophrenia	75–83% overall accuracy	Takayanagi et al., 2010
13	sMRI	GM, white matter, and CSF density maps	Schizophrenia	91% overall accuracy	Fan et al, 2007

14	sMRI	GM density	Schizophrenia, schizophreniform, or schizoaffective disorder	86.1% overall accuracy	Sun et al., 2009
15	fMRI	Activated voxels in DMN and temporal network during AOD task	Schizophrenia & bipolar	70–72%	Arribas et al., 2010
16	fMRI	Activated voxels in DMN and temporal network during AOD task	Schizophrenia & Bipolar	90–95%	Calhoun et al., 2008
17	fMRI	Functional connectivity during the resting state	Schizophrenia	93.75% for schizophrenic patients, 75.0% for healthy controls	Shen et al., 2010
18	fMRI	Functional network connectivity	Schizophrenia	67–100% overall accuracy	Arbabshirani et al., 2013
19	fMRI	DMN and temporal network from ICA and GLM activation map	Schizophrenia	95% overall accuracy	Castro et al., 2011
20	fMRI	ICA components	Schizophrenia	98% overall accuracy	Du et al., 2012
21	fMRI and genetic	fMRI activation maps and SNP	Schizophrenia	87% overall accuracy	Yang et al., 2010

DMN, Default mode network.

prediction of neural activation associated with the meaning of words (Mitchell et al., 2008). We believe automatic prediction methods will have a longer path compared to diagnostic methods to reach the clinical environment.

After a number of successful studies on automatic diagnosis of chronic schizophrenia from healthy controls, now researchers have moved toward discriminating schizophrenia subtypes (Takayanagi et al., 2010, 2011) as well as other overlapping brain abnormalities such as bipolar disorder (Calhoun et al., 2008). Although only recently started, these studies have shown that high-accuracy classification of schizophrenia subtypes and overlapping disorders is plausible. Recruiting a large number of patients with these specific disorders is one of the practical challenges in these studies. The hope is that, given enough data, all major subtypes could be diagnosed with similar frameworks as used previously but probably with different features (or different weight for the features).

Although we focused on schizophrenia in this chapter, similar methods are applicable to a wide range of mental disorders, such as Alzheimer's disease (Greicius et al., 2004; Li et al., 2002; Supekar et al., 2008; Wang et al., 2006) and mild cognitive impairment (Fan et al., 2008; Haller et al., 2010; Machulda et al., 2009; McEvoy et al., 2009; Petrella et al., 2011).

We believe that a combination of MRI-based neuroimaging biomarkers, along with other biomarkers from modalities such as EEG and MEG and genetics, can provide a robust framework for diagnosis and prognosis of various mental disorders with high accuracy in a reasonable time. Such a framework can alleviate the socioeconomic burden of mental illnesses as well as helping patients with early diagnosis, which can significantly improve treatment response and reduce associated costs.

REFERENCES

Arbabshirani, M. R., Kiehl, K. A., Pearlson, G. D., & Calhoun, V. D. (2013). Classification of schizophrenia patients based on resting-state functional network analysis Frontiers in Brain Imaging Methods, in press.

Ardekani, B. A., Bappal, A., D'Angelo, D., et al. (2005). Brain morphometry using diffusion-weighted magnetic resonance imaging: application to schizophrenia. *Neuroreport, 16*(13), 1455–1459.

Ardekani, B. A., Tabesh, A., Sevy, S., et al. (2011). Diffusion tensor imaging reliably differentiates patients with schizophrenia from healthy volunteers. *Human Brain Mapping, 32*(1), 1–9.

Arribas, J. I., Calhoun, V. D., & Adali, T. (2010). Automatic Bayesian classification of healthy controls, bipolar disorder, and schizophrenia using intrinsic connectivity maps from FMRI data. *IEEE Transactions on Biomedical Engineering, 57*(12), 2850–2860.

Bhugra, D. (2005). The global prevalence of schizophrenia. *PLoS Medicine 2*(5). e151; quiz e175.

Biswal, B. B., Van Kylen, J., & Hyde, J. S. (1997). Simultaneous assessment of flow and BOLD signals in resting-state functional connectivity maps. *NMR in Biomedicine,* *10*(4–5), 165–170.

Biswal, B., Yetkin, F. Z., Haughton, V. M., & Hyde, J. S. (1995). Functional connectivity in the motor cortex of resting human brain using echo-planar MRI. *Magnetic resonance in medicine : official journal of the Society of Magnetic Resonance in Medicine / Society of Magnetic Resonance in Medicine, 34*(4), 537–541.

Bluhm, R. L., Miller, J., Lanius, R. A., et al. (2007). Spontaneous low-frequency fluctuations in the BOLD signal in schizophrenic patients: anomalies in the default network. *Schizophrenia Bulletin, 33*(4), 1004–1012.

Bokde, A. L., Lopez-Bayo, P., Meindl, T., et al. (2006). Functional connectivity of the fusiform gyrus during a face-matching task in subjects with mild cognitive impairment. *Brain: A Journal of Neurology, 129*(Pt 5), 1113–1124. doi: 10.1093/brain/awl051

Buchsbaum, M. S., Schoenknecht, P., Torosjan, Y., et al. (2006). Diffusion tensor imaging of frontal lobe white matter tracts in schizophrenia. *Annals of General Psychiatry, 5,* 19. doi: 10.1186/1744-859X-5-19

Caan, M. W., Vermeer, K. A., van Vliet, L. J., et al. (2006). Shaving diffusion tensor images in discriminant analysis: a study into schizophrenia. *Medical Image Analysis, 10*(6), 841–849.

Calhoun, V. D., Adali, T., Pearlson, G. D., & Pekar, J. J. (2001). A method for making group inferences from functional MRI data using independent component analysis. *Human Brain Mapping, 14*(3), 140–151.

Calhoun, V. D., Kiehl, K. A., Liddle, P. F., & Pearlson, G. D. (2004). Aberrant localization of synchronous hemodynamic activity in auditory cortex reliably characterizes schizophrenia. *Biological Psychiatry, 55*(8), 842–849.

Calhoun, V. D., Liu, J., & Adali, T. (2009). A review of group ICA for fMRI data and ICA for joint inference of imaging, genetic, and ERP data. *NeuroImage, 45*(1 Suppl), S163–172. doi: 10.1016/j.neuroimage.2008.10.057

Calhoun, V. D., Maciejewski, P. K., Pearlson, G. D., & Kiehl, K. A. (2008): Temporal lobe and "default" hemodynamic brain modes discriminate between schizophrenia and bipolar disorder. *Human Brain Mapping, 29*(11), 1265–1275. doi: 10.1002/hbm.20463

Caprihan, A., Pearlson, G. D., & Calhoun, V. D. (2008). Application of principal component analysis to distinguish patients with schizophrenia from healthy controls based on fractional anisotropy measurements. *NeuroImage, 42*(2), 675–682.

Castro, E., Martinez-Ramon, M., Pearlson, G., et al. (2011). Characterization of groups using composite kernels and multi-source fMRI analysis data: application to schizophrenia. *Neuroimage, 58*(2), 526–536.

Cordes, D., Haughton, V. M., Arfanakis, K., et al. (2000). Mapping functionally related regions of brain with functional connectivity MR imaging. *AJNR. American Journal of Neuroradiology, 21*(9), 1636–1644.

Cordes, D., Haughton, V., Carew, J. D., Arfanakis, K., & Maravilla, K. (2002). Hierarchical clustering to measure connectivity in fMRI resting-state data. *Magnetic Resonance Imaging, 20*(4), 305–317.

Csernansky, J. G., Schindler, M. K., Splinter, N. R., et al. (2004). Abnormalities of thalamic volume and shape in schizophrenia. *American Journal of Psychiatry, 161*(5), 896–902.

Davatzikos, C., Shen, D., Gur, R. C., et al. (2005). Wholebrain morphometric study of schizophrenia revealing a spatially complex set of focal abnormalities. *Archives of General Psychiatry, 62*(11), 1218–1227.

Davis, C. E., Jeste, D. V., & Eyler, L. T. (2005): Review of longitudinal functional neuroimaging studies of drug treatments in patients with schizophrenia. *Schizophrenia Research, 78*(1), 45–60.

Demirci, O., Clark, V. P., & Calhoun, V. D. (2008a). A projection pursuit algorithm to classify individuals using fMRI data: Application to schizophrenia. *Neuroimage, 39*(4), 1774–1782.

Demirci, O., Clark, V. P., Magnotta, V. A., et al. (2008b). A review of challenges in the use of fMRI for disease classification/characterization and a projection pursuit application from multi-site fMRI schizophrenia study. *Brain Imaging and Behavior, 2*(3), 147–226.

Du, W., Calhoun, V. D., Li, H., et al. (2012). High classification accuracy for schizophrenia with rest and task FMRI data. *Frontiers in Human Neuroscience, 6*, 145.

Esposito, F., Scarabino, T., Hyvarinen, A., et al. (2005). Independent component analysis of fMRI group studies by self-organizing clustering. *NeuroImage, 25*(1), 193–205. doi: 10.1016/j.neuroimage.2004.10.042

Fan, Y., Batmanghelich, N., Clark, C. M., & Davatzikos, C. (2008). Spatial patterns of brain atrophy in MCI patients, identified via high-dimensional pattern classification, predict subsequent cognitive decline. *NeuroImage, 39*(4), 1731–1743.

Fan, Y., Shen, D., & Davatzikos, C. (2005). Classification of structural images via high-dimensional image warping, robust feature extraction, and SVM. *Medical Image Computing and Computer Assisted Interventions, 8*(Pt 1), 1–8.

Fan, Y., Shen, D., Gur, R. C., et al. (2007). COMPARE: classification of morphological patterns using adaptive regional elements. *IEEE Transactions on Medical Imaging, 26*(1), 93–105.

Fox, M. D., & Greicius, M. (2010). Clinical applications of resting state functional connectivity. *Frontiers in Systems Neuroscience, 4*, 19.

Fox, M. D., Snyder, A. Z., Vincent, J. L., et al. E. (2005). The human brain is intrinsically organized into dynamic, anticorrelated functional networks. *Proceedings of the National Academy of Sciences of the United States of America, 102*(27), 9673–9678. doi: 10.1073/pnas.0504136102.

Friston, K. (2002). Beyond phrenology: what can neuroimaging tell us about distributed circuitry? *Annual Review of Neuroscience, 25*, 221–250. doi: 10.1146/annurev. neuro.25.112701.142846.Friston, K. J., & Frith, C. D. (1995): Schizophrenia: a disconnection syndrome? *Clin Neurosci, 3*(2), 89–97.

Frith, C. D., Friston, K. J., Herold, S., et al. (1995). Regional brain activity in chronic schizophrenic patients during the performance of a verbal fluency task. *British Journal of Psychiatry, 167*(3), 343–349.

Garrity, A. G., Pearlson, G. D., McKiernan, K., et al. (2007). Aberrant "default mode" functional connectivity in schizophrenia. *American Journal of Psychiatry, 164*(3), 450–457. doi: 10.1176/appi.ajp.164.3.450

Georgopoulos, A. P., Karageorgiou, E., Leuthold, A. C., et al. (2007). Synchronous neural interactions assessed by magnetoencephalography: a functional biomarker for brain disorders. *Journal of Neural Engineering, 4*(4), 349–355.

Greicius, M. D., Srivastava, G., Reiss, A. L., & Menon, V. (2004). Default-mode network activity distinguishes Alzheimer's disease from healthy aging: Evidence from functional MRI. *Proceedings of the National Academy of Sciences of the United States of America, 101*(13), 4637–4642.

Haller, S., Nguyen, D., Rodriguez, C., et al. (2010). Individual prediction of cognitive decline in mild cognitive impairment using support vector machine-based analysis of diffusion tensor imaging data. *Journal of Alzheimer's Disease, 22*(1), 315–327.

Havlicek, M., Jan, J., Brazdil, M., & Calhoun, V. D. (2010). Dynamic Granger causality based on Kalman filter for evaluation of functional network connectivity in fMRI data. *NeuroImage, 53*(1), 65–77.

Heinrichs, R. W., & Zakzanis, K. K. (1998). Neurocognitive deficit in schizophrenia: a quantitative review of the evidence. *Neuropsychology, 12*(3), 426–445.

Honea, R., Crow, T. J., Passingham, D., & Mackay, C. E. (2005). Regional deficits in brain volume in schizophrenia: a meta-analysis of voxel-based morphometry studies. *American Journal of Psychiatry, 162*(12), 2233–2245.

Jafri, M. J., Pearlson, G. D., Stevens, M., & Calhoun, V. D. (2008). A method for functional network connectivity among spatially independent resting-state components in schizophrenia. *NeuroImage, 39*(4), 1666–1681. doi: 10.1016/j.neuroimage.2007.11.001

Josin, G. M., & Liddle, P. F. (2001). Neural network analysis of the pattern of functional connectivity between cerebral areas in schizophrenia. *Biological Cybernetics, 84*(2), 117–122.

Kawasaki, Y., Suzuki, M., Kherif, F., et al. (2007). Multivariate voxel-based morphometry successfully differentiates schizophrenia patients from healthy controls. *NeuroImage, 34*(1), 235–242.

Kingsley, P. B. (2006). Introduction to diffusion tensor imaging mathematics: Part II. Anisotropy, diffusion-weighting factors, and gradient encoding schemes. *Concepts in Magnetic Resonance Imaging, Part A, 28A*(2), 123–154.

Kubicki, M., McCarley, R., Westin, C. F., et al. (2007). A review of diffusion tensor imaging studies in schizophrenia. *Journal of Psychiatric Research, 41*(1-2), 15–30.

Lee, K., Yoshida, T., Kubicki, M., et al. (2009). Increased diffusivity in superior temporal gyrus in patients with schizophrenia: a diffusion tensor imaging study. *Schizophrenia Research, 108*(1-3), 33–40.

Li, S. J., Li, Z., Wu, G. H., et al. (2002). Alzheimer disease: Evaluation of a functional MR imaging index as a marker. *Radiology, 225*(1), 253–259.

Liang, M., Zhou, Y., Jiang, T., et al. (2006). Widespread functional disconnectivity in schizophrenia with resting-state functional magnetic resonance imaging. *Neuroreport, 17*(2), 209–213.

Lowe, M. J., Mock, B. J., & Sorenson, J. A. (1998). Functional connectivity in single and multislice echoplanar imaging using resting-state fluctuations. *NeuroImage, 7*(2), 119–132. doi: 10.1006/nimg.1997.0315

Machulda, M. M., Senjem, M. L., Weigand, S. D., et al. (2009). Functional magnetic resonance imaging changes in amnestic and nonamnestic mild cognitive impairment during encoding and recognition tasks. *Journal of the International Neuropsychological Society, 15*(3), 372–382.

McEvoy, L. K., Fennema-Notestine, C., Roddey, J. C., et al. (2009): Alzheimer disease: quantitative structural neuroimaging for detection and prediction of clinical and structural changes in mild cognitive impairment. *Radiology, 251*(1), 195–205.

McKeown, M. J., Makeig, S., Brown, G. G., et al. (1998). Analysis of fMRI data by blind separation into independent spatial components. *Human Brain Mapping, 6*(3), 160–188.

Meyer-Lindenberg, A. S., Olsen, R. K., Kohn, P. D., et al. (2005). Regionally specific disturbance of dorsolateral prefrontal-hippocampal functional connectivity in schizophrenia. *Archives of General Psychiatry, 62*(4), 379–386. doi: 10.1001/archpsyc.62.4.379

Michael, A. M., Calhoun, V. D., Andreasen, N. C., & Baum, S. A. (2008). A method to classify schizophrenia using inter-task spatial correlations of functional brain images. *Conference Proceedings IEEE Engineering in Medicine and Biology Society,* 5510–5513.

Mikula, S., & Niebur, E. (2006). A novel method for visualizing functional connectivity using principal component analysis. *International Journal of Neuroscience, 116*(4), 419–429. Doi: Doi 10.1080/00207450500505761

Mitchell, T. M., Shinkareva, S. V., Carlson, A., et al. (2008). Predicting human brain activity associated with the meanings of nouns. *Science, 320*(5880), 1191–1195.

Nakamura, K., Kawasaki, Y., Suzuki, M., et al. (2004). Multiple structural brain measures obtained by three-dimensional magnetic resonance imaging to distinguish between schizophrenia patients and normal subjects. *Schizophrenia Bulletine, 30*(2), 393–404.

Narr, K. L., Hageman, N., Woods, R. P., et al. (2009). Mean diffusivity: a biomarker for CSF-related disease and genetic liability effects in schizophrenia. *Psychiatry Research, 171*(1), 20–32.

Omori, M., Koshino, Y., Murata, T., et al. (1995). Quantitative EEG in never-treated schizophrenic patients. *Biological Psychiatry, 38*(5), 305–309.

Pardo, P. J., Georgopoulos, A. P., Kenny, J. T., et al. (2006). Classification of adolescent psychotic disorders using linear discriminant analysis. *Schizophrenia Research, 87*(1-3), 297–306.

Pereira, F., Detre, G., & Botvinick, M. (2011). Generating text from functional brain images. *Frontiers in Human Neuroscience, 5,* 72.

Petrella, J. R., Sheldon, F. C., Prince, S. E., et al. (2011). Default mode network connectivity in stable vs progressive mild cognitive impairment. *Neurology 76*(6), 511–517.

Rice, D. P. (1999). The economic impact of schizophrenia. *Journal of Clinical Psychiatry, 60*(Suppl 1), 4–6; discussion 28–30.

Salvador, R., Sarro, S., Gomar, J. J., et al. (2010). Overall brain connectivity maps show cortico-subcortical abnormalities in schizophrenia. *Human Brain Mapping, 31*(12), 2003–2014. doi: 10.1002/hbm.20993

Shen, H., Wang, L., Liu, Y., & Hu, D. (2010). Discriminative analysis of resting-state functional connectivity patterns of schizophrenia using low dimensional embedding of fMRI. *NeuroImage, 49*(4), 3110–3121.

Stein, T., Moritz, C., Quigley, M., et al. (2000). Functional connectivity in the thalamus and hippocampus studied with functional MR imaging. *AJNR. American Journal of Neuroradiology, 21*(8), 1397–1401.

Stevens, M. C., Kiehl, K. A., Pearlson, G. D., & Calhoun, V. D. (2007). Functional neural networks underlying response inhibition in adolescents and adults. *Behavioral Brain Research, 181*(1), 12–22.

Stevens, M. C., Kiehl, K. A., Pearlson, G. D., & Calhoun, V. D. (2009)/ Brain network dynamics during error commission. *Human Brain Mapping, 30*(1),24–37.

Sun, D., van Erp, T. G., Thompson, P. M., et al. (2009). Elucidating a magnetic resonance imaging-based neuroanatomic biomarker for psychosis: classification analysis
using probabilistic brain atlas and machine learning algorithms. *Biological Psychiatry,*
66(11), 1055–1060.

Supekar, K., Menon, V., Rubin, D., et al. (2008). Network analysis of intrinsic functional
brain connectivity in Alzheimer's disease. *PLoS Computational Biology, 4*(6): e1000100.

Szeszko, P. R., Robinson, D. G., Ashtari, M., et al. (2008). Clinical and neuropsychological correlates of white matter abnormalities in recent onset schizophrenia.
Neuropsychopharmacology, 33(5), 976–984.

Takayanagi, Y., Kawasaki, Y., Nakamura, K., et al. (2010). Differentiation of first-episode
schizophrenia patients from healthy controls using ROI-based multiple structural
brain variables. *Progress in Neuro-Psychopharmacology and Biological Psychiatry,*
34(1), 10–17.

Takayanagi, Y., Takahashi, T., Orikabe, L., et al. (2011). Classification of first-episode
schizophrenia patients and healthy subjects by automated MRI measures of regional
brain volume and cortical thickness. *PLoS One, 6*(6), e21047.

Turner, G. H., & Twieg, D. B. (2005). Study of temporal stationarity and spatial consistency of fMRI noise using independent component analysis. *IEEE Transactions on*
Medical Imaging, 24(6), 712–718. doi: 10.1109/TMI.2005.846852

van de Ven, V. G., Formisano, E., Prvulovic, D., et al. (2004). Functional connectivity as
revealed by spatial independent component analysis of fMRI measurements during
rest. *Human Brain Mapping, 22*(3), 165–178. doi: 10.1002/hbm.20022

Wang, K., Jiang, T. Z., Liang, M., et al. (2006). Discriminative analysis of early Alzheimer's
disease based on two intrinsically anti-correlated networks with resting-state fMRI.
Lecture Notes in Computer Science, 4191, 340–347.

Wyatt, R. J., Henter, I., Leary, M. C., & Taylor, E. (1995). An economic evaluation of
schizophrenia—1991. *Soc Psychiatry Psychiatr Epidemiol, 30*(5), 196–205.

Xiong, J., Parsons, L. M., Gao, J. H., & Fox, P. T. (1999). Interregional connectivity to primary motor cortex revealed using MRI resting state images. *Human Brain Mapping,*
8(2-3), 151–156.

Yang, H., Liu, J., Sui, J., et al. (2010). A hybrid machine learning method for fusing fMRI
and genetic data: combining both improves classification of schizophrenia. *Frontiers*
in Human Neuroscience, 4, 192.

Yoon, U., Lee, J. M., Im, K., et al. (2007). Pattern classification using principal components of cortical thickness and its discriminative pattern in schizophrenia.
NeuroImage, 34(4), 1405–1415.

Zhou, Y., Shu, N., Liu, Y., et al. (2008). Altered resting-state functional connectivity and
anatomical connectivity of hippocampus in schizophrenia. *Schizophrenia Research,*
100(1–3), 120–132. doi: 10.1016/j.schres.2007.11.039

INDEX

f denotes figure; *t* denotes table; n denotes note